WOMEN
OF
BRITISH
COLUMBIA

WOMEN OF BRITISH COLUMBIA

Jan Gould

Hancock House Publishers

ISBN 0-919654-42-8

Designed by Nicholas Newbeck Design

This book was designed and first produced in Canada
by Hancock House Publishers Limited, 3215 Island
View Road, Saanichton, British Columbia, Canada.

Printed in Canada by D. W. Friesen & Sons Ltd.
Altona, Manitoba

Canadian Shared Cataloguing in Publication Data

Gould, Jan
Women of British Columbia

1. Women — British Columbia — Biography.
2. Frontier and pioneer life — British
Columbia. I. Title.
F
[LC: F1086.8.G69]
ISBN 0-919654-42-8

hancock

house

HANCOCK HOUSE PUBLISHERS LTD.
3215 Island View Road
Saanichton, B.C., Canada

CONTENTS

DEDICATION

For the men in my life,
My husband Ed, and my son Jay

FOREWORD

The women included in this book came to my attention through research, interviews, and Fate. I believe that the women who are not shown in these pages are just as important as those I have written about. What I hope is that others who read this book will identify with some of the women described: perhaps they too wrapped themselves in cheesecloth to protect themselves from northern blackflies as they raked hay, or marched in weather 40° below zero to open a rural school, or campaigned in some way to bring about full human rights for others.

In my search for material, I found numerous diaries or journals known to have been written by women had been burned or lost: a few had been thrown out because relatives did not realize their importance. The Provincial Archives of British Columbia will make a copy of pertinent documents; museums are interested in them, while college and university women's studies also will find them of value. Both my publisher and I welcome any correspondence.

JAN GOULD

ACKNOWLEDGEMENTS

I owe special thanks to Catherine Salter for aiding me with early historical research and to J. Robert Davison, Archivist, Provincial Archives of British Columbia who has written a Foreword. Others to whom I acknowledge my appreciation for assistance or suggestions are: Provincial Archives of British Columbia staff including Brian Young, Karen Ramsden, Terry Eastwood, Len DeLozier and Barbara McLennan; the staffs of R. Atkinson Museum, Penticton, the Kamloops Museum, Princeton Museum, Ladner Museum and Prince Rupert Museum and members of the Queen Charlotte Historical Society. My thanks also to Jessie Wharf for co-ordinating material while I travelled, Sylvia Keith, Betty Emery, Delta; Jo Fitzsimmons, Kamloops; Marguerite Davies, Peace River Country; Al and Marg Leveridge, Prince George; Lillian Horsdal, Salt Spring Island.

I acknowledge help and kindness of all the organizations which opened files for my perusal, also the assistance of staff of Vancouver City Archives and University of British Columbia Special Collections Division. Material came from sources named in bibliography as well as from private sources. Unpublished letters and diaries from the Provincial Archives of British Columbia were used. For taped background information on Mallardville and on Chilcotin, I acknowledge aid of Aural Division of Provincial Archives and Dick Scales, College of New Caledonia, Prince George. For supportive encouragement, I thank all my friends, the staff of University of Victoria's Creative Writing Department, Ivy Michelson and Ada Severson.

Old totem at Kitwancool. Until the 1950's, this Indian village in forested country near Hazelton, was used for winter social and ceremonial affairs, and was accessible only by trail.

8

The wild cherries were falling when the woman went to the meadow to work on her land. She carried a large clam shell, the tool she could use to cut off dry or dying foliage and the exposed portion of the clover roots. She would return once the preparatory work had been done, bringing a yew dibble with which she would dig the precious roots. She would be careful not to damage or take the central root-stock. This species of clover was highly prized for its health-giving qualities.

She was a Kwakiutl woman and this land was her property; she could lease it but she could not sell it, neither could she give it away. To give up meant that she would deprive her descendants of her inheritance that had been in her family for generations. The roots were her security and her insurance. Her descendants, too, could eat the cooked roots or use them in trade.

Berry patches, fishing areas, sea lion rookeries, mountain goat pastures, even stands of timber, often were the property of specific households or lineages of the first people to live in British Columbia. Other inherited rights could apply to the ownership of songs and stories, the right to carve a totem pole, to wear certain masks, or perform a particular dance. Just as the environment differed throughout the land, so the social structure and organization of the people varied from group to group. Philip Drucker, former member of the Smithsonian Institution's Bureau of American Ethnology, states in his *Indians of the Northwest Coast* that among the apparently varied patterns of structure there are two basic principles of areal society which can be traced: an autonomous local group consisting of a *lineage* (a formalized, named group of relatives tracing descent to a common ancestor through one line), or *an extended family* (a social division less rigidly formalized and defined, in which descent may be reckoned through either the male or the female line, or both).

Authorities have classified the Indians of British Columbia into ten major groups, divisions set by language: the Haida, Tsimshian, Kwakiutl, Nootka, Bella Coola, Coast Salish, Interior Salish, Kootenay, Athapascan, and Inland Tlingit. Within these groups, numerous dialects exist, although some languages are extinct. Various attempts are being made to preserve these. In 1972, Vancouver Island Hesquiat Band hired linguist Dr. Barbara S. Efrat to work with Band elders to record this dialect of the northern Nootka and to create graded language lessons for younger band members. Now Curator of the Linguistics Division of the British Columbia Provincial Museum, she continues her research and directs the collection of languages by groups in native communities. The government-sponsored British Columbia Indian Languages Project, coordinated by linguist Randy Bouchard with researcher Dorothy Kennedy, also works to preserve Indian languages.

In all groups it was considered woman's work to prepare and preserve food, and often to obtain it. She collected berries, roots and the bulbs of plants. At seasonal camps, she cleaned cod, salmon, herring or

Root-digging was considered women's work. Various roots could be steamed or roasted; they also were trade items.

A

Nicola Indians pose for an early photographer.

halibut, cutting off their heads and tails for traditional boiled dishes. Fish skins were removed from the flesh, dried and roasted; the flesh itself was thinly sliced so it could be smoked and dried. Eulachon oil was a major staple and the large amount of it included in their diet probably helped to fortify the people against the cold. The eulachons were boiled in canoes and other wooden containers by adding hot stones to keep the water near boiling point. Once the fish were well cooked their oil either seeped out or was pressed from them. It had numerous uses: foods were dipped into it, it was used as a food preservative, newborn babies were anointed with it, women in labor had it smoothed over their stomachs, and Chiefs were known to burn huge amounts of it at potlatches, wasting it, and thereby showing their wealth. As a valuable trading item, it was packed in large kelp bulbs and transported in wooden containers from group to group, along with other food commodities. Game and fowl were also included in the diet.

Those taking the first salmon or the first berries of each season showed their appreciation to the gods by observing certain rituals. They also practiced ecology: when a woman took bark from a tree to use in her baskets or clothing, she took only enough for the item at hand, never damaging the tree so much it would die. She also asked the tree's understanding of her act. Bark for baskets was carefully prepared. Interior women among the Athapascan and Interior Salish used birchbark which they folded into shape, stitched with willow strips, and rimmed with a wooden hoop. At the coast, a non-weaving technique known as coiled basketry was practiced by Coast Salish. Others wove with spruce roots and cedar bark; the weave varied according to the purpose of the basket. A tightly woven basket could be used as a cooking utensil, with heat provided by red-hot stones which were thrown into the cooking water; loosely woven baskets were used to carry preserved food which needed aeration, or to hold fish that required draining.

Kwakiutl woman shredding bark. The inner bark was taken from trees in July and soaked for ten days in salt water.
A

Preparing the salmon was women's work, and the first salmon of the year was acknowledged by ritual.
B

Inside of Nootka house. Note fish drying from rafters.
D

Salish summer encampment on the banks of the Fraser. Fishing sites also could be rented to others.
C

Split spruce roots were used for basketry. A

The baskets of this Tachie Lake mother and child were used for food gathering. B

This Yale basketmaker's products would vary according to their eventual use. C

Salmon trap for narrow streams, Kwakuitl. D

A woman's skilled hands could fashion traps and nets; she also wove mats as bedrolls. Rank indicated which natural fibres would be used as material for Nootka hats—spruce roots were used for the headgear of high-ranking officials, while commoners' hats were made from cedar bark. Raincapes were woven by Nootka and Kwakiutl women, who also traded their cedarbark to other groups.

Mountain goat wool was traded down to the coast by northern groups, whose menfolk hunted the goats with the aid of small tracking dogs. Of all the robes woven from goat hair, the most famous were the Chilkat "blankets," which still can be seen when they are worn at today's ceremonies. The blankets were desired items of wealth for nobles of all groups. Chilkat women wove them, but Drucker points out that the technique may have been borrowed from the Tsimshian, who once made dancing aprons and half-leggings using the same techniques:

According to one tradition . . . a Chilkat bride of a Tsimshian chief learned the art. At her death, a dance apron she had woven was sent to her home, where her relatives studied the weave, loosening and unravelling it bit by bit until they understood how it was done.

The men painted the design of each blanket on a board so that the women could follow it when they had completed all the preparatory work of spinning the wool, dyeing it, then setting up the loom. The colored designs on the robes contrasted with the wool's natural shade. Blue-green yarn was obtained by steeping copper in urine, then boiling natural wool in the liquid. Black came from the liquid in which hemlock bark had been soaked, and yellow was made from tree moss.

Chief Maquinna, Nootka Sound. Chiefs wore distinctive hats. D

11

Designs on Chilkat blankets.   *A*

Woman spins mountain goat wool using primitive but efficient spindle.   *B*

Sheep's wool used in Cowichan sweaters drying at Duncan.   *C*

Modern Cowichan Indian knit Fair Isle-styled sweaters, using their own designs. Ruby Peters displays one of her products.   *D*

Detail of 'Ksan weaving.   *E*

The Coast Salish had several weaving techniques, and used a wider variety of materials than other groups. As well as importing a small amount of mountain goat wool, they used the wool of dogs kept especially for the purpose. Down from geese and ducks was utilized, as was the papus of cat-tail reeds and fireweed. Interior groups fashioned clothing from deer and moose skins. Coastal women wore shredded bark clothing, while Tlingit dancers chose to wear the buckskin dance aprons made by their women.

The woman's ornaments were chosen according to her status or rank. Trade goods from other groups supplemented the choice of materials from her own area. Dentalium shells decorated ears as did pieces of abalone shell. Heiltsuk, Haisla, Tsimshian, Haida and Tlingit women wore bone or wooden labrets which pierced their lower lips. Kwakiutl and Nootka women used fern or hide bracelets, while anklets of hide were reputed to keep ankles slim. Face painting became elaborate for ceremonial purposes but was usually a protective device against the weather. Both the Coast Salish and Kwakiutl practiced some head deformation by binding babies' heads so they became elongated or sloped, although the custom was never extended to include the children of slaves. Although most Indians used quiet forest pools as mirrors, the Tsimshian saw their reflections in pieces of slate over which they ran water.

If childhood was a time of joy for Indian children, who were pampered with cradles softly lined with shredded bark and moss, puberty was fraught with numerous taboos with the girl kept from others lest she contaminate food supplies. However, a daughter's coming of age was a joyful event and celebrated by some groups. The Nootka, for example, held a potlatch for a girl of high rank when her puberty was evident.

Marriage was subservient to rules and restriction and usually had to be among partners of the woman's own social class. Her role spun around that of her husband, as the late George Hunt recounted when he described a lifestyle reported to him by a Clayoquot whaler:

When they were near the village, the people heard the whalers singing the towing songs, and that showed them that they had killed a whale; and they put four canoes into the water, and nine men in each of them went to meet the whalers. As soon as they came up the whalers stopped and cut from the back of each whale's neck a piece of blubber one span long and a span and a half wide, and one of the four canoes paddled back to the village with them as fast as they could. And as soon as they came to the beach, one gave it to the whaler's wife, and she cut it into strips.

In a few minutes she spread on the floor a small new mat, removed the kettle from the fire; and laid the cooked blubber on the mat. She kept one piece for herself, and the man carried the mat with the blubber on it to the canoe; and they paddled back and gave it to the whaler. . . .

It was the wife's job to go down to the beach as soon as the whale or whales were grounded. She carried a horn rattle in her right hand and some eagle down in her left hand; silently, she sang her secret bathing song. Still singing and shaking her rattle, she stepped into her hus-

Kwakiutl woman with abalone shell earrings and the bracelets. Note cedarbark robe.　　　　A

Baby carriers were made of various materials depending on location.　　　B

Kwatiutl woman with elongated head caused by binding in childhood, a mark of status.　　　C

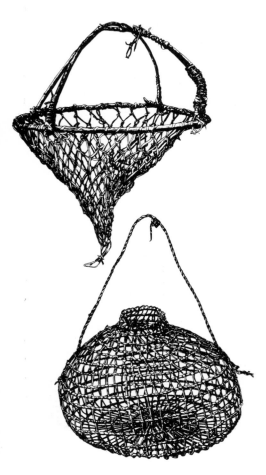

The Nootka fish baskets.   *A*

Today's Indian children in a Quamichan Lake sports event.   *B*

band's canoe and put the down on his head, then sprinkled it over the blowholes of the dead whales. After this, she made a speech to tell everyone that she and her husband had observed strict preparatory rituals for eight moons, had slept in separate beds, and prayed for strength and power.

If her life was rigidly defined, it was to undergo gradual, then abrupt changes as the sea explorers and traders and the land traders came west. The first Europeans seen by coastal Indians were Spaniards who came in 1774 with Juan Perez who had been sent from Mexico to explore the coastline. In 1775, two more Spanish ships came north, then, in 1778, Captain James Cook arrived with his vessels, the *Resolution* and the *Discovery*, staying at Nootka to acquire spars and masts. In his diary of April 19, 1778, he noted:

Having now finished most of our heavy work, I set out the next morning to take a view of the Sound. I first went to the west point, where I found a large village, and before it a very snug harbor. . . . In most of the houses were women at work, making dresses of the plant or bark before mentioned, which they executed in the same manner that New Zealanders manufacture their cloth. Others were occupied in opening sardines. I had seen a large quantity of them brought on shore from canoes, and divided by measure amongst several people, who carried them up to their houses where the operation of curing them by smoke-drying is performed. They hang them on small rods at first, about a foot from the fire, afterward they remove them higher and higher to make room for others, until the rods, on which the fish hang, reach the top of the house. When they are completely dried, they are taken down and packed close in bales, which they cover with mats.

Captain Cook also noted the "bashfulness and modesty" of the women and the Indians' disgust on first tasting liquor. Europeans admired the fine lines of the seaworthy canoes and the superb craftsmanship of the Indians' finely wrought boxes, rattles, and houses.

In the summer of 1787, the *Imperial Eagle* (originally the *Louden*) sailed to the northwest coast, putting down anchor off Nootka Sound. By the time the vessel left the area, she had swept it clean of furs, acquiring many of the 800 sea otter skins that were to be taken to China. Fur was brought to the traders in exchange for iron, brass, copper, rum and blankets. Trading introduced European guns and clothing, augmenting the wealth around which ceremonial life pivoted. Potlatches had been given by chiefs to proclaim a name, to introduce a presumptive heir to a chieftainship; sometimes they included announcements of claims and rights, and some groups, such as the Tlingit, used a potlatch ceremany to announce a chief's death. Newcomers failed to perceive what was behind such ceremonies; those in a group who helped their chief assemble wealth found insurance in their gifts, for they would be cared for in hard times. Europeans could not comprehend that the destruction of property—the burning of blankets, the breaking of a copper— demonstrated both the power and the wealth of a chief. With the approval of some missionaries, the Canadian Government banned the potlatch in 1884, a ban not rescinded until 1951, and ceremonies went underground.

From painting by Paul Kane, Clal-lum woman weaving a basket with another woman spinning at Esquimalt near Victoria.   A

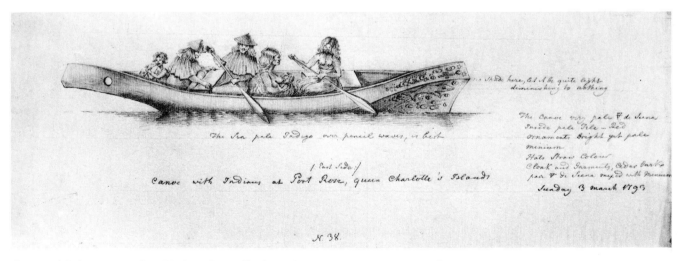

Canoe with Indians at Port Rose Harbor, Queen Charlotte Islands, 1793.   B

Traditionally hunters and gatherers, Indians turned to trapping after European traders arrived. These well-dressed Indians were photographed at Ashcroft.
A

At Cranbrook these St. Eugene Indians proved horse-riding skills in 1902.
C

European clothing replaced traditional clothing worn by Chief Chilliheetza's daughter and her children.
D

European "wasp-waists" influenced this Kamloops' maiden's fashions.
B

Inter-tribal warfare affected population levels, and disease made claims too. Smallpox broke out among the Haidas in the 1780's, according to local histories, and in 1862, when a white miner from San Francisco sailed to Victoria bringing the disease with him, it immediately affected anyone near. The smallpox raced through the encampments of visiting Indians who had come to Fort Victoria to trade furs. The camps were burned in an effort to prevent the disease spreading, but it was too late; the people paddled away, carrying smallpox with them to the mainland and further afield. Journals of the time recorded the situation and cited the numerous dead found in beached canoes, the stiff bodies in tents, the temporary snow graves of Cariboo victims, and the corpses found in pools and lakes where victims had sat trying to slake the fever that raged so wildly through their bodies. Missionaries and doctors carried out some vaccinations, but not enough could be done to save thousands from dying.

Tlingit grave house. Burial methods varied from group to group. A

Federal government land policies concerning Indian territory are complex and still are being clarified today. The policies of the Colonies of Vancouver Island and British Columbia in the era before amalgamation in 1866, and again before Confederation in 1871, were set as settlers arrived to take up land. Some groups, such as the Nass River area Indians maintain an attitude they expressed in 1887, considering that their land was never conquered and still is properly their own. Hunting and fishing rights were given to the native people, but the distribution of reserve lands proved restrictive. In time, the woman going to her bushes in late summer found that a settler now occupied what had been her land. Sometimes when she went for spruce roots, the trees had been felled and the land cleared. Her Indian name was not understood by the impatient newcomers who distributed their own names, so she became Mary, Annie, or Minnie.

Her grandmother's clothes had been made of natural materials, and were replaced whenever necessary. Now her European clothing needed washing, ironing and sewing; nobody thought to show her what was required but she learned to cope. Because she so often cooked over small fires and her face showed the evidence of smoke, ash and heat, she sometimes was described as a "savage" by settlers to whom she sold baskets or berries.

Residence of Chief John Chilliheetza, powerful chief of the Quilchena and Douglas Lake Indian bands in the 1860's. B

Susan Allison, pioneering in Princeton in the 1860's, described the first visit made by an Indian woman who came into her home dressed in mid-Victorian clothing. The Indian obviously had the impression that settlers sat stiffly, their hands clasped, their eyes directed at a certain part of the wall: she, too, attempted to maintain this position. Later, Mrs. Allison realized that she had failed as a hostess and should have served tea. She made up for this later, and befriended the women who came to see her, trading her own butter for their fish.

In the Okanagan, in 1890, Evelyn Blackman unpacked a trousseau that included too many red flannel nightgowns, so she gave a dozen gowns to the Indian women who came to visit; the women wore the gowns when they were riding, the flash of their clothing signalling their arrival everywhere.

Indian families listened to missionaries who preached equality for all, but who allowed segregation to be practiced. In Hazelton, settlers were

Early hospitals and clinics had one door for Indians and one for whites in northern areas; today it's one door for all. Here, Hazelton hospital is visited by local Indians waiting for medical attention.

separated from Indians by a rope slung across the pews of the Anglican church. Northern hospitals and doctors often had two entrances for patients—one for settlers, the other for Indians.

Not all settlers thought of Indians as a race to be set apart, and Indian women were particularly noted and admired for their industry. Jessie Ann Smith, the Scottish immigrant who arrived at Spences Bridge in 1884, wrote that Indian women worked side by side with their men who were building the wooden flumes to irrigate local orchards. The women carried the flume boards on their backs to the mountain side, and collected water from the Thompson River so their men could use it to cool the tools that had to be handled in an area where the temperature often rose to 100 degrees Fahrenheit in the shade. In 1860, the Anglican Bishop Cridge visited the Songhees reserve near Fort Victoria and wrote to England, recording his observations:

. . . the women were making a rope, in other lodges women were making mats, weaving rushes and grass . . . . I was struck with the industrious character of these poor people.

Indian women married to traders often served as interpreters; in small posts they substituted for their husbands while they were away on business and they adapted well to their new way of life. The women married to settlers often intervened to prevent hostility when local Indians and resident settlers failed to understand one another. At L'Anse au Sable, later known as Kelowna, the Indian wives of some settlers saved everyone from starvation by finding sources of food during a lengthy and severe winter in the 1880's. Some proved to be excellent businesswomen as did Tenas Catherine of the Okanagan; when her husband, settler John Lutz died, she made shrewd business negotiations and successfully ran a ranch in the Kettle Valley area. Some women learned new languages: Helene, a Cariboo girl, daughter of the local chief, learned French after her marriage to French-Canadian trapper Joseph Dussault and her daughter Angelique was tri-lingual, speaking her mother's language, as well as fluent French and English. Angelique helped her husband William Lyne to operate a stopping house when he expanded his smithy, and she assisted with the management of the ranch they developed some nine miles south of Soda Creek.

Madame Savona, wife of the ferry owner Francis Savona, a daughter of Joseph Bourke and an Indian woman, was mentioned in the Hudson's Bay Company Kamloops Journal in the 1860's:

December 29, 1860:

Cold weather. Two Indians of Bout du Lac arrived and traded 1 marten, 1 fisher and 2 sm. black bears for ammunition. Mrs. Savonah *(sic)* also paid us a visit. She purchased ½ lb. seed beads at $4.00 per lb.

November 8, 1861:

. . . Thomas, the man who sold the goods to St. Paul arrived. It appears that he is not the man who shot another at Cariboux and reported to have run . . . for life. It was only one of the tricks of the murderer making use of his name in order, more easily to get assistance from Savona's wife to facilitate his escape.

The church with the steeple, a landmark of numerous Indian villages after the missionaries arrived: this is a Tahltan village.　　　　　A

Women's work was never done and moose hide was used to make moccasins, a "rope" and clothing.　　　　　B

Chief William Sopass and family of the Sardis area.　　　　　C

As canneries were built, employers found skilled workers among Indian women.
A

Fraser River cannery.
B

At Alert Bay mending nets and replacing old wooden floats with fiberglass ones is women's work today.
C

Totem poles were raised to celebrate name-giving ceremonies and to mark the death of important people. This is what Masset used to look like; today, Robert Davidson is one of the best known carvers and one of his poles stands near the Haida village church.
D

Going to school often meant leaving family and other relatives for months at a time and not being allowed to speak anything but that new language, English.
E

January 31, 1862:

Dupuie Snr. arrived from Bout du Lac stating that Savona's wife had received some injury from a horse and required the immediate appearance of Madm. Bourke, her mother, to take care and nurse her injury.

Madame Savona was able to operate the ferry, something she must have done well, since she continued to do so for some years after her husband died in the early 1860's. She had a reputation for "driving a hard bargain when ferrying for the Hudson's Bay Company."

Seasonal patterns still dominated lives. Indian women found work in canneries when the fish were running, in orchards when the fruit was ripe for picking, and in fields when flowers were unfolding their petals. With their fish, their berries, and their baskets, they visited the settlers accepting tea, a small amount of cash, or old clothes in exchange for what they offered. In northern areas, their skilled fingers fashioned intricate beadwork and moccasins.

Residential schools separated children from parents for long periods of time. Some schools forbade the children to speak to their friends in their own language during free time; the punishments for breaking this rule were severe. Boys often were trained for an agricultural future—a career which failed to interest many of them; girls were expected to learn domestic skills—to cook, sweep and sew. Being sent away to school was traumatic for children used to the close-knit Indian family life. Josephine Edenshaw, now Josephine Nash of Masset, recalls how hard it was to leave her family. She was sent to Metlakatla, where heavy seas sometimes prevented her family from visiting her. "I missed everyone so much. It was hard." Vitalena Patrick of the Stoney Creek Reserve, tried to hide whenever it was time to be sent away to Le Jaq Residential School. "I cried and cried and cried. No. I did not want to go. They had to have the policeman come to get me."

Reserve schools meant adjustments for teachers, parents, and students. It was difficult for a white teacher to understand that the reserve home was so small and crowded that a student might have problems doing homework on a table she shared with others. Faced with compulsory schooling for her children, a mother might recognize the benefits that education would provide, but she herself had to consider a new way of life. By staying home to make sure the children did go to school, she no longer was able to be a working partner on the trapline; she no longer could go along to cook or to scrape and prepare skins. A man had to evaluate this, too; his frustrations at change often spilled over into family life.

In Indian homes a grandmother was a very important person, giving love and teaching family history as well as telling stories. Usually she knew the full value of herbal medicines. Lillian Collier of Williams Lake recalls that it was her Indian grandmother who would take her to the Riske Creek meadows to collect the bright gold flowers that had healing qualities.

Granny Edenshaw, who had come to her husband's village with several slaves, the measure of her noble status, was known for her weaving abilities. She made cedarbark baskets which could be washed and shaken out. She also made large loosely woven sacks strong enough to carry potatoes from family potato patches.

Fraser Lake Indians cooking berries. Hot stones heated the water.   A

Hot and dry, the sun often raised temperatures to over 100 degrees at this Kamloops reserve in summers.   B

21

Childhood was a good time with games and fun although Josephine remembers working in a cannery, stacking cans, one summer when she was 12. Other children had to sit with stoic patience while their mothers stood beside them, cutting and packing fish. At Stoney Creek, Vitalena Patrick's favorite game was "sliding down the mooseskins. That was what I did."

Teresa Cheeky of the Doig Reserve outside Fort St. John did not go to school. She can recall the bad winter when the family ran out of food when they were on the trapline. They looked for live game desperately. "Nothing. No squirrel, nothing." Starving, they killed one of the packdogs in order to survive. Happier times came later in life when Teresa, well into middle age, was offered a child by another family. She accepted the little girl, then adopted a boy who had known several foster homes. Raising them has been the happiest time of her life, and her eldest child is studying at college now. "I was the mother," she explains. "Yes, same thing as their mother. It was good when they came to me."

Sarah Hindle, lady of many talents, at Hazelton.   A

Hazelton Band Chief Jane Mowatt sees education as an aid to developing self-awareness in bringing people back to pride in the past.   B

Mary Leonard, Band Chief at Kamloops, also has been mother to more than 30 foster children, as well as her own family. She and her husband operate a dude ranch, a project sparked by some of the foster children. "There we were with a houseful of teenagers who didn't know what to do with themselves, so we bought them horses and saddles. So many people came to ask if they could ride that we saw we had a business here." Aggressively concerned for the welfare of the Kamloops Band people, she believes that Indian children should be returned from foster homes outside the reserve to reserve homes. She is campaigning for more jobs for young people and she also wants to continue traditional medicine interests, the herbal medicines in which devil's club and balsam bark were used for specific ailments. Another priority in her interests, besides land claims, is the establishment of a senior citizens' nursing home on the reserve, so that elderly ailing members of the band can remain close to home.

Sarah Hindle of Hazelton is postmistress alongside her postmaster-artist husband, a job she has held for 16 years. As a girl she stayed often with her blind grandmother who told her stories and legends, including her own memories of the last inter-tribal raid in that area. "She remembered that the people had come to visit with their Chief who sat in his canoe with a toy, an umbrella. Everyone went down to see what he had, and they were killed. My great-grandmother ran and ran, then hid in the bushes." Sarah's grandmother also taught her to appreciate the medicinal value of herbs; she found her first work at the Hazelton hospital. Later she became forelady at a cannery. With others, she helped Bruce Rigsby, a University of Mexico linguist, and her son Lonnie, then a student at the University of British Columbia, to compile a *Short Practical Dictionary of the Gitksan Language.*

Jane Mowatt, the young Band Chief at Hazelton, foresees a time when everyone in her area will know not only Gitksan and English, but French as well. A firm advocate of higher education, she believes in opportunity for youth. Youth work is a major interest, one she plans to develop when her two-year term as Band Chief is completed. As Band Chief she directs a female band manager and eight male councillors. When

Old crafts and new ways of using them: Haida designs learned from her ancestors were utilized by Roberta Olson as she did liquid embroidery in her Quamichan Lake home in the 1960's.   *A*

Kitwanga, an old Gitksan village on the Skeena River, and some of tomorrow's citizens.   *B*

Group of Indians in Vancouver early 1900's.   *A*

Events at the commemorative ceremonies of the 'Ksan Village.   *B*

24

the British Columbia Union of Indian Chiefs met to discuss refusal of government funds, Jane Mowatt thought over the matter thoroughly, then decided that funds still were needed in her own area.

"I knew this job would be demanding. When I took it, I found myself thinking of an old legend about a young chief, very young, and he had a lot of spirit power. He used to go to a cave and meditate, then call upon his power. He always knew what to do for his people. One day, he became so self-righteous that he didn't go to the cave, nor did he call upon his power, and along came some people who almost wiped out his village. . . . I've learned that I need the power. Spiritual power."

Jane Mowatt's tutor was a beloved grandfather whom she visited often. He had once owned a packtrain, and when he injured himself in an accident, losing a leg, he calmly fashioned himself a new one made of wood. Her parents lived off the land, with her father supplementing their income by logging. She was in high school when she began to appreciate the full value of her own heritage. When the 'Ksan project was underway, establishing a pre-European Gitksan village with its Fireweed House of Treasures, Today House of the Arts, The Frog House of the Distant Past, and the Wolf House of the Grandfathers, a new surge of pride in heritage threaded through local people. Researching the project, Jane came to new understanding about her own life. "I suddenly realized that I was part of it all." With her carver husband, she has a sense of destiny, a belief that everything is set out for them. "It is all planned." When a woman recently gave a feast in the Band Chief's honor to give her the name Rainwater, Jane accepted it eagerly. "There are times when I feel a different name," she says with quiet humor. "Sometimes I call myself Mud Puddle."

The Frog House in the historic 'Ksan village at Hazelton where Gitksan guides now answer questions from the tourists.

First sawmill at Sooke owned by the John Muir family who with their children and nephew, landed at Fort Victoria in June, 1849, from the sailing ship Harpooner *The men of the family were under a standard three-year company contract to work in mines.*

CHAPTER TWO

THE LONG VOYAGE OUT

December 11, 1848:

The women are all in bed sick except for Marion Smith. John, also the rest of the company are squeemish.

December 14, 1848:

. . . . went on deck and sat in the galley. A fearful squall came on. Frightened me out of my wits almost. I thought the galley was away . . . some would give all they possess to be in Dreyhorn and Daly again. The women are still bedfast. Mother gets a little wine for nourishment. Mrs. Smith got a little today, too.

February 11, 1849:

The women went on deck to air themselves . . . till a fine sea came over our weather bulwark and right on them which sent them downstairs in a fine hurry, wet, but nothing the worse of it.

Andrew Muir's Journal

The Muir family had boarded the *Harpooner* in London, leaving England on December 5, 1848, to sail "Vancouver's Island" via Cape Horn, a voyage that might take anywhere from four to seven months, since sailing times depended on winds and weather. It was six months before the family arrived at Fort Victoria, Vancouver Island, on June 1, 1849, with all the passengers heartily relieved to step on land once more. The Muir men, John and his four sons, were with others who had been hired under a three-year Hudson's Bay Company contract to work in the Fort Rupert mines, Beaver Cove. Travelling with his parents, brothers and sister, Andrew Muir kept a journal, now the property of the Provincial Archives of British Columbia, which gives a glimpse of the women's life on board ship. On Sundays, provided the weather was good, they assembled on deck for prayers. Saturdays usually were set aside for washing clothes. Crises occurred when the beef supplied to passengers proved to be bad. There was a brief mutiny when the crew's cask of beef proved to be bad, too; the sailors refused to reef the sails, complaining that they could not be expected to work long hours without a good meal of meat. New casks were opened and the journey continued. It was three months before the passengers walked on land: on March 22, 1849, everyone ignored the squally weather to turn out on deck from which they looked for the Juan Fernandez Islands, a small group some 400 miles off the coast of Chile.

March 27, 1849:

This is a fine morning after a fine run . . . land appeared ahead of us about 6 oc a.m. a glorious sight when understood it was our promised watering place, the Island on which poor unfortunate Robinson Crusoe was cast . . . . Men, women and children all turned out in a hurry to get once more a sight of land after a lapse of 3 months without such a sight. Breakfast was taken very hurriedly, all in confusion, some preparing the boats, some the water casks, and others passing remarks on the land. About 11 oc a.m. he came quit *(sic)* to it so that we could see the goats running on the side of the hills . . . . We came to anchor in the best bay in it about 100 yards from shore, just as we were entering the bay, we perceived some signs of one or 2 huts and shortly after a boat making for us. They pulled alongside of us and came on board. 4 men, Spaniards, not bad looking chaps very civil, one head one got in talk with me . . . he said there was just 7 of them on the Island . . . 3 of them was married. He gave me a napkin full of peaches to give to the women, and invited me to his hut and said we could get as many peaches as should fill the boat in no time . . . one half of us was to get ashore on pleasure the first day, the other half the 2nd day . . . .

March 31, 1849:

Fine morning, had fresh fish for breakfast. This is another washing day . . . one of the Captain's turkeys went overboard today and was lost . . . . I have got another old hen.

April 1, 1849:

This is a beautiful day again, had worship after breakfast . . . had a fine dinner today of peach tarts. . . .

The lumber market provided income for early settlers such as the Muir family who completed a Hudson's Bay Company Vancouver Island mining contract, then took up land at Sooke; this scene shows lumber-loading from Vanouver's Hastings Mill.

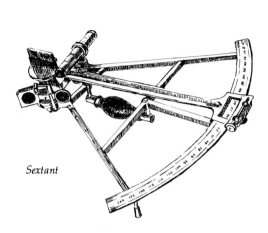

Sextant

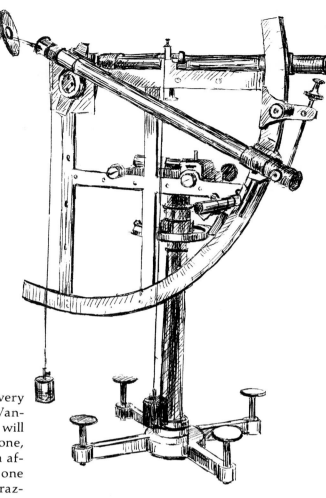

Quadrant

May 2, 1849:

We altogether had a fine mess of Turtle soup which was very nice indeed. We are all beginning to weary now to get to Vancouver's. It is a rare place on board this craft, anything will be made for you if you give a notion of what you want done, such a general shop I never saw. It would be too tedious an affair to mention all the Trades carried. I shall just put down one or two of them. Smiths, Wrights, Tailors, Shoemakers, Braziers, Bookbinders, Shelldressers, etc., etc. . . .

The Muir family served their three-year contract at the company mines, then became settlers, farming at Sooke, Vancouver Island, where they also operated a mill that supplied lumber to Chinese and Japanese markets.

Frances Hornby Trevor Barkley, known to be the first European woman to set foot on the northwest coast after her husband's ship anchored near Friendly Cove off Nootka Sound, saw Vancouver Island in 1789, 60 years before the arrival of the Muir family. Unlike women married to Hudson's Bay Company servants or to independent settlers who came to the island after it was declared a colony in 1849, she sailed to its virtually unknown shores as wife of Captain Charles William Barkley, master of the *Imperial Eagle*, formerly the *Louden*. What her impressions of the momentous event were at the time it happened are unknown for unfortunately she did not keep a journal, neither is there any record from the ship's log, which was surrendered to shipping company officials who wanted to keep the area's rich fur harvest a secret. In her *Reminiscences*, now property of the Provincial Archives of British Columbia, Mrs. Barkley deplores the fact that she did not maintain a daily diary, and noted that she was writing some 50 years after the events. She recalled that her husband, who obtained from the region

Captain James Cook's arrival at Nootka with the ships, Discovery and Resolution .   A

Early views of Greer's Beach (Kitsilano).

30

most of the 800 sea otter skins he took to China, learned key words of the area's Indian language; he also charted local coves, bays, islands, and designated the name "Wickianish Sound" in honor of the chief who seemed to possess great authority there. Mrs. Barkley claimed that Captain John Meares later claimed her husband's discoveries of Barkley Sound, Frances's Island, Hornby Peak, and other areas, as his own. The Strait of Juan de Fuca, named after an early Greek sailor who claimed to have visited the area, was given this name by Captain Barkley, who located it on a clear day. Fog had probably kept it hidden from Captain James Cook when he sailed with the *Discovery* and the *Resolution*, reaching Nootka area in March, 1778.

Mrs. Barkley was a first-class sailor and rarely was ill. She could remember the first voyage she had made as a child, when she left her native Somersetshire to sail from London to Rotterdam with her family and servants on a stormy crossing during which she slept while everyone else was violently ill. On her first voyage with her husband, she recorded that he fell ill with rheumatic fever:

My situation was very critical at that time from the unprincipled intentions of the Chief Mate supported by the Second Mate, who being a Lieutenant in his Majestie's service ought to have had more honor.

Usually, Mrs. Barkley was accompanied by a maid, and she acquired Winee, a Hawaiian girl, on that first journey with her husband. On a later journey made to the northwest coast on board the *Halcyon* in 1792, she travelled with her two children and "two black girls" who were servants. She made the decision to make this journey although she was offered the choice of staying in a bungalow in Bengal, India. When the *Halcyon* left the area:

. . . . on board a small vessel indifferently officered, and worse manned the sailor being chiefly Lascars unused to cold climates or the dangers and difficulties to be anticipated in such an undertaking, with this crew we once more were doomed to circumnavigate the Globe.

Her young daughter Patty fell ill with colic and died at sea. The child's body was put in a leaden box, and kept for a burial at the Dutch settlement on the Island of Celebes, in the Straits of Makassar. Patty was buried "under a grove of cocoa nut trees." As the Dutch colonists would not permit her parents to stay on shore for the burial, they had to watch from the ship's decks.

The few women coming from overseas to the northwest Pacific coast before 1840 were likely to be the wives of missionaries. Jane Beaver, wife of the tempestuous Reverend Herbert Beaver, a chaplain hired in England to take up duties at Fort Vancouver, sailed with him on the *Nereid* on a seven-month voyage from London, arriving in September, 1836. The Fort was the western headquarters for Hudson's Bay Company trade; it was located in the Columbia valley, an area shared by British and American traders until 1846 when the Oregon Treaty, sparked by increasing American settlement, divided the land, leaving Fort Vancouver within American borders. The traders and company laborers mostly had Indian wives: company men did not expect European women to come to an area that was "considered wild," or which lacked "civilized settlement."

Emma Tahourdin Staines, who was to tutor the children at Fort Victoria where her husband, Reverend Robert John Staines, became chaplain, sailed with him and their ten-year-old nephew on the *Columbia*, arriving in March 1849, the year Vancouver Island was declared a colony. Women missionaries arrived in 1858 when gold had been found on the lower reaches of the Fraser River. The first four nuns, teachers and nurses from the Order of Ste. Ann, Lachine, Quebec, sailed down the Atlantic coast, took a train across the Isthmus of Panama, a boat to San Francisco, then sailed on board the *Sea Bird*, along with some 1700 miners, to Fort Victoria where they arrived in June 1858.

Women travelling alone in the sailing ship era were enough of a rarity to pique the interest of fellow passengers. No exception were the two ladies travelling cabin class on the *Ganymede*, which left Gravesend, England, in mid-September, 1832, bound for the Hawaiian Islands. Here they disembarked, leaving other passengers to continue the voyage to Fort Vancouver where the vessel arrived in May, 1833. Dr. William Fraser Tolmie, who gained fame as an agriculturist, physician and educator in the land that became British Columbia, was on board sharing his cramped cabin quarters with "G", the aloof Dr. Grainger. During the long voyage to Fort Vancouver, and later during his days as a physician and trader, Dr. Tolmie maintained a diary, now the property of the Provincial Archives of British Columbia. In the diary he provides answers to some of the questions concerning conditions under which women travelled, sometimes as far afield as the northwest Pacific coast: What did women on board ship do with their time? What about mail? Were cabins comfortable?

Dr. Tolmie recorded that he loaned books by Goldsmith and Shakespeare to a Mrs. Taylor, and described what happened to her as she was reading one day:

Wednesday, March 28, 1833:

While sitting, reading, on the locker close by the window, an immense body of water dashed in the window frame and struck right against her drenching her thoroughly and then inundated the floor of both cabins. Mrs. T. sat motionless as a statue screaming hysterically until G. and I laid her in bed when she trembled violently and continued insensible for some time. Spt. Lavnd: Conf: was administered. She soon recovered and now laughs at her misfortune.

Letter-writing, using the day's quills and bottled ink, took time. Dr. Tolmie mentioned that letters could be mailed in Oahu, from there were sent to England via Mexico, a process that took about three months. Letters could be given to homeward-bound vessels, too.

November 27, 1832:

At Trignometry *(sic)* till 10 when a homeward vessel in sight about an hour's sail from us. Laid aside my book and wrote my father a brief epistle. As we met the vessel at 11, the letter was necessarily short . . . . I shall begin another letter, so as to have it in readiness.

Among problems encountered by all passengers, mildew was hard to avoid, and even the physician's books would mildew if not handled constantly. As he noted on November 12, 1832, the cabins were damp: "the sea has washed the Quarter(deck) several times and has entered

Lumber-loading sailing vessels.   A

General views of New Westminster. "Old Colonial era" before 1871.   B

Edward Langford residence at Colwood, one of the Puget Sound Agricultural Company's farms.   *A*

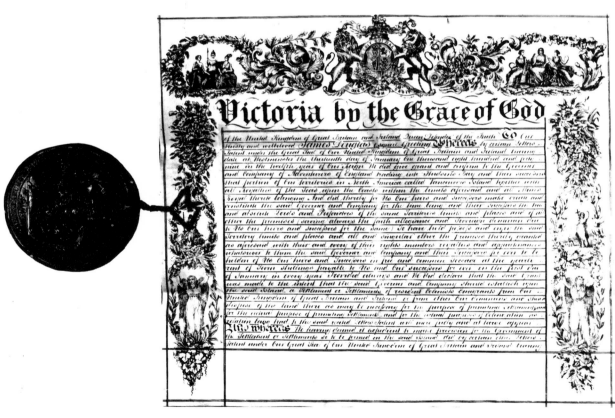

Sir James Douglas' Commission as Governor of Vancouver Island.   *B*

my berth by the floor." The women on board travelled without servants and presumably did a small wash on board. Most boats supplied a set amount of drinking water for passengers; rainwater collected in containers spread out on the deck could be used for washing. A wash could be done also at stop-over ports. At Oahu, the meticulous Dr. Tolmie sent out his laundry to be washed while he visited the women passengers, met their families, then spent some time collecting plants to take to Fort Vancouver. Meanwhile, the *Ganymede's* crew "rounded up hogs, goats, turkies *(sic)*, ducks, fowls, and a bullock."

The physician's journal maintained on board the *Ganymede* showed that weather shaped all events and provided a variety of squalls, gales, and calm periods. The creaking and groaning of timbers, and the violent lurching of the ship meant that it was hard to sleep and almost impossible to walk on deck. When the weather was calm, an abundance of life centred on the ship; pods of whales knifed through the wake that trailed the *Ganymede*; birds wheeled over the masts, and butterflies fluttered around the rigging.

The observant Dr. Tolmie, whose detailed accounts of life aboard ship in that long-gone era so vividly illustrate for today's readers the difficulties passengers then encountered, founded one of British Columbia's most interesting families. His marriage to Jane Work, daughter of John Work and his wife, the former Josette Legace, blended Indian and white heritage; the couple's seventh son, Simon Fraser Tolmie, became a premier of the province, serving from August 7, 1928, to November 15, 1933.

Craigflower Manor in later years. One of the Puget Sound Agricultural farms affiliated with the Hudson's Bay Company. Cooking had to be done on outside ovens until the buildings were completed for the Bailiff and his family and for workmen and their families.

When the *Norman Morison* made the first of three voyages from Gravesend, England, to Vancouver Island in 1850, company surgeon Dr. J. S. Helmcken was on board, bringing with him his canaries and packets of flower seeds. He had to work day and night to keep an outbreak of smallpox under control. The same vessel brought 35 passengers when she arrived in June, 1852; on her third voyage she arrived in January, 1853, with 53 workmen and their families, and Bailiffs Thomas J. Skinner and Kenneth McKenzie, all personnel under contract to The Puget Sound Agricultural Company, a subsidiary of the Hudson's Bay Company. The Skinner group was to operate the Constance Cove Farm while the McKenzie party was to manage the Craigflower Farm. A third bailiff, Captain Edward Edwards Langford, and his wife Flora, had already arrived on the barque *Tory* in May, 1851, bringing with them five daughters and a son, servants, a piano, trunks full of crinolines, a goat and a dog. They were to operate the Colwood Farm.

The ships that followed brought out company employees, settlers, and aspiring miners. Numerous miners sailed from San Francisco, too, leaving the California goldfields for the gold in the lower reaches of the Fraser which had been highly publicized by the English *Times* correspondent, Douglas Fraser, a former member of the Council of Vancouver Island. James Douglas, Chief Factor of the Hudson's Bay Company, who was also Governor of the Colony of Vancouver Island, realized that the influx of immigrants could create problems and wrote to the British Government pointing out the necessity of establishing law and order. Plans were made to send several detachments of the Royal Engineers, who were to serve not just as military personnel, but also were to improve and colonize the mainland area.

Mrs. Richard Clement Moody attended all social events and was used to such entertaining as her husband previously had been Governor of the Falkland Islands.

The 165 noncommissioned men and officers chosen were selected for their character as well as their skills; among them were surveyors, astronomers, draughtsmen, printers, carpenters and tailors. An advance group of surveyors and carpenters was split into two groups, with 20 men under the command of Captain Robert Parsons and 12 under Captain John Marshall Grant. The groups left England in September, 1858, travelled via the Isthmus of Panama, reaching Esquimalt in late October and early November. The main body of engineers, consisting of 118 noncommissioned men, with 31 women and 34 children, sailed on the *Thames City*, leaving England on October 10, 1858, and arriving in Victoria, via Cape Horn, in April, 1859. Colonel Richard Clement Moody, who had served as Governor of the Falkland Islands, was placed in charge of the Royal Engineers and appointed Chief Commissioner of Lands and Works in British Columbia. He and his family arrived on Christmas Day, 1858.

The two advance groups of Royal Engineers arrived just in time to participate in the ceremony for the inauguration of the new Colony of British Columbia. With James Douglas, Governor of the Colony of Vancouver Island, and other officials, they sailed for Fort Langley where the ceremony was held in one of the Fort's large rooms. James Douglas, now appointed Governor of the Colony of British Columbia, retained his position as Governor of the Colony of Vancouver Island but finally severed connections with the Hudson's Bay Company. Newly arrived Matthew Baillie Begbie was named judge. On that rainy day, November 19, 1858, English law was declared, and the exclusive privileges of the Hudson's Bay Company were revoked.

The main body of Engineers, with their wives and children, found that entertainment was provided on board the *Thames City* and a band played for balls and concerts. A printing press on board was used to produce *The Emigrant Soldier's Gazette and Cape Horn Chronicle*, the newspaper that was read aloud each Saturday night, and carried extensive articles on natural history and military intelligence, as well as poetry, puzzles and songs. It recorded two births on the long voyage, as well as the death of Elizabeth, "wife of Sapper George Newton," while the final edition included "A Farewell Ditty" that described conditions on board:

Farewell thick biscuits and thin pea soup,
Farewell the suet, grog, and junk,
One was weak, the other stunk.
Farewell to the hen coop, and lonely duck,
Farewell to Longboat Square and muck,
Farewell to Laundry Lane and Galleys,
We'll cook our grub in glades and valleys....
Farewell to the hammocks, farewell to the clews,
Farewell to the would-be Irish stews,
Farewell to the cockroaches and thieving cats,
And a long farewell to those horrible rats.

On board everyone discussed their plans, printing their aspirations in the newspaper. They expected to build homes and "a grog shop or two, some stores, a Government House, a bank, a church, a burial ground, a hotel, a jetty, and finally a street." They were to achieve all that. As they sailed westward, excitement trailed them like the wake of a ship.

Family of Colonel Richard C. Moody of the Royal Engineers.　　　　　A

COLONIZATION OF VANCOUVER'S ISLAND.

THE grant of Vancouver's Island to the Hudson's Bay Company formed the subject of a very striking debate in the House of Commons on Friday evening, It appears that the Governor having requested of Government the grant of the British territory west of the Rocky Mountains, and specially of Vancouver's Island, lying along its southern coast, the Colonial Secretary has favoured the application, the justification being that " the island in question has not advantage enough to ensure its voluntary colonization, and that if we did not make provision for occupying it in some manner or other, we should probably be anticipated in such proceedings by parties ready to avail themselves of our neglect."

On Friday, Mr. Christy called the attention of Parliament to the proposed grant, which was opposed by Mr. Gladstone, on the ground that investigation, deliberation, and caution were demanded before the confirmation of the charter Mr. Hume was of the same opinion ; but, eventually, the hon. member's motion for an address to the Crown, to stay the grant of the charter, was lost by 58 to 76.

During the debate, the importance of the island as a field for colonisation was geographically illustrated by more than one of the speakers. Mr. Wyld observed that Vancouver's Island stood in a peculiar position : it was the sentinel of the Pacific Ocean. Its local position, with reference to China, Australia, New Zealand, and other important places, made the possession of it a matter of great moment. Its numerous harbours made it also of great value in that part of the world ; and the time, he believed, was not far distant when Vancouver's Island would command the trade with China. Again, its agriculture was by no means to be despised, and it produced spars of the finest quality. Mr. Hume quoted a report from Mr. Douglas, a public officer of the Hudson's Bay Company, which stated there to be an abundance of timber on

Report in "Illustrated London News," August 26, 1848.　　　　　B

Early Victoria after settlers had arrived.　　　　　C

37

There was no entertainment on board the brideship *Tynemouth*, which docked at Esquimalt on September 17, 1862. The greatest attraction aboard, 60 girls described as marriageable, had been kept below deck in a dark portion of the vessel amidship throughout the entire voyage. The women had been brought out to the Colonies by the British Columbia Emigration Society with the aid of funding supplied by Baroness Angela Burdett-Coutts, whose wealth also provided salaries for the Church of England clergymen sent to the new territory. Life for the girls below deck must have been dull. They were supervised constantly by a clergyman and by a matron, Mrs. James Robb. Charles E. Redfern, a passenger on the *Tynemouth*, wrote about the journey, leaving his manuscript to the Provincial Archives of British Columbia. He claimed it was a wonder that the 1500-ton steamer had made the journey at all since the very first night after leaving harbor she had run into a terrible storm; a cow on deck was killed and several live pigs were washed overboard. After the storm passed and the weather cleared, the passengers were surprised to find the steamer was motionless; the coal passers had refused to work and the ship's captain had put them in irons. He gave the travellers a choice: either the men could fuel the engines until the vessel reached the Falkland Islands, or he could return to England there and then. For an entire month, the male passengers filled wheelbarrows with coal, pushing them to the bunkers while another mutiny erupted and more men were put in irons. Fortunately, there were good trade winds in the South Pacific, so steam was shut off and, this time, volunteers were called to man the sails.

Just before the ship sailed into the Falkland Islands, she ran headlong into another violent storm during which the seas washed over her decks, some empty iron tanks in the hold broke loose from their moorings and clattered over stacks of railway rails, striking the ship's side all night long. There were nearly 400 passengers on board, a few travelling as first-class passengers, some as second-class, and a large number sailed as third-class in the fore of the ship. Several women were included in the group of prospective settlers and miners, including sisters Louisa and Charlotte Townsend who planned to teach. They brought along a piano, a sewing machine, and trunks full of fine lingerie, dresses and hats.

All the passengers had been provided with a passenger contract. Contract Number 13, issued to two brothers, Charles Frederick Green and his brother Robert, who eventually took up land at Ladner, is in the Provincial Archives of British Columbia, and points out that in addition to any provisions the passengers themselves took on board, they would be supplied with three quarts of water daily, and a weekly allowance of provisions would be made of the following:

Printing press used by the Royal Engineers who used it to print their Emmigrant Soldiers' Gazette and Cape Horn Chronicle *as they sailed to"the colonies".*

5¼ lb.	Biscuit	½ lb.	Rice
1 lb.	Preserved Meat	1 lb.	Raw Sugar
½ lb.	Soup & Bouilli	1¾ lb.	Tea
1 lb.	Mess Pork	3½ lb.	Coffee
1½ lb.	Indian Beef	6 oz.	butter
½ lb.	Preserved & Salt Fish	2 oz.	Salt
2 lb.	Flour	½ oz.	Mustard
1 lb.	Oatmeal	¼ oz.	Pepper
6 oz.	Suet	1 gill	Vinegar

½ lb. Raisins & Currants	6 oz. Lime Juice
2/3 pint Peas	21 qts. Water
½ lb. Preserved Potato	

When Fresh Beef is issued, 1 lb. to each Adult per day will be allowed; there will be no Flour, Rice, Raisins, Peas, Suet or Vinegar, during the issue of Fresh Meat. 1 lb. of Fresh Potatoes may be substituted for ¼ lb. Preserved Potatoes.

Meals were not prepared for third-class passengers. Their rations were served to a representative from each third-class cabin, and these had to be prepared by the passengers themselves, who then took the food to the galley where the ship's cook did the cooking. The cook also supplied hot water for tea, coffee, or drinking purposes. Any food that required constant attention, such as oatmeal porridge, had to be cooked by the people who would eat it.

The *British Colonist*, noting the arrival of the 60 "marriageable" women described them as if they were freight, writing in an edition in September, 1862:

We are highly pleased with the appearance of the 'invoice' and believe they will give a good account of themselves in whatever station of life they may be called to fill—even if they marry lucky bachelors from the Cariboo.

The newspaper continued to comment on the plans for the women who were to be brought from Esquimalt to Victoria harbor by the gunboat *Forward*. It must have been frightening for the women when they did reach Victoria, where hordes of men jostled against one another to ogle the arrivals. Not surprisingly, a few women became hysterical. Some did not want to leave the gunboat. The Townsend sisters had been smart enough to wear old clothes on board ship which they calmly pushed through the portholes when the *Tynemouth* docked. They arrived in their best clothes. The 60 girls being studied so intently by crowds of men used the laundry buckets and packets of soap that had been placed near the Parliament Buildings. They stood there washing their clothes, trying to ignore the gawking miners, and glad to be standing in fresh air at last.

Eventually they were marched to Christ Church, where the Reverend Mr. Scott exhorted them to remember their religious duties and to shape their conduct so that they might prove a credit to their mothers.

It was not the first nor the last shipment of women to be sent from England to British Columbia. Perhaps the publicity given to the *Tynemouth's* passengers had been too great, for only one year later, when the *Robert Lowe* arrived in January, 1863, the local press paid scant attention to some 36 girls from Manchester, noting only that there had been no deaths on board, and that "these poor, friendless creatures" would be welcomed as servants by local families. Their journey had not been broken anywhere and the ship's captain had gambled on having enough supplies of food and water to last throughout the voyage. There were no parades.

Josette Work with members of her family. When she died, the B.C. Legislature sent a special message of sympathy to her children and grandchildren.

CHAPTER THREE:

THE TRADER TAKES A WIFE

> I have as yet said nothing about my wife . . . . She is not indeed exactly fitted to shine at the head of a nobleman's table, but she suits the sphere she has to move in much better than any toy, in short she is a native to the country.

Charles Ross, Factor of Fort McLoughlin, near Bella Bella, was describing his wife Isabelle—also known as Isabella—in a letter to relatives in Guelph, Ontario, in 1843. Isabella, who claimed Spanish ancestry through her father's lineage and whose mother was Indian, probably could have shone at any nobleman's table, since women of Indian heritage had proved their worth long before. Europeans coming west had noted the adaptability of these women, and had found them strong, industrious, reliable and capable.

Many an explorer owed his very life to their abilities to gum a canoe or to make showshoes. It was the women's work to prepare pemmican, the dried meat that was a major part of provisions for any long distance travel, and without this staple explorers such as Simon Fraser and Alexander Mackenzie might have starved on their arduous explorations of the Pacific northwest. Route-paver and geographer David Thompson had a wife whose father was Canadian-Irish and whose mother was Canadian-Indian. She proved her worth superbly: she and their children accompanied Thompson on some of the most hazardous journeys ever known. Loving and loyal, she stayed with him to the end of his life, when he was so impoverished that he was forced to sell his clothing to others. Finan McDonald and Pierre Legace, who came to the West Coast via the Rocky Mountains, met their wives while they spent a harsh winter with an Indian chief on the coast of what later became Washington State. Both women, who were reputed to be "strong and elastic as steel", later lived with the two traders at various postings in British Columbia.

Traders of the North West Company, and its competitor, the Hudson's Bay Company, soon came to realize the benefits of liaisons with local women: their own Indian people would bring furs and offer them protection when it was necessary. Love and a longing for female companionship accelerated such relationships, too, as an April, 1896, entry in the Calumet Journey, the log maintained by the Hudson's Bay Company settlement near Fort Kamloops, noted:

Dusseau, one of my men, fallen desperately in love with a young Indian woman and intends trying to win her as soon as possible.

Traders Archibald McDonald and Duncan McDouglas lived with women who were sisters, daughters of a northwest coast chief. Dr. John McLoughlin, the stalwart Chief Factor of Fort Vancouver, the prestigious western headquarters of the Hudson's Bay Company trade in the Co-

An old Hudson's Bay Company fur press at Fort St. John. For convenience, furs were pressed into an 80 lb. packhorse load which minimized possible losses when transported across rivers. Even so, horses often lost their footings on narrow mountainous passes. The cross pieces of fur were taken out and the fur positioned after which the bars were replaced and tightened by driving wedges into the peg holes shown.

41

Josette Work, wife of trader John Work. She was the daughter of Pierre Legace and a Nez Pierce Indian woman. No one had taught her how to read or write but she proved to be capable of dealing with anything and everyone; she ran the Hillside farm property in Victoria and entertained V.I.P.'s.   *A*

lumbia Valley, had an Indian wife whom he revered. "Little Yale" at Fort Yale, and numerous other traders, had Indian wives, too. In time, heritage blended: John Work married Josette, Pierre Legace's daughter; Roderick Finlayson, Hudson's Bay Company officer, Dr. William Fraser Tolmie, physician, trader, and agriculturist, and the Honorable Edward G. Prior, Premier of the Province from November, 1902 - June, 1903, and Lieutenant-Governor from December, 1919 - December, 1920, married daughters of the Works.

Even Daniel Harmon, the intense New Englander Nor'Wester trader, who earnestly and successfully planted one of the first gardens in the west at Stuart Lake Fort, had to change his mind after announcing that he did not intend to marry a Canadian-Indian. In his journal dated October 10, 1805, he noted:

This day, a Canadian's daughter, a girl of about fourteen years of age, was offered to me; I have finally concluded to accept her, as it is customary for all gentlemen who remain for any length of time in this part of the world to have a female companion with whom they can pass the time more sociably and agreeably.

He recorded that the acceptance of an offer of a wife was formalized by a presentation of gifts to the bride's father, gifts of a horse, a gun, or rum. Harmon and his wife were considered married after he had given these gifts to his bride's father, an arrangement commonly accepted and one referred to as "the custom of the country." His wife was reputed to have a quiet, even disposition, and she must have been strong, too, for she gave him 14 children. Even so, when he was

The old Company post at Fort George, B.C.   *B*

The Honourable Simon Fraser Tolmie who could claim Indian heritage.   *C*

Interior of Fort Langley. Drawing by E. Mallandain.

preparing to leave New Caledonia to return to his native New England, he wondered if she would be happier left at the fort. Again he changed his mind, reasoning that since they had shared so much, including the sorrow of the death of several of their children, she should accompany him back to his home.

Indian women were used to isolation and could accept a simple life; they were willing to move wherever the men were posted, and they accepted company rulings which forbade men to eat with their wives. They bore their children easily and devoted their time to child-raising. The women sometimes spoke several languages since they often came from other areas, although the Chinook trading language, used by Indian and quickly adopted by traders, proved an effective means of communication, too.

Domestic life inside the forts was not always harmonious, as the Fort Langley Journal noted in March, 1828:

. . . . As late as 10 o'clock last night our eleven women in the Fort created a most unconscionable noise, and 2 couples proceeded to actual blows . . . the heroines, on this occasion, are the enlightened ones imported from the Columbia—'tis impossible to learn the precise cause of their quarrels.

While "Little Yale" was second in command at this post, which had been established by the Hudson's Bay Company in 1827, he was offered a wife whom he soon found out was already married. He dismissed her, but she explained that she was not happy away from him, so he accepted the situation, and her. Women of this post made their men aware of their value, as the fort journal noted:

July 3, 1828;

Our family connections among the Indians here being a subject on which much stress is laid, it behooves us to watch its tendency with the strictest attention to keep these dames under control.

Provisions were a major concern at all posts and this one was no exception:

October 4, 1828:

Trades 10 Beaver skins from two different Indians of this neighborhood—we also have upwards of 300 salmon, at which the women and 4 men have been employed all day . . . hauled from the Lower field, 58 barrels [of potatoes] including eight of the red.

October 25, 1828:

Traded another canoe today and no less than 500 salmon. The women and 5 men cleaning and salting them the whole day.

Forts were rectangular in shape and flanked by bastions. Some consisted of an eight-foot high quadrangle which contained a store and living area for the trader. The palisades usually were made of split cedar logs fastened together with wooden pegs inserted in holes bored through logs. Metal nails were not available until about 1843. Fort Langley had been built with considerable difficulty as local Indians resented the intruders, trying to drive them out by setting fire to nearby woods. Factor McDonald noted:

The Fort is 135 feet by 120 feet with two good bastions and a gallery four feet wide allround. [There is] a building of three compartments for the men, a small log house of two compartments in which the gentlemen themselves now reside, and a store . . . there are two other buildings, one a good dwelling house with an excellent cellar and a spacious garret . . . the other a low building.

At night, the gates of the fort were closed; a watchman patrolled a walkway inside the walls, and a bell signalled the early beginning and end of the working day. It also rang for meals and for special occasions such as a birth or a wedding. In smaller posts, the wife of a company man found herself dealing with numerous situations. She might have to receive a distinguished guest if her husband was absent, she might have to act as interpreter, and sometimes she might have to oversee the trading, giving out axes, rings, combs, knives, and tea in exchange for furs brought to the fort by local Indians.

On one of his periodic inspection trips across the country, George Simpson, the Governor of the Hudson's Bay Company, recorded in his journal that he had been impressed by Isabella Ross, wife of the Fort McLoughlin Factor Charles Ross.

The wife of Mr. Ross of this fort lately displayed great courage. Some Indians, while trading in her husband's absence with her son drew their knives upon the boy. On hearing this, the lady, pike in hand, chased the cowardly rascals from pillar to pillar, till she drove them out of the Fort.

Isabella married Ross in 1822 and bore him nine children. In a letter written to his relatives in 1833, her husband confided that business at

Fort Fraser, one of the company posts of Hudson's Bay Company, with barley field in fore-ground.

A

Southwest corner of the Bastion at Fort Victoria.

B

45

Gossip and snobbery trailed her but towards the end of her life, she reclaimed pride in her past; Amelia Douglas, later Lady Douglas, had married James Douglas when he was a young company clerk in Fort St. James.   A

Amelia Douglas at a happier time in her life, as a grand-mother.   B

46

the small fort took up only a small portion of his time, and was limited to receiving furs and giving goods in exchange. He described the environment:

By way of recreation and change we are frequently shifted from one Fort to another . . . the Fort is situated on the shores of the North Pacific, the country around here is extremely wild and rugged and instead of frost . . . we have almost constant rains for two thirds of the year.

Foreseeing changes in the Columbia-Willamette Valley, the area known as Oregon Country by the fur-traders and their rivals an ever-increasing number of American farmers, Governor Simpson began to consider the establishment of a new Hudson's Bay Company headquarters on Vancouver's Island. John McLoughlin, Chief Factor of Fort Vancouver, sent his second in command, James Douglas, to select the site. In 1843, three years before the signing of the Oregon Treaty, which established the 49th parallel as mainland boundary between British and American territory and left Fort Vancouver in the American sector, the construction of Fort Victoria began. Charles Ross was sent to supervise the building, but was taken ill and died of stomach pains, probably appendicitis, before the fort was completed. By 1846, Fort Victoria had become a busy trading post, but Isabella Ross had missed out on her long-earned role of chatelaine.

This is how a woman posed for the photographer—and Amelia Douglas shows in her eyes what she had endured.

Amelia Connolly, Mrs. James Douglas, became chatelaine of the fort in 1849. She was a quiet woman who, at first glance, seemed ideally suited to a life she probably expected to end in the customary way, spending her last days with her husband near the fort from which he had retired. Her life was different from all expectations, however, and she ended it as Lady Douglas. It was an unusual life in which the sensitive Amelia knew the full ugliness of snobbery, snubs, and gossip.

She was the eldest daughter of Nor'Wester William Connolly and his Canadian-Indian wife, Suzanne Pas-de-Nom. Connolly and his wife, the daughter of a Cree chief, had been married in "the custom of the country" at Rat River House, Manitoba, in 1804. Amelia was named Amelie, a name sometimes changed to Amelia, and more often to 'Nelia. She had reddish-brown hair and grey eyes with a fair skin which prompted the French-Canadian workmen and Cree nursemaids to refer to her as "Little Snowbird." She spoke fluent French and Cree before she learned English. As was customary, Connolly and his family moved from post to post. In 1824, he was Chief Factor of the important Stuart Lake post and in the employ of the Hudson's Bay Company; union between the two rival fur-trading companies had taken place three years earlier.

Fort St. James, at the southern end of Stuart Lake was an important trading post in a territory dotted with lakes and known for its bitterly cruel winters. Myth and fact both proved that local Indians had known periods of starvation when game was scarce and snows were deep. In that harsh and beautiful land, it was possible to grow gardens such as Daniel Harmon, the Nor'Wester, had done when he was stationed on the lake. The provision of supplies was a major concern and when Amelia Connolly's husband, James Douglas, was sent to the fort in 1825, he was put in charge of the salteries, supervising the drying and storage of whitefish and salmon.

Douglas was a serious young man with a rich loyalty to the "Honorable Company." The son of a Scot and a West Indian woman, he was educated in Scotland. He was straight-laced, intelligent, sensible, and extremely earnest in carrying out his duties; he was also human enough to notice the attractiveness of the Factor's daughter Amelia, although her parents suggested the couple wait a little. Amelia was 16 when the couple married in April, 1828. There were no priests in the area and they married "in the custom of the country."

Two months later, Douglas found himself in temporary charge of the fort. Connolly was away on the annual fur round-up, collecting furs to take to Fort Vancouver, company headquarters in the Columbia Valley. On August 6, 1828, Douglas made a brief entry in his journal: "Tumult with the Indians." Those four words were an immense understatement of what had happened, for he had come close to losing his life—and he gained enough insight into handling people that the incident served to sharpen future judgments. He owed his life to Amelia. Numerous versions of what actually happened have been written. Perhaps one of the most reliable accounts is that given by Father Morice, the Oblate missionary who was stationed at Fort St. James until 1885. Even so, there is a gap of many years between the date of the actual event and the retelling of it. What is known is that an Indian who had taken part in the murder of a company official at Fort Langley had come to the northern area. Douglas and his men apprehended the man, and in the resulting scuffle, the Indian was beaten and killed, an action that brought immediate hostile reprisal from the local Indians, who stormed into the fort. Douglas was held at knife-point and threatened with death. It was only the quick-thinking actions of Amelia that saved his life: she and the interpreter's daughter quickly tossed trade goods from the fort. The Indians relented and accepted the goods as retribution for the loss of a life.

Connolly was still away when Douglas received a visit from George Simpson, the Governor of the Company, a man so aware of his own importance that he chose to arrive on horseback with plenty of fanfare— the pipers playing and the cavalry preceded by flagbearers. It was an impressive arrival and, in turn, the Governor himself was impressed for it was on his recommendation that young clerk Douglas was transferred to the Fort Vancouver headquarters in 1830.

Amelia was pregnant when her husband left, and stayed behind to await the birth of her child, a sickly infant who soon died. Then she had to wait until summer when the annual fur brigade made its way south. She described the journey to her grandchildren years later: she was dressed in a broadcloth skirt with buckskin leggings embroidered with porcupine quills and numerous beads. Her long hair was braided, and little bells hung from the harness of her horse. The group had been travelling for three weeks when Amelia's horse lost its footing and slipped into the turbulent waters where the Okanagan and Columbia rivers angrily meet. The horse was swept away with Amelia clinging to the saddle, but they were lucky; a large rock held them briefly, keeping them from being swept into the rapids.

"Tenez-vous, restez-tranquille," ordered the horse-keeper, who instructed the scared woman to throw him the bridle as he came towards her. She had a double rein and did as he asked; soon, the horse-keeper guided horse and rider to the opposite shore. She glanced back

Fort St. James, loading the brigade horses on the Stuart River ferry in 1912.   A

Ready to leave Fort St. James for Fort McLeod in May, 1914. The building to the left was
for fish storage.   B

Old Square-toes, stiff Sir James Douglas who revealed a softer side in his famous letters to his daughter, Martha, to whom he wrote when she was receiving the finishing steps of education in England.

at the furious current and the roaring rapids, then fainted.

The words of her husband's greeting, when they met after the arduous journey, always remained in her mind. He expressed his disappointment at seeing her so sun-tanned—he had been boasting about "Little Snowbird's" fair skin. Perhaps his insecurities stemmed from his own background, for he was believed to have had a Creole mother while his father was a Scot, a situation not regarded favorably by the Europeans who still held mid-Victorian attitudes that maintained that a white skin was superior to any other. Amelia had a friend in the wife of the Chief Factor, Dr. McLoughlin, who also had mixed heritage and was revered by her husband.

If Fort St. James presented a stark, beautiful, but often harsh environment, Fort Vancouver had the appearance of prosperity and safety. With its 20-foot palisade, two inner courts, the acres of tilled land, lush pastureage for sheep and cattle, orchards, a flour mill and a threshing machine, as well as the settlement of some 30 houses where fort employees and their families lived, it represented a haven for the Douglases. Life was pleasant, and in May, 1836, the S.S. *Beaver* made her first appearance. She was the first steamship on the North Pacific coast and had been built to replace the sailing vessels that so often were lost or wrecked in the narrow coastal fjords. *Beaver's* captain made several pleasure excursions along the Columbia River, and the fort women went along as passengers.

All harmony was shattered soon after the arrival of another Beaver. This time, it was the Reverend Herbert Beaver who came with his wife, Jane, and with the trappings of the Church of England, an altar cloth, silver communion chalice, bibles, and even register books for the school the couple expected to run. Courageous as Jane Beaver had been to undertake a seven-month journey under sail, she lacked the ability to change herself. Around her she saw the Chief Factor and his second in command, both with Indian women to whom they had not been married in a church. How shocking! How sacrilegious! She could not rid herself of the mid-Victorian idea that the values of other cultures were not as valid as her own. Soon Beaver discovered that he had located himself "in the stronghold of Popery," and he wrote to company officials in London, expressing his chagrin. He had 60 young students whom he described as "half-bred boys and girls" and he was not allowed to interfere with their Roman Catholic teachings. After the Beavers had made complaints to the Chief Factor, they resorted to personal attack. Jane held herself aloof from the women; Beaver stormed around angrily. Sometimes, the tension between company personnel and the English couple flared into angry shouting matches.

Presumably many of the Beavers' complaints were justified. They complained of "poor living quarters, or working men invading their house at all hours of day and night; of inadequate wine supply; of incompetent servants; too few vegetables and too little fresh fruit, and of mud around their door where pigs were allowed to run." The main contention arose from Beaver's expectations that, as Fort Chaplain, he should be allowed to instruct the children in the Church of England faith, but since most of the fort employees were Roman Catholics, McLoughlin refused to allow this, and took away the school from Beaver. Two women, wives of visiting missionaries, Mrs. Whitman and Mrs. Spalding, were invited to teach instead.

Clucking around like a hen trying to find a chick, Beaver made enough noise to attract fort personnel into considering the "sinful" state of their alliances. In February, 1837, Beaver performed a double wedding, re-marrying James and Amelia Douglas, whose 1828 marriage had been perfectly satisfactory and acceptable until then, and marrying the McLoughlin's youngest daughter, Maria Eloise, to company employee William Rae. McLoughlin refused to consider such a ceremony for himself; he had married his wife both in the custom of the country and, shortly after Beaver's arrival, had had James Douglas officiate at a civil ceremony. Beaver refused to consider either of these marriage ceremonies legal, and wrote to London, referring to Mrs. McLoughlin as a "female of notorious loose character, and kept mistress of the highest personage in your service." This was a cruel and spiteful attack on a woman whom Mrs. Spalding and Mrs. Whitman found perfectly pleasant and hospitable. Beaver's rage was fired by the Factor's refusal to build a church as he was supposed to do.

All this must have been disturbing to the sensitive Amelia Douglas who already had unhappy family news to consider as she had received word of her parents' separation. Her father, William Connolly, who had retired to Montreal where he had introduced his Canadian-Indian wife Suzanne around the city, suddenly ended their marriage. He put Suzanne in the Red River convent, and married Julia Woolrich, the daughter of a wealthy Montreal merchant. It was upsetting news to the young wife and mother, who had other griefs to consider: several of her children had died; her favorite son had died in a freak accident when his father, returning from a trading trip, swept the child into the air, and caught him, with the boy crying out in pain. He died a few days later, probably of a broken neck. More and more, Amelia concentrated her attention on her surviving children.

Fort Victoria was a community of some 200 people when James Douglas arrived to take command in June, 1849. When the Reverend Robert John Staines, his wife, Emma, and their 10-year-old nephew arrived on the *Columbia* in March, 1849, he to take up duties as fort chaplin, and she to teach the fort children, Roderick Finlayson, then in charge of the Fort, noted their arrival with some concern, leaving this description of the community:

At the time there were no streets, the traffic cut up the thorough-fare so that every one had to wear sea boots to wade through the mud and mire. It was my duty to receive the clergyman, which I did, but felt ashamed to see the lady come ashore. We had to lay planks through the mud in order to get them safely to the Fort. They looked around wonderingly at the bare walls of the buildings and expressed deep surprise, stating that the company in England had told them this and that and had promised such and such.

Dr. J. S. Helmcken, the company surgeon hired in London, who had arrived at the fort in 1850, noted that Mrs. Douglas and Mrs. Staines were not friends, "there being too much uppishness about the latter, she being the great woman—the great complaining." If Mrs. Staines was haughty, she also had other qualities that drew praise from the surgeon. She was an excellent teacher, and won the interest of the children at the fort. She spoke several languages, and perhaps it was unfortunate that French was not one of these since that language came

Agnes Douglas who later became Mrs. A. T. Bushby.   A

Jane Douglas, later Mrs. Alexander Grant Dallas. She and the
youngest sister, Martha, both married Victoria men who were
well known. Martha married Dennis Harris.   B

Fort Victoria after it had become part of
a boom-town. A good rainfall made the
'streets' into a sea of mud.   C

Cecilia Douglas whose untrained but beautiful voice was noted by company surgeon John Helmcken when he arrived in the Fort in 1850. She married him later in a ceremony held in the Fort.   B

Alice Douglas (later Mrs. Charles Good).   A

"A Fashionable Wedding," reported the Colonist in March, 1878: "The Reformed Episcopal Church was yesterday densely crowded by a brilliant assemblage of ladies and gentlemen to witness the nuptials of Dennis R. Harris with Martha, youngest daughter of the late Sir James Douglas, K.C.B. . . . . It was the same day that R. B. McMicking, superintendent of the British Columbia telegraph lines received a shipment of telephones. 'Remarkable,' he said, as he told reporters that persons standing fifteen miles apart could hear each other." C

easily to Amelia. In his Reminiscences, now in the files of the Provincial Archives of British Columbia, Dr. Helmcken noted that "Mr. Douglas was coldly affable—but he improved vastly on acquaintance afterwards":

.... at the windows stood a number of young ladies, hidden behind the curtains, looking at the late important arrivals, for visitors were scarce here but we were not introduced. Anyhow before going away, the room of Mr. Douglas partly an office and partly domestic, stood open and there I saw Cecilia his eldest daughter flitting about, active as a little squirrel, and one of the prettiest objects I have ever seen; rather short but with a very pretty graceful figure—of dark complexion and lovely black eyes—petite and nice. She assisted her father in clerical work, correspondence and so forth—in fact, a private secretary.

He noted that Amelia led a quiet life, putting her interest in her children ahead of the social life in the fort and that she was inclined to fuss and be possessive of the children. He described her as an auburn-haired woman of considerable activity, "orderly and very neat and cleanly," adding the Mrs. Douglas always made time to visit anyone who was sick:

She visited them when ill, and in part nursed them . . . and I remember she remained for a long time with Mrs. Yates when her child was born, making her kneel down at the bedside, which Mrs. Yates considered did her a great deal of good.

If Mrs. Staines had neither the time nor the inclination to be friendly, Amelia found good company in Josette Work, the former Josette Legace, who proved to be as "strong and as fine as steel," as her mother reputedly had been. She had a strong sense of friendship, although her husband, trader John Work, seemed wary of the opinion of newcomers since he married her for the third time with the Reverend Robert John Staines officiating at the ceremony. The first ceremony had been the standard "custom of the country" marriage, the second a civil ceremany. Josette was as lively and as intelligent as any woman in the area, but nobody had thought to teach her to read and write English, so she signed her name with an "X" on official records. Her friendship with Amelia Douglas lasted throughout their lives.

Amelia's family increased while she was at the fort; her son James was born in 1851, the year her husband succeeded Richard Blanshard as Governor of the Colony of Vancouver Island. Three years later, in 1854, when she was 42, she gave birth to her last child, a daughter, Martha, who was born in the fashionable Governor's House in the Victoria area known as James Bay. Life also was expanding beyond the fort, which was now a supply store. The Works had taken up property and operated a Victoria farm known as Hillside. Victoria itself was growing steadily, with naval officers giving balls on visiting ships, and horseracing in the Beacon Hill area. Nonetheless, while staples were available from the local stores, anything beyond the ordinary had to be ordered from abroad. James Douglas wrote to England, giving precise details of the clothing he wanted for his family:

.... the following orders for goods on my private account which please forward by the first safe conveyance, insured

The south front of the residence of Sir James Douglas, K.C.B., and Lady Douglas. She and her brother are standing on the veranda.

against the risk of capture and seizure in addition to the ordinary sea risks. Forty yards good black Merino, six pieces assorted Linings for ladies' dresses: four ounces Eau de Cologne: six pieces white muslin for ladies' dresses.

John Work also wrote to England, ordering the latest fashions for the women of his family, for whom he also ordered "surprise parcels" of gold watches.

Amelia Douglas' quiet life received a setback in 1858. By then, gold had been found on the lower reaches of the Fraser River and hundreds of miners, reading of the strikes in reports published by American and English newspapers, began to arrive in Victoria where they bought supplies for their newest venture. James Douglas made his own inspection of the gold area, then advised the British government that, beside the need for some sort of law enforcement, an official declaration should be made that all mineral wealth belonged to the Crown. The British government, following some of his recommendations sent officials to provide "Law and Order." The Royal Engineers were despatched to clear and survey land, and to build a mainland city. On November 19, 1858, in a ceremony conducted in one of the large rooms at Fort Langley, the Colony of British Columbia came into being, with newly arrived Judge Matthew Begbie swearing in James Douglas as its Governor. He retained his Governorship of the Colony of Vancouver Island, but his connections with the Hudson's Bay Company were revoked.

Douglas's public enemy was Amor De Cosmos, a Nova Scotian who had come to Victoria via way of the California goldmines in May, 1858, changing his name enroute from Bill Smith to the name that meant that he was "A Lover of the Universe." He was a great believer in the idea of Confederation, and when he began printing the *British Colonist* in the winter of 1858, he immediately began to attack the Hudson's Bay Company "family compact," saying that colony officers were "filled with toadyism, consanguinity and incompetency." Governor James Douglas made the mistake of trying to suppress the newspaper, an action that brought De Cosmos public support, and fired his enthusiasm for a series of outpourings attacking not only Douglas, but also his wife.

De Cosmos pointed out that Mrs. Moody, wife of Colonel Richard Clement Moody, who had been named Chief Commissioner of Lands and Works in British Columbia after he arrived there to supervise the work of the Royal Engineers, always graced New Westminster social events. In Victoria, Amelia Douglas was conspicuous by her absence at social affairs. In February, 1860, he fired some vicious remarks at the Douglas family, after stating his objections to Douglas' governorship role:

Were a good Indian agent required, over whom could be extended "a reign triumphant", it would not be too difficult to discover a suitable incumbent, qualified by long experience and intimate associations.

When Douglas retired in April, 1864, he was honored at a Victoria banquet which his wife did not attend, although she did go with him to New Westminster where he received equal homage. They both held new titles, for he had recently been knighted. After this, Lady Douglas was seen occasionally at the theatre; she went for rides with the child-

Fort St. James. Donald Tod and children hauling wood.   *A*

Fort St. James—a modern view of the Fort where James Douglas and Amelia Connolly first met in 1825.   *B*

ren, she visited the John Works and the Roderick Finlaysons. Then, in 1867, an abrupt change took place: she no longer appeared outside, and was reported to be "unwell." At that time in Eastern Canada, the higher law courts were considering an appeal from an earlier decision upholding the legality of William Connolly's marriage to Suzanne Pas-de-Nom. Connolly, Amelia's father, had died and with the death of his second wife, Julia Woolrich, John Connolly, Amelia's brother, contested the will, claiming his share of the estate to which his late mother had been entitled. The legitimacy of all the Connolly children came under review, and since so many people could own to similar situations, with marriages made "in the custom of the country" now under scrutiny, the case became a popular topic of conversation.

By 1869, the earlier court decision had been reaffirmed. Connolly's first marriage was considered to be legal, and neither Amelia's legitimacy, nor that of her brother John, could be questioned. Her health improved, she began to receive guests, and she was seen in public once again. When her husband died in 1877, her daughter and son-in-law, Martha and Dennis Harris, came with their children to live with her. She continued to do church work, buying fish and berries from local Indians who beached their canoes at the foot of her garden, giving this food to the poor. Best of all, she gained new pride in her heritage. She told her grandchildren Indian legends, and a Chief of the Songhees Band, who lived in Victoria, was invited to visit her home to tell his stories.

Fort St. James, where Amelia and James Douglas first met, was also the setting where the Traill sisters enjoyed a carefree childhood in the late 1880's. Their father, William Traill, was born in Ontario, the son of the famous settler and writer Catharine Parr Traill, author of *The Backwoods of Canada*, as well as other books. Traill had married Harriet McKay, daughter of a Manitoba trader, who had been educated at a Winnipeg private school, but whose childhood experiences with her family at different forts had taught her how to cope with isolation.

Hudson's Bay Company trading post, Takla Lake, still a fairly isolated area today, trapped by Indians and some whites with hunting and fishing camps in the area.

58

Eighty years later, these sisters retired to the site of a happy childhood at Fort St. James where their mother was "the lady of the Fort," and their father was Factor. Mary Traill on the left, Anne Traill on the right.　　　　A

Victoria Theatre and New Driard Hotel where socially prominent officials took their families to concerts and plays.　　B

Mary and Anne Traill, who live in Victoria today, remember happy days running around the soft beaches that rimmed Stuart Lake. Mary was five when the family of five girls arrived at the fort; the two boys had been sent away to public schools. Two more girls, including Anne, were born during their parents' stay at the post. Registration of the births was made at Quesnelle, as it was known then, and it was from this town that the "packet," the mail, was collected twice a year by the Fort St. James employees. "Occasionally, some trusted person might call at the Quesnelle post and be allowed to bring up the packet," Mary remembers. Clothing was ordered from England, and took months to arrive. Food was local. The fort had a big garden and a chicken pen with a high fence so that no bird would fly into the jaws of dogs belonging to visiting Indians. A major part of the diet was dried salmon, as it always had been at the fort.

Both parents taught the girls whenever they had time to spare. "Kinzie," Mr. McKenzie, a retired company employee, took it upon himself to be their chaperon, taking them for walks and inviting them to the house where he lived with his Indian wife. He had studied medicine for a time in Scotland before joining the company, and acted as 'midwife' when the last two Traill girls were born.

Christmas at the fort during the years from 1889 to 1893 was an experience never to be forgotten. A huge tree decorated with lighted tapers dominated one room; Mrs. Traill made gifts for the women at the fort, sometimes collars or other fancy work, and there were numerous gifts of toys for the children. New Year was a big day too, when local Indians arrived by dog-team to visit all day, and to accept a glass of lime juice.

When their term of duty was over in 1893, the Traill family left as numerous other traders' families had departed—by riverboat.

Rosanna Swanson.
Born at Kamloops, in the year 1862
John Innes
1927

The gift at the end of an arduous four month journey overland, Rosanna (Rose), daughter of Catherine Schubert. Catherine had made one of the most remarkable journeys ever made by a woman when she travelled West in 1862.

CHAPTER FOUR:

SAME COUNTRY, DIFFERENT ARRIVALS

Gold was the lure, pulling people from all over the world. They came by steamer, on horseback and on foot, following various routes that all led to the same goal: Cariboo gold. Those who made the long journey across Canada were aptly named Overlanders. Three small groups already had won the right to that title in 1859, when they trekked across the land, then traversed the Rocky Mountains and the Interior ranges that led them to Kamloops, where they rested briefly before hurrying on to the goldfields.

In June, 1862, the first large expedition of Overlanders, men from many small villages, gathered at various towns in Upper Canada, travelling from there to Fort Garry where a group from St. Paul, Minnesota joined them. Divided into three brigades, one led by the expedition's organizer Thomas McMicking, another by Stephen Redgrave, and the third by Dr. Symington, the contingent anticipated some 60 days of travel. About 200 men, one woman, Catherine Schubert, who was about to make a name for herself in the West's history, and the Schuberts' three children, set off in Red River carts, driving their stock along with them.

When they joined the Overlanders, Irish-born Catherine and her German husband Augustus, had a six-year-old son August, and two other children—Mary Jane, just under three years, and the baby James Anthony, a year and 10 months—both of whom spent much of their time sleeping in baskets slung on either side of a packhorse. The Schuberts were also expecting another child, though they planned to be at their destination before its birth.

It was summer when the travellers started out; they crossed the prairies under a strong and relentless sun, beginning a journey that was to be beset with problems, the first of which was a lack of fresh water; then their thirsty oxen began to stampede. Indian hostilities were feared; each night as the groups fuelled the campfires with dried buffalo dung, the wagons were placed in a protective triangle around the people, with the slats pointing outwards. Before too long, misunderstandings caused the first hired guide to desert the party. There were also good times when the travellers caught fish fresh from the lakes or shot duck in the quiet marshes; some evenings the men brought out fiddles and mouth organs for impromptu concerts. By July, however, there were new concerns as they reached Saskatchewan: torrential rains caused creeks to overflow and rivers flooded the plains. The prairie, that vast flat plate of earth, was transformed into a sea of mud. The carts had to be disassembled and the cattle driven through the rising waters. At times, Catherine was unable to ride a horse through the now raging currents; the men carried her children while she waded in water up to her waist. Hours were spent pulling the cattle from mud in which they were mired, and sometimes the Red River carts were placed end to end to form a bridge across rivers, while the cattle had to be encouraged to ford them by swimming.

Everyone realized the worth of packhorses by the time the group reached Alberta and was nearing Fort Edmonton. There was frantic bargaining with fort employees and nearby settlers to trade oxen for horses and packsacks. The Schuberts halved their belongings by trading part of them; they also sold one of their two cows, purchasing supplies from the fort with the cash. Not far away was St. Ann's Mission where Catherine and the children accepted an invitation to spend the night. The nuns, anxious about the family's future, pleaded with Catherine to stay with them at least until her baby was born, but no amount of persuasion would make her change her plans. There was no way she wanted to split the family, and she expected to be in the goldfields long before the baby's arrival.

Ahead of her were thick woods, marshes, creeks and steep tracks winding through the mountains. Trails had to be blazed through the woods and bush. More time was spent rescuing the cattle from boggy areas. At one river, Catherine had the men tie her youngest child to her back while she swam the horse through icy waters. The new Metis guide, Andre Cardinal, was reliable and competent, but the terrain was harsh. Dismounting from her horse to inch the way up a treacherous, narrow trail that wound around the mountains, Catherine could hear the screams of terrified horses, then their screams reverberating through the canyons as horses lost their footing, and fell over the edge of the precipice. Underfed, overtired, and well behind schedule, the Overlanders finally reached Tete Jaune Cache.

Fraser Canyon.

62

Kamloops Livery Stables, 1917.   *A*

There they bartered goods with local Indians, trading various items for fresh salmon and dried berry cakes. New decisions had to be made: the majority planned to raft down the tumultuous rivers of the Fraser. The Schuberts also considered this, as Catherine was finding the trails difficult, but nobody wanted the responsibility of helping the family raft down the dangerous river. The Schuberts, therefore, made plans to travel with a group of 36 men from Queenston to the North Thompson River, and to winter their 130 head of cattle and horses at Kamloops. They began this lap of the journey on September 2, 1862, three months to the day after they left Fort Garry. At first, the trail was good, but after a few miles they had to hack their way through dense bush and were lucky if they travelled five miles a day. They had no guides with them now, and when they reached the Albreda confluence, the woods thickened still more. A new reality emerged: treacherous as it was, they had to ford the river. There was no way they could transport their livestock across the tumbling, roaring waters, so the faithful horses were turned loose to fend for themselves, while the men set to work slaughtering the oxen and cattle, making pemmican from the meat, and preserving it in fat. Laboriously they also made rafts and canoes. Ropes were fashioned from cowhide.

Kamloops country—the Shuswap Lake area.   *B*

The air was crisp, and there were hints of fall approaching when they launched the rafts and canoes on September 22. The river proved to be as dangerous as any they had encountered, and almost immediately a raft was dashed to pieces, its two occupants left clinging to the rock that precipitated their disaster. One would-be rescuer drowned in the rapids, but eventually the two were pulled from the rock onto a raft. At Hell's Gate, the furiously churning waters defied everyone, and the group was forced to portage for nine miles. A few probably continued on foot for the remaining 140 miles, but the others used their rafts and canoes, swept along by the turbulent river.

It was difficult to keep spirits high; and they were tired and hungry. A neglected potato field near an Indian village, deserted because of smallpox, offered them food. Ignoring unburied corpses, the men began to dig for the food that saved their lives. They reached an Indian settlement near the Kamloops fort when Catherine's labor pains began. An Indian woman who hurried to Catherine's aid brought Rose Schubert into the world.

Catherine Schubert's bravery in fording rivers, wading through swamps, climbing mountain trails, and fording the tumultuous North Thompson River by raft failed to impress Hudson's Bay Company officials. They did not see the birth of a child as significant either, for their journal entry simply stated:

October 11, 1862:

A party of men have come down the North River by Raft, they are from Canada and the States and have come via Red River, Saskatchewan, and Jasper House to Tete Jaune Cache thence to the source of [the] North River and down to this point.

Gold was not the only lure that brought men and women to the new country that would become known as British Columbia; the promise held by vast tracts of land was another great attraction, and many dreamed of carving a home from the wilderness, as did one young couple, the Allisons.

Governor Seymour in New Westminster issued the license, Archdeacon Woods travelled all the way to Hope to perform the ceremony, and on September 18, 1867, Susan Louisa Moir was married to John Fall Allison. The guests included her sister, whose husband, Edgar Dewdney, was to become known for his survey and supervision of the Hope-Princeton Trail; Peter O'Reilly, who was to become the first Gold Commissioner of the Cariboo, as well as a stipendiary magistrate; and the enterprising Mrs. Langvoit, an ingenious woman who had not blanched when her husband revealed that they had neither money nor future. She had calmly used what flour and fat she had left to make pies which she sold to miners at 25¢ a slice, gaining enough security in time to open a small store which she and her husband developed into a large business.

Susan admired women who were strong and adaptable. She herself had known a sheltered, genteel life, pampered by servants on the Colombo, Ceylon plantation where she was born. When her father died, the family moved to England, moving to Canada in the early 1860's when Susan's mother remarried. Now she was going off to the wilds, to the ranch her husband owned in partnership with another man. There was a small store at the Princeton ranch, but in winter all the mountain passes would be closed, and her nearest neighbors then would be the Hudson's Bay Company employees 40 miles down the valley at Keremeos.

The Allisons were accompanied by a pack-train carrying supplies on the three-day journey from Hope to their new home. Susan was introduced to three Indian men who became family friends: Johnny Suzan was the packer who rounded up the horses, mended saddles, and made sure that ropes lashed around the supplies were dry; Yacum Tecum was bell boy and cook, leading the horses; Coqshist was cargodore, who looked after the supplies, distributing them so each animal had a

S.S. "Aberdeen", caught in winter ice.

Gold drew the Overlanders on their journey west, then north. Goal for some was Quesnel, then Barkerville. Here is Quesnel waterfront after most of the gold excitement had died down—1913.   A

Where most prospective miners went first—Victoria—for supplies and where one dollar bills were issued in December, 1859. (Bank of British North America.)   B

Susan Allison who coped so admirably with all those children as well as visiting soldiers.   C

Susan Allison saw the wild flowers still in bloom as she crossed mountain bluffs on her honeymoon ride to her home.   A

Interior spring sunflowers.   B

Gastown, Vancouver, 1886, where others were settling.   C

Lytton, at the junction of the Fraser and Thompson rivers, 57 miles above Yale. Taken by the Maynards in 1884.   D

Those first roads, Great Bluff Thompson River, some 28 miles above Yale.   E

66

fair load, then stowing them under shelter when he removed them from the horses. The packtrain forged ahead, with the bride and groom riding behind. It was dusk when they arrived at the first night's camp. The bride looked around and saw that the tents were already erected and that the campfire was lit. Canvas had been spread on the tent floors and the beds had been made with "mountain feathers"—spruce boughs—with fur robes for coverings. She hurried down to the creek and slowly washed the dust out of her hair. Then she returned to a gourmet meal she never forgot: baked grouse, trout, bacon and bannock "all washed down by cups of delicious tea."

The young couple and their Indian friends left at daybreak in order to get the packtrains over the Skagit Bluff before dark. At noon they took a break to eat lunch, then took the "zigzag," the trail over the mountain, meeting on the way a black settler, Mr. Richardson, who told them he had been removing rocks from the Bluff, clearing it of slides. The bride was in luck, he said, for the wildflowers were still blooming; soon the party came to the wild rhododendrons, their full blossoms matching the colors of the sunset. They ate by the fire that night, but the mosquitoes were hungry too. They were glad to rise early to continue their journey to Princeton.

Susan made a good rancher's wife. She lived in several homes on the property, but after a few years, in 1873, she and her family moved to Sunnyside, a ranch on the shores of Okanagan Lake, sending their 900 head of cattle to feed on the bunch grass of the Similkameen area. She was burned out of one house, and in 1883, the family prepared to return to their property outside Princeton. When William Tecumseh Sherman, the famous Union general in the American Civil War, visited the Allisons' home in 1883, he noted that she seemed to be happy:

Allison's place was a comfortable dwelling with a few outbuildings. In one of the latter was a small store. Allison was at Victoria but his courteous wife received us with hospitality. She was a rosy cheeked woman of about 25, born in Ceylon, and she had 10 children, healthy, handsome urchins which goes to show that the more distant, the difficult of access the place, the more prolific are the human inhabitants.

General Sherman had underestimated Susan's age; she was 38 years old when he met the family, and was to bear four more children. She noted:

The General had obtained leave to pass through B.C. to the coast with an escort. We had plenty of oats that we had bought at Keremeos but no hay. The bunch grass field was flourishing, knee deep in grass as it was August. The new house was not finished and we could not accommodate anyone so when the general came they all camped in the big calfpasture and turned their horses into the field.

She modestly omitted to mention that the American general had been so impressed by the family that he left them a special gift: he gave them his long silver sword with the brass hilt.

The story of Sylvia Stark, who wrote, "I see the hand of God, guiding me through all my troubles, guiding me to the higher life," is different from that of either Catherine Schubert or Susan Allison, although she was no less courageous.

Mrs. Edgar Dewdney, Susan Allison's sister-in-law whose husband won fame for surveying and establishing the Dewdney Trail.

Born in slavery in Clay County, Missouri, in 1839, Sylvia Estes, daughter of slaves Howard and Hannah Estes, was only nine years old when she had to care for one of her master's children. Sick with fever herself at the time, she commented on her situation, saying, "a little sick girl to look after a big child like that. Such things should not be."

Freedom came to the family when Howard Estes obtained a job driving cattle west, going with his owner's permission to purchase his own freedom and that of his family. In California, he found work in the goldfields, and sent back $1,000 which his owner, a Scottish immigrant, claimed. He sent another $1,000, and this, too, was claimed. Hannah's owner, a German immigrant, a baker named Charles Leopold, instigated a court case on Howard Estes' behalf, and while Estes' money was drained by the court cases, it was agreed that he had full rights to purchase his freedom. He remained in California long enough to earn the money which would purchase the freedom of his wife and children, though his wife, Hannah, worried about him, wondering if he would ever return. When her daughter Agnes fell sick, she listened to the little girl recount a dream: father would return wearing a grey suit, with a panama on his head, and a soldier's overcoat on his arm. Agnes died before she saw her dream fulfilled, but a year later Howard Estes arrived, dressed in the clothing his daughter so accurately had described.

Freedom meant that the family was able to purchase about 40 acres of land in Clay County, but it was a short-lived experience. The Ku Klux Klan visited a neighbor, threatening to kill him if he did not move out. The Howard Estes family decided that they would not await trouble, so when Charles Leopold, Hannah's former owner, told them he was taking livestock across the plains to California, Howard willingly accepted a job as herder; Hannah was hired as a cook. In April, 1851, they began the long trek that was to take six months, less three days.

Sylvia, then aged 12, never forgot the ride, and described it in detail to descendents who live on Salt Spring Island today. She remembered the herds of buffalo that stampeded ahead of the wagons, the night that an Indian arrowhead shot into camp, an incident that meant a hasty departure one early morning, with Indians in pursuit whooping and hollering to scare the cattle, which were too bone-tired to plod anywhere. Flour, other provisions, and some horses appeased the Indians. The wagon moved forward, with the travellers constantly searching for sources of fresh water, but the creeks often were full of cattle carcases. Sylvia never forgot the sight of pregnant ewes which were abandoned to the wolves because they could not keep up with the other stock.

Howard Estes once again found work in the goldfields when the family arrived in California in September, 1851. The free mining population was opposed to slavery, and had their own trade union. Others, fearing that wages would be lowered if newcomers accepted minimum amounts of pay for their work, helped spark the 1850 legislation that proclaimed no black, mulatto, or Indian person should be permitted to give evidence against a white man. Seven years later, Negro children were barred from public schools, and attempts were made to prohibit Negro immigration into California.

Sylvia Stark who began life as a slave and ended it as a respected member of a Canadian community. Her favorite book was the bible but it took some years before she found that "good land flowing with milk and honey." She died on Salt Spring Island where some of her descendents still live today.

Vesuvius Bay where early pioneers were taken by Indian canoe from schooners to beach.

Although life in California had been pleasant enough until hostilities towards the blacks increased, Negroes there faced their future with uncertainty. About this time, Governor James Douglas made it known that any Negro immigrants to the colony would be welcomed, and that they would have the same right to purchase land as other immigrants. The Estes, along with their daughter Sylvia, who was now married to Louis Stark, mulatto son of a slave owner, joined the Negro exodus from California, and headed north to Vancouver Island.

Sylvia, her two small children, and her mother stayed on the Saanich Peninsula, while the men cleared land on nearby Salt Spring Island, where a group of Negro settlers already had begun to found a community. When the Stark cabin was near completion, with a quilt hanging over the space left for a door, Louis returned to the Peninsula for his wife, and for the cattle he had brought from the United States. Sylvia's first view of the island was from the decks of the schooner *Black Diamond*. Disembarkation was achieved with care: Sylvia, pregnant for a third time, climbed down the ship's swaying rope ladder, and sat patiently in the waiting Indian canoe until she was joined by her husband, the two children, and Mr. McCauley, a Hudson's Bay Company employee. The family belongings were piled into a second canoe, handled by an Indian woman from Kuper Island, and the Starks' cattle, which had been lowered from the ship into the water, swam ashore. As soon as the family reached land, Louis hurried off to get help from the settlement, so that Starks' possessions could be carried to their property, about two miles from Vesuvius.

Sylvia sat looking around her. It must have seemed like a paradise, with the orange-barked arbutus trees leaning limply from the steep cliffs, the dark green of the fir trees, the tangle of salal and Oregon grape, and the bay itself, cool and as calm as a piece of jade green silk. Suddenly the two Indians who had handled the canoes stiffened. The woman stood up, pushing her canoe further down the beach, and hiding behind some bushes. Sylvia watched while seven large canoes manned by northern Indians, and loaded with furs, came into sight. The canoes were beached, and the occupants hurried out, looking over the belongings on the sand, while their leader drew out a knife which he held against McCauley's throat. Sylvia noticed that the Kuper Island woman was paddling quietly away towards her home. She looked at McCauley who had turned very pale when the Indians asked him if he was afraid. He shook his head, forcing a smile. Sylvia held her children close, and began to pray: "Please God, do not let them kill my children. Let them be safe. And what would happen to the children if anything happened to me?"

The local Indian pilot sat by his canoe, not daring to look at the intruders. Then Sylvia heard the men offer to carry the goods to their property, and McCauley's explanation that Louis Stark already had gone for help. The men left, and Sylvia sat wondering what life would be like.

The land was benevolent, although life was not easy. The local Indians, who had used the island as a summer camping ground for years, naturally did not want settlers there, so they harrassed both black and white pioneers. When Ebenezer Robson, the Wesleyan Methodist, visited the Starks in 1861, he noted that they had a good farm, with wheat, huge turnips, and more:

Quiet Gulf Island scene.

His wife, who was converted about 2 months ago filled my sacks with good things—4 lbs. fine fresh butter, 2 qt. bottles new milk; Mr. Stark gave me some of his large turnips.

As time went on, Indian hostilities intensified, and Louis decided to try the advantages of another area, so the family moved to Extension, near Nanaimo, on Vancouver Island. There, Louis was found one day, his body broken and propped at the foot of a cliff. A court case produced no evidence of foul play, although family descendents on Salt Spring Island today claim they have evidence to prove that he was murdered. Willis, the Starks' son, returned to farm on the island, where his widowed mother joined him.

Sylvia lived to the age of 105. She was a deeply religious person and considered that a religious power had shone through her life, guiding her through all her troubles. She helped bring numerous Salt Spring Island children into the world, working as a volunteer midwife and nurse at times. If she had begun her life in the full degradation of slavery, she ended it in the glowing respect and affection of others.

Quiet farm scene, Fulford, Salt Spring Island, 1960's.

Mayne Island, B.C.

Galiano Island.

The John Fall Allison residence, the first home was a shack down the river. His bride's first home was built for her but the house burned down in 1881. The next house was washed away in a flood before these buildings were constructed. Susan liked the area, just outside Princeton.

A

Camping out while the Esquimalt was being built. Left to right (adults) Winifred Grey, Miss Barton, Isabel, Mabel and Edith Fenwick. 1910.

B

At John Miller's stopping place on Pemberton Trail, August, 1911, Mile 34½ on the railway from Squamish. Mrs. Alex Philip who built Rainbow Lodge to extreme right, beside Miller, with Charles Barbour of Pemberton in rear and a land - seeker, bound for Pemberton on foot.

C

CHAPTER FIVE: HOMEMAKING

Settlers, for whatever reasons they journeyed to the land that became British Columbia, were faced with situations requiring enormous adjustments. The relatives and friends who might have helped in the process often had been left behind in Britain and Europe; beloved possessions, once a part of life elsewhere, were now thousands of miles away. The creation of a warm, pleasant atmosphere to sustain the family was of utmost importance, and courageous homemakers used whatever was handy to achieve success.

It was almost snowfly when Susan Allison arrived in Princeton in the 1860's. Her husband and his partner just had time to drive their cattle to the New Westminster market before the mountain passes were snowed in. As for the town itself, which had the thriving appearance of a settled community, the new arrival soon discovered that most of the cabins were empty. The inhabitants had been drawn away by those two strong magnets, Cariboo and Rock Creek gold. Alone in her new house, she began to unpack her belongings, wondering what she could do to turn the place into a home. In a series of recollections written for mainland newspapers in the 1920's, Susan recalled:

When I looked around the bedroom, I thought it would look better with a toilet table. There was a plain wooden table about three feet long and two feet wide standing under one of the windows. I found some pink stuff and covered the table with that, over the pink I gathered a white muslin skirt and threw a white dimity cover on top. This, with a fairly good mirror, made a beautiful table. The room was papered already so I hung my pictures on the wall. When my husband returned he was delighted with the changes I had effected.

The kitchen in Point Ellice House Museum, Victoria, home of Peter O'Reilly and his family in early days.

She spent most of the long winter inside the house, while her husband, John, did some outside chores and ran the small trapline that stretched around the ranch. Susan did not mind the long winter evenings, nor the silence and loneliness: the Indians had left for the season and the nearest neighbors were snowed in some 40 miles down the valley at Keremeos. She read a lot and she helped her husband make furniture. They used lumber left from the construction of the house and the wooden sides of teachests, from which they made chairs, a rocker, a desk, and a bureau. Susan made padding for seats. Some of the lumber had rough surfaces which she smoothed by sticking over them wrapping paper, using a glue she had made by boiling cows' feet and deer hooves: a final coat of varnish completed the work. It was home now, no longer just a house. She was a little better off than most women who went pioneering in the wilds: she and her husband had some money, and the land was cleared. Still, she did what other settlers were learning to do: she made use of whatever happened to be available. Every pioneering woman knew all about that.

Pioneering women in rural areas had to be able to sew, quilt, make soap, bake bread, churn butter, pluck and draw chickens, preserve meat, put down fruit, and care for the sick. They did outside chores

when their husbands were away—and the men were sometimes absent for long periods of time, cutting hay, working on the roads, making railway ties, all for that rare commodity, *cash*. The cash was exchanged for the yearly or semi-annual purchase of staples, for the flour, tea, and sugar that no woman could produce magically. In parts of the Peace River District, where roads often were a series of bogholes, roots and stumps, some money was obtained from selling produce to the trappers who came by in spring and fall. Cash was so scarce at Little Prairie that the postmaster there accepted weasel and squirrel pelts in exchange for stamps.

Berry picking was considered the work of women and children. There were plenty of berries: blackberries, huckleberries, salmonberries, blueberries, saskatoons, and those sweet succulent strawberries that dotted the mossy slopes. Indian women showed settlers the value of other berries such as the fruit of salal and Oregon grape. Buckets and lard pails made good berry containers, and it was pleasant work, even if numerous mothers did have a scare the first time they faced a bear on the other side of the bushes. Women made enough jam to last the family through the winter, and finding containers took some ingenuity until glass jars were available, and even after that, because some people lacked the money for such luxuries.

"We used whisky bottles," recalls Granny Peterson of Ruby Lake, north of Prince George. She was Mabel McLarty back in 1911 when the family pioneered in the log cabin at Fort George. "My father would go to the local hotels and saloon and ask for all the empty whisky bottles. We had to sterilize them just as they were for sauces and ketchups. To make the containers for jam, we tied a string around the bottom of the neck of each bottle, dipped that in coal oil and set it alight, then plunged the bottle into a pail of cold water. Usually, the neck snapped off neatly."

Sealing jams and preserves was another task; settlers could use the hard, glutinous substance in which store-bought bacon was preserved. "It was so hard you had to chip it off, then melt it down," remembers Florrie Evans of Vanderhoof. "We used pieces of cloth, cheesecloth or paper to cover the jars."

Dried fruit could be purchased from the store, although some women dried their own fruit, slicing pears and apples, leaving them in the sun, then in the oven, until they were dried. Meat was salted, then weighted down in huge crocks or 45-gallon barrels. In the Cariboo, settlers built ice-houses, wooden structures with numerous shelves supporting chunks of ice from lakes or rivers. In spring, the meat would be taken to a home-made smokehouse. Beef was a precious gift. Venison and bear meat made good roasts. As the land was cleared in northern areas, the moose came inland, so another food source became available. Fowl—partridge, grouse, and duck—were canned, too. People fortunate enough to own a cow sometimes canned extra supplies of butter.

Susan Allison learned to go one step further: she stored butter in barrels and sold it whenever she could. She traded the butter for fish brought to her by local Indian women. When she had a spare barrel, she used the butter with other scraps of fat which had been saved, and made soap.

Pioneer women who didn't know how to make butter, and who had no neighbor to teach them could rely on ancient cookbooks. Sometimes, provided all the newspapers had not been used for house insulation or for leg-wrapping to ward off blackfly and mosquito bites, a recipe, then described as a "receipt" might be wedged between news. In February, 1860, the *British Colonist* blithely advised its readers to make butter *without* a churn:

After straining the milk, set it away for about twelve hours, for the cream to rise. (Milk dishes ought to have good strong handles to lift them by.) After standing as above, set the milk without disturbing it, on the stove, let it remain until you observe the coating of cream on the surface assume a wrinkled appearance, but be careful it does not boil, as should this be the case, the cream will mix with the milk and cannot again be collected. Now set it away till quite cold, and then skim off the cream, mixing it with as little milk as possible. When sufficient cream is collected proceed to make it into butter as follows: Take a wooden bowl or any suitable vessel, and having first scalded and then rinsed it with cold spring water, place the cream into it. Now let the operator hold his hand in water as hot as can be borne for a few seconds, then plunge it into cold water for about a minute, and at once commence to agitate the cream by a gentle circular motion. In five minutes, or less, the butter will have come, when, of course, it must be washed and salted according to taste, and our correspondent guarantees that no better butter can be made by the best churn invented.

Early sewing machine.

Settlers often poured milk into a series of pans and covered them with cloths. The cream would rise to the top of the milk where it could be skimmed off. Any unused cream that wasn't mixed with morning cereals, or given to the new calves, could be made into butter. The sweetness of the butter varied, depending on what the cows had been chewing out there in the meadow. Milk might be tainted if the cows had been in a patch of seasonal weeds, or had munched some wild onion. Settlers who allowed their cattle to graze freely had to know the territory well themselves. When the Wilkin family moved to Lake Cowichan from Saskatchewan in the 1920's with a prize herd of Holsteins, they overlooked the poisonous qualities of the wild lupin that had spread in one corner of the field; one by one, the entire herd died.

Some housewives kept hops in a crock to provide a ready supply of yeast, and potato "starter" was also used a lot, while packages of dry yeast cake could be purchased at the store. Making bread was a lengthy business as the dough had to be left to rise overnight. Many a woman, new to that fine art of bread-making, quickly hid the failure of dough that refused to rise, only to have one of the children take her to see the failure later when it had the appearance of a huge mushroom suddenly dominating the compost pile, or had dared to rise in ostentatious splendor in the dirt behind the barn. Some people ground flour, putting wheat through a small coffee grinder, or crushing it between two large rocks.

Soapmaking was another new venture for most women; it could mean an all-day production with varying dramatics. Some women made soap from bear fat, but usually all scraps of any fat had been collected for

Without wood and handhewn logs, a farmer wouldn't have been able to shelter his cattle. This old barn is in Fort Steele, B.C. A

When a cabin fell in ruins, this is what was left in the Duncan, Vancouver Island area. The newspapers were dated late 1800's. B

the occasion. The lye came from wood ashes which had been placed in a wooden barrel with three holes in the bottom. This container was set over the wash boiler; water was poured on top of the ashes, and the liquid which seeped into the boiler was pure lye. Boiled with scraps of fat, it produced a lumpy but commendable soap.

Pioneer women usually had a large wash, not because their families were dirtier than anyone else's, but because they probably had a large family. Fertility was linked to land production and a sign of success in early days. All that grubbing around, digging out stumps, cleaning barns, and making brush fences, meant that clothes needed more than one good scrub. They could be washed in a large boiler, a huge utensil that was put directly onto the stove; more frequently, however, water was heated in many small containers, then poured into a family wash-tub where clothes were scrubbed on a tin or wooden washboard. Later, those new-fangled contraptions, washboards made of ridged glass could be purchased. Some of them were taken to the Gulf Islands by "drummers," or travelling salesmen, at the turn of the century; pioneer Winifred Grey told her children that it was a difficult place for a salesman to insist he had only one of the latest washboards and butter churns left to sell—after all, pioneers could watch him as he hurried over to the neighboring farm.

Wash tub night invited individual family dramatics when the more portly family members tried to squeeze into the tub, knees right under elbows, hands close to toes. If it was a nippy winter night, when the tub was placed right beside the woodstove, you had to check to see nobody fell asleep, or they would be roasted on one side, for there wasn't room to turn around.

Settlers were fortunate if they had their own well to give them clear water, or if they had a stream or creek snaking through their property. Others collected rainwater from the roof, letting it drip into large wooden barrels. It made the skin soft, so grandmothers claimed, and it gave a woman's hair a musty, attractive smell, as if she had been stretched out in a meadow all day. Cedar roots in woodland areas gave washwater a rusty hue and stained clothes. Sometimes, obtaining water involved a journey, as it did for some Sunrise mothers in the Peace River District; they tied syrup cans to the saddles of their horses, and led them a couple of miles to the river, then back home. In winter, in northern areas, a hole had to be chopped in ice for water, or snow could be thawed. Snow could also be used as a refrigerator, and sometimes a well helped to prolong the life of durable produce, such as butter or eggs, which could be suspended in a bucket over the cool water during warm spells in spring and summer.

"I used to carry water from the creek in old coal oil cans that had handles made of bailing wire," recalls Florrie Evans, who pioneered in the Nechako Valley area. Her wash was done in a large boiler on the stove. At Milne's Landing, where she and her husband spent 1913 as employees of the ferry operator, they met a man trailing a blanket behind a boat. "He said he wanted to surprise his wife, and he towed that blanket down the river to wash it—it was a white Hudson's Bay blanket, too. It must have been a surprise all right—by the time he was through, all he had was a bit of wool ruined by mud and silt."

Coal oil succeeded candlelight, which was hard on the eyes but which lent a soft and pleasant glow to interiors. Candles, made in small tin

Florrie Evans arrived in the Vanderhoof area and went further east to pre-empt her own homestead in 1911.

moulds from tallow, to which a wick was added, lit the way to bed, or to the outhouse at night. Barn lanterns, made of perforated tin which enclosed a candle, threw strange frescoes on walls. An even more basic lighting system could be improvised by putting grease into a saucer and setting a small wick into the centre. Coal oil could be bought at the store, usually in two five-gallon cans which were packed in one sturdy box, a double blessing as the box could be used as a child's seat or as kindling. The coal oil can had a tap and a spout at one corner so lamps could be filled easily. With one end removed, and a wooden or wire handle inserted, the can became a useful pail for berries, animal feed, or water. It could be cut down the middle of one side, and rolled up at the ends to become a tiny baby or foot bath, perhaps even a cooking vessel. Several pieces could be overlapped to make a drain; single pieces would fix a leak in the roof, and some settlers, usually those considered eccentric, sometimes constructed cabins of wood and pieces of coal-oil cans. Cat-tail rushes, dipped in coal-oil and lighted, provided instant lanterns for the guests of one Gulf Islander so that they could safely follow a dark woods trail to their home.

Woodstoves, which had a gargantuan appetite for fuel, usually were the only heat source in the home, besides being used as cooking ovens. A husband often started the fire early in the morning, so the house would be warm when his wife and children arose. In families, it was usually the children who had the responsibility of keeping the kindling box filled with the bark and woodchips used as fire starters. Learning which chips were best was a traumatic experience for Jane Wilkin, who spent part of her childhood at Lake Cowichan in the 1920's; it was her turn to keep the fire burning when the midwife tending her mother shouted that she needed plenty of hot water. "All night long I worried, wondering if I had put the right chips on the fire."

The kitchen or food box became standard equipment for Indian families, who took them on seasonal jobs in the 1920's. Vitalena Patrick, of Stoney Creek Reserve near Vanderhoof, used to pack the box with all the staples—flour, sugar and tea—that would supplement fresh game and fish. She helped cut railroad ties, working side by side with her husband. She cooked on an open, outdoor fire, and her kitchen box was kept inside the tent.

Settlers frequently lived in a tent for a while, and often used one while they were travelling. They would follow the trail as far as it led, then obtain wagons and tents as the Reid, Gilbert, and Armishaw families did, leaving Vancouver for Ashcroft, then taking wagons to the land they pre-empted near Chilco in 1913. It was almost three weeks before their journey was completed, and they enjoyed it all. Cans filled with pebbles were tied around the children's necks, so they could be heard if they wandered off into the bush. Game and fish supplemented their diet. The women took advantage of an empty miner's cottage to heat water which they then used for baths, laughing at the thought of the man's face if he chose to return at that moment.

Pioneers' homes usually were log houses chinked with moss. The floor might be made of poles neatly levelled by an adze. Cloth or paper, and sometimes deerskin, hung over the windows at night until glass was available and could be afforded.

Our house was about 20 by 24 feet, and we lived in a tent while

Of course, Granny had to ride—and this horseshoe became part of the tree that grew around it in Victoria Cedar Hill area.

Knowlton and Lawrence Reid and Eric Armishaw with young chicken hawks. At the Chilco homestead, 1913.   A

Homestead near Goodlow, outside Fort St. John, Peace River District.   B

The end of the Journey but the beginning of work: Jim, Lyle and Jessie Gilbert, Eric and Joe Armishaw with birds; Margaret and Olney Reid with Leona Gilbert in front; Knowlton Reid sitting.   C

81

David, Blanche, Sadie and Barnett Dopp with their horses in 1926 and outside their home at Bear Flat, Peace River District in 1934. Sadie was postmistress and the only local telephone was in her home; when urgent messages came, family members would help her deliver them, sometimes as far as twenty-two miles—by horseback. It was 1922 when the family heard their first gramophone and in 1926, young brother David and Blanche would walk three miles in 20 below weather to hear the radio, using earphones at a friend's house. Blanche remembers good memories were made of "simple things such as bird songs in the morning, and a frothy pail of fresh milk."
A

Sybil de Bucy, Queen Charlotte City, holds up her tray cloth made from a linen Fisheries Department notice used in the thirties. Sometimes it covers her bread today.
B

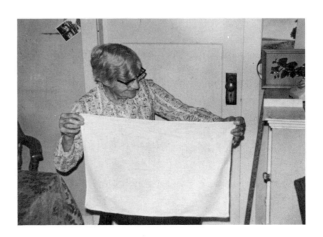

it was built. We were still in the tent in September when the snow came, so our shoes were ruined, and we slept several days just sitting on the beds. There wasn't much lumber available, and Dad had never learned the art of whipsawing lumber, so we had a hay floor," recalls Mrs. Hipkiss of Fort St. John, remembering her family's pioneering days at Bear Flat, Peace River Country. "Mom would sprinkle down the hay from time to time, and take out the trampled hay, which Dad would replace with fresh hay. It smelled so nice. It was the perfect setting for the first Christmas tree I ever saw."

Blankets were a necessity, and usually flannelette sheets were used. Mattresses could be made from cotton ticking filled with hay, goose or duck down. "Slough hay was best," in the opinion of Florrie Evans. "It smelled so sweet." Mosquitoes and blackflies plagued everyone and everything night and day in some northern areas. "You had to have cheesecloth," Florrie says. "I draped it around the bed. And long skirts didn't stop those mosquitoes from biting. We wrapped newspapers inside stockings." In northern areas, smudge pots had to be made for the cows, and cotton flaps protected the horses' ears from the plague of insects.

Early irons were heated on the stove.

In the thirties, flour sacks saved homesteaders from nudity when they were poor—and, during that era, most people lacked ready cash. There usually was enough to buy essentials, such as flour, and the sacks in which the flour came were used in every imaginable way: children's clothes, patches for coveralls, often so many of them that it was hard to tell where the material stopped and the patches began, table cloths, sheets, and tea towels were fashioned from the sacks. Viola Wood of Queen Charlotte Islands recalls that she made most of her trousseau from them. "Lots of people did. I think the sacks were from Five Roses Flour." Fishing notices, outlining fishing regulations and restrictions, were not wasted either. Sybil de Bucy, who pioneered in the Queen Charlottes during the Depression, still has one fishing notice she used years ago. Washed a few times, and pressed, then embroidered, it became a traycloth she still uses today.

Catalogue shopping was popular if cash was available, and sitting under the shade of the apple tree, or in the privacy of the outhouse, if that was the only time available, women could study all the latest fashions in the store catalogue. Shoes, a wedding suit for a man, and bolts of material came from city stores. Sometimes orders were mixed, as young Violet Shaver of Barriere found out when she wrote to the Robert Simpson Company in Regina in the twenties:

Violet Shaver, Barriere district, liked to study the department store catalogues. Here are the boots that the Robert Simpson Company, Regina, advertised in the 1920's.

On receiving my order today, I found it unsatisfactory. In the order I sent you, I ordered a yd. of white which I received, also 3 yds. of blue and only received one yet. So instead of sending me the remaining two yds. of blue please send me 3 yds. of the same kind of cloth but sending me the color helio. The 1 yd. of blue you sent is of absolutely no use to me as I wanted it to be for a whole dress.

Freight costs had to be considered when women made out an order. There was no point in ordering anything if the nearest railroad station was miles away.

Nobody wasted anything. Old clothing became a quilt, or could be braided into floor mats. Until mills operated in local areas, settlers cut trees and whipsawed their own lumber; boxes provided the wood for shelves. Some concerns and duties of women did not change over a 100-year period, as the extracts from the diary of Martha Beeton Cheney, who pioneered at Metchosin, some 20 miles from Victoria, with relatives Thomas and Anne Blinkhorn, in the 1850's, show when they are compared with those of Nancy Hoff, who pioneered in the 1950's with her husband Dunning, and their children at Chief Lake, 30 miles northwest of Prince George:

That all-important household necessity, the family stove where sad irons were warmed, father bathed in the tub near it, and mother hovered around it much of the time, all the children magically reappeared when the bread was ready. This stove is at Point Ellice House, Victoria.   A

Life often was a communal one among Doukhobor families with mothers teaching daughters crafts. Here a young weaver demonstrates her skills at Brilliant Museum.   B

October 29, 1853:

Aunt still at Mrs. Langfords. I had to churn and make butter all the day.

November 21, 1853:

Washing all day.

November 22, and 23, 1853:

The same.

November 24 and 25, 1853:

Ironing all day, in the evening of the 25th we felt a shock of the Earthquake, which shook the whole house which nearly took us off our feet; it was about five o'clock.

February 21, 1854:

Uncle gone to Fort per canoe. Aunt and self alone with Indians until the 25 which was Saturday.

March 29, 1854:

Snow, Hail, Rain and Blowing a hurricane at time[s] all day. Mr. and Mrs. Langford, Mrs. Skinner and her babe, Constance Langford Skinner, came over walking from Colwood that miserable day to see us. They were almost frozen as they stayed all night, went back the next fine day but very wet. We set the Goose on five eggs. . . .

March 26, 1952:

Goose laid again.

April 12, 1952:

Twin ewes born this morning.

February 19, 1953:

Zero, Nice and bright. I washed clothes.

March 25, 1953:

Thawed a lot today. I went to town. The game warden out to set poison bait for coyotes.

March 27, 1953:

Dogs got loose. Poisoned with coyote bait.

February 13, 1954:

Eight degrees below and blowing. The men went to mill but no work; our road drifted.

June 20, 1954:

We saw a big bear on hill. Washed clothes and baked bread.

January 21, 1955:

Twelve degrees above and dull. The men went to work. Mill broke down again. Connie had a bull calf. The kids went sliding.

December 2, 1955:

We all went to a pie social.

Somehow Grandmother managed to do all the housework and find time to pose for this family portrait of the Tuttle family at Yale, B.C. *A*

How you and the freight were delivered in early days. The stage at Yale. *B*

As the communities grew, so churches mushroomed throughout the province. *D*

Patricia Vant Haaff of Saanich, Vancouver Island, taught herself to preserve foods and won all these ribbons and awards in 1970 at the Pacific National Exhibition, Vancouver, and the Saanich Fall Fair on Vancouver Island. *C*

Where shall we settle? Even today there's plenty of space between ranches in the Chilcotin district.

A

Homestead at Surrey Centre, B.C.
B

CHAPTER SIX:

The land the settlers found was vast and full of beauty. Already it wore the silent shroud of past mythologies and the quiet footprints of early inhabitants. Wild as it was, with muskeg, mountains, rain forests, woods, rushing rivers and rapids, it also possessed lakes, sleepy sloughs, peaceful valleys and meadows. Its sun-drenched soil needed only to be mated with water before it became some of the finest fruit ranching and cattle grazing land in the world.

The gifts of the land had been acknowledged by those early inhabitants. Using elaborate rituals, the Indians had given thanks for the berries, bark, fish, and roots Nature had so generously bestowed on them. No rituals—not a single one—could be found to appease another force, a malevolent one, which brought famine and flood upon the land. The newly arrived settlers came to know this, too, for settling was not always a wonderful adventure. Sometimes, in spite of hours of back-breaking labor, loneliness, deprivation and sickness, settlers paid a toll for transplanting themselves. It came unexpectedly and drastically: a plague of grasshoppers in the Okanagan; a flood in the Fraser Valley; or an overlong winter which diminished crops and cattle, or piled deep snow on shores where octopuses, flounders and starfish quickly froze and died.

Women who accepted isolation often had to learn the art of killing. They had to shoot the bear that preyed on the calf, the hawk that preyed on the chickens, and the cheeky raccoon that ate an entire crop of corn. Often with no medical assistance for miles, with roads blocked by snow, or no neighbor near enough to help, a woman gave birth to her child alone. Sometimes complications meant that she lost her life or that of the child. In sickness or in accidents, home nursing skills were not always enough to save a life. Poverty could be handled. Human sacrifices never could be forgotten. Now and then, the land made settlers pay such tolls.

Eli and Marie Lequime paid that toll soon enough. Gold had drawn them from France to the California goldfields and then, in 1859, it pulled them further north to the lower reaches of the Fraser. They took the five-day steamer voyage from San Francisco to Victoria, another passage to the burgeoning community of Sapperton on the mainland, then they walked to Fort Hope. The winter they spent at Strawberry Island.

In spring, the Lequime family set off for Rock Creek. Travelling with other miners to protect themselves against rumored Indian hostilities, they followed the old brigade trails to Tulameen, then the paths by the Similkameen River to Princeton, going into the valley at Keremeos, thence to Rock Creek. The two Lequime boys sat perched on top of the family belongings, carried by two packhorses, while Marie walked with the men, travelling 180 miles on foot.

At Rock Creek, their arrival made little impression on the 4,000 men who already were taking out most of the gold. The new group found work sharpening picks and axes. Marie washed clothes and cooked.

Celebrations, Hastings Mill in 1876. The settlers going to rural areas relied on occasional get-togethers, such as pie socials or barn-raising days.

One clear morning, she noticed that young Gaston had slipped out of sight, and she hurried through camp to find him. Frantic with fear, she ran to the mining operations, but it was already too late: Gaston had fallen into a sluice box and drowned.

Soon the Lequime's five-year-old son Bernard was the darling of the camp, but Marie watched him constantly, even while she was busy cooking, washing, and milking the cow she had acquired. One day, tired, and still drained of energy by the enormous grief she was experiencing, she saw Bernard being lifted onto the horse of a man who had admired her son. She cried out for help as the man and the child rode away. The kidnapper was apprehended just as he was about to cross the border into American territory and in the ensuing skirmish, he was killed. Young Bernard was returned to camp unharmed.

News of gold strikes in the Cariboo brought hope to anyone left in Rock Creek, and it enticed the Lequimes and their friends to leave for the North. This time, the family belongings were carried by the family's cow, with Bernard perched on top. Marie, who was pregnant, walked with the others. They had passed Penticton Mountain when they saw a bearded, tanned man in a buckskin suit riding towards them. He was Father Pandosy, the Roman Catholic missionary, who greeted them in their own language, inviting them to settle in the area. He promised little hostility from Indians and a good future. The Lequimes needed little persuasion to forsake their journey, going instead to the location Father Pandosy had described. Before long, a settlement grew there; Marie's oppression lifted when she gave birth to her new son, whom she named Gaston, in honor of the child she had lost in the new country.

The Lequimes lived on the outskirts of an area that became known as Kelowna, where some retired Hudson's Bay Company clerks had settled with their Indian wives. Others came too. When official reports were filed to Colonial Secretary W. A. G. Young in August, 1862, Provincial Constable W. C. Cox noted:

There are five occupied farms of 160 acres each. There are 130 acres of cultivated ground of which 68 represent cereals. There are two substantial and excellent dwelling houses and materials on the premises for a third.

The settlers are composed of Canadians, Frenchmen, and half-breeds; and are all Roman Catholics, and I am sorry to add, paupers, comparatively speaking. They have not enough funds amongst them to have a flour mill constructed; this is discouraging as their wheat crops look very promising.

In 1865, a different report would have shown that the L'Anse au Sable settlement was flourishing and was known for its fine beef and sheep. Wheat rippled in the fields like the waves of a carefree sea. In 1871, the settlers acquired their flour mill.

The men whipsawed lumber for the cabins, dovetailing the corners. Wagonwheels had been made from huge tree trunks and attached to roughhewn axles with wooden pins; the hubs and bowings were the only parts brought from outside. Plows were handmade; the wide crotch of a tree made an excellent harrow with wooden or iron teeth fitted into it. The women cooked in open fireplaces, using heavy-lidded iron pots that were buried in the hot ashes. They used tin cups and plates, had broad-bladed knives and three-pronged forks. They served

Kamloops in early days.

as midwives to one another, and Marie Louise Lequime acquired a reputation for her home-nursing skills. When all the work was done, sometimes the people listened to the music provided by fiddlers, other times they held spontaneous square dances.

The very first settlers to come to what later became known as British Columbia, arrived in 1849 under the leadership of Captain W. Colquhoun Grant. Fearing American expansion, and with her wounds still smarting from loss of territory in Oregon, Britain had named a new colony, Vancouver Island, previously rented to the Hudson's Bay Company for the scant sum of seven shillings a year. Settlement was encouraged, but settlers trickling into the new colony found that the company still considered that it occupied the land, and continued to give advice. Terms of land purchase were set: no sale could be made of less than 20 acres of land, the price was to be one pound per acre, and five single men or three married couples were expected to occupy a land parcel of 100 acres. The company retained one-tenth of the revenue from timber, mineral and land sales; nine-tenths of this revenue went to the building of roads, the support of the church, and education of children. Numerous complaints about the company were filed to the British Government by the settlers. Douglas, who had been made Governor in 1851, a position he held while still acting as Chief Factor and Trader, was ordered to hold elections for a House of Assembly, which meant that in 1856 the first parliament west of the Great Lakes came into being. Dr. J. S. Helmcken, company surgeon, was Speaker of the House, and there were only seven members: one each for Sooke and Nanaimo, two for Esquimalt-Metchosin area, and three for Victoria. The Governor-Trader still retained a veto over all legislation.

By spring 1858, Victoria's population had mushroomed from 300 to 5,000. Many of the newcomers were miners, headed for the gold strikes on the lower Fraser, who planned to make the town their headquarters. Among these eager fortune-hunters was a group of prospective settlers who arrived on the *Commodore* in April that year. Negroes who had worked in the California goldfields, they came to consult Governor Douglas about the possibility of establishing a segregated settlement. Their proposal was turned down, but they were welcomed into the community and soon sent appraisals to California, where other blacks were suffering under the new anti-Negro legislation.

Wellington Delaney Moses had written: "All the colored man wants here is ability and money." The blacks who responded to his assessment were as heterogeneous as any other group of settlers. Some were teachers, some were businessmen, and some had no trade. What they shared was the common knowledge of prejudice and repression. In Victoria, they found acceptance and a little prejudice. Some settled, while others roamed the mining camps. Prejudice came from Colonial whites who felt that their own skin color somehow gave them superiority over other races; it came also from American Southerners who had no time for people they regarded as slaves "back home." A few blacks were barred from saloons, there were squabbles at the theatre, and the first militia group of the Colony of Vancouver Island, Victoria Pioneer Rifles, a unit of 60 black men, had to disband when Governor Douglas's support did not include financial aid.

Individual families fared better. Mifflin Wistar Gibbs and his partner,

Charles and Nancy Alexander whose descendents live in Victoria and Vancouver today.

Sylvia Stark who posed for this Salt Spring photograph when she was in her nineties and kept her apron on since she always had been a working woman and was proud of that.

A

Nicola Valley pioneers Mrs. Chapman and daughter with friend.   B

Peter Lester, opened a dry goods store that rivalled the trade of the Hudson's Bay Company. Gibbs, with his wife Maria, lived in a fashionable James Bay house, choosing to ignore any prejudice. Maria left Victoria in 1867, but her husband remained three more years. Gibbs eventually returned to the United States where he was made that nation's Ambassador to Madagascar. Gibbs helped to found Queen Charlotte Mining Company, was elected to city council, and studied law. The Lesters became well known, also. Peter helped build the business with Mifflin Gibbs; Sarah gave piano tuition.

Two sisters who stayed in the area were the Hermandez girls, Julia and Mary, who became known for their fine foods. They each made $100 a month cooking in Victoria in 1859. In the 1860's, another black cook, Josephine Sullivan, helped her chef-husband prepare meals for the workers at Moody's Mill on the mainland. After she was widowed, Josephine opened a successful restaurant in Gastown. Charles Alexander left his wife, Nancy, and two children in Victoria, accepting the offer of another immigrant, an Englishman, who offered a share of the gold he expected to find in the Cariboo. Strike they did, and Charles returned to the coast a richer man. He bought a large farm in Saanich, where he and Nancy raised a large family and attended all local community and church events.

In 1859 and 1860, Negro and white settlers took up land on Salt Spring Island. Among them were Fielding Spotts and his wife Julia, who lived on the Saanich Peninsula after taking up land on the island. Their Saanich cabin was made of handhewn logs which dovetailed, and which were held together by wooden plugs. Fielding Spotts became a Saanich school trustee, while Julia attended community events. No racial prejudice existed, with one exception which the Wesleyan Methodist Ebenezer Robson noted in his diary after a meeting with white pioneer Mrs. Lineker:

February 21, 1861:

Mrs. Lenniker *(sic)* says Mr. L nor herself will come to any meeting when the colored people might associate with the white. Poor woman she says some people might do it but she has been brought up so that she cannot—was the daughter of a church of England clergyman.

Robson mentioned settlers Louis and Sylvia Stark, too, noting that they were farming good land for which they had paid one dollar an acre.

If Salt Spring Island appeared to be that promised land of milk and honey, also bestowing clams, fish, fruit, and game upon its settlers, it also offered cause for alarm. An occasional bear appeared, as did wolves and cougars. The major fear uniting settlers was Indian hostilities; Indians had been using the island as a summer camp for years; and were outraged to see the land taken. They were believed responsible for the murder of settlers Robinson and Curtis, and for the slaying of the white doctor who tended the community.

Salt Spring Island today.

In 1866, the two Pacific Colonies amalgamated to ease economic problems, both being absorbed by the separate colony of British Columbia. New Westminster was capital for about two years, but in 1868, Victoria became the seat of government. Throughout British Columbia new roads were built to mining areas. They attracted not just miners,

Nicola, the old mill.

but people willing to farm or ranch. Women travelled on these roads to join husbands in mining towns, or to go into business. They worked as cooks, hotel owners, in saloons, and as dressmakers or milliners. Some had come to the colonies under immigration plans; they were expected to work as domestic servants .

Some men who found work or gold returned to their former homes to wed sweethearts, as did John Smith, bringing his bride Jessie Ann back from Scotland to British Columbia in 1884. In Port Moody, John Smith asked the engineer in charge of the Canadian Pacific Railway lines being laid to Yale if they could travel on the railroad "as far as it is built." The engineer hesitated, but finally gave permission provided the couple took along only one suitcase each. The train swayed, rocks fell to smash windows, and the bride, fresh from a secure life in Scotland, began to wonder just what she had undertaken. It was four in the morning when they reached the end of the line at the community of Cisco. The bridge that was to lead the railway lines across the turbulent Fraser to the east bank was under construction, so they waited on the mountainside for transportation. Lightning was filling the sky when a man driving a horse appeared. The animal was towing a huge basket that was attached to a cable crossing the river. A man sitting in the basket shouted out a welcome to British Columbia, announcing that he had come to take them across the river.

Jessie Ann climbed into the basket with her husband while the operator suggested that she close her eyes as he let go of the rope. "If that rope breaks, I would like to see where I am going," she said resolutely. The rope was released and the basket sped across the river, sliding down a cable, and depositing everyone in a pile of hay. After breakfast was served in a small roadside restaurant that catered to the railway construction workers the final laps of the journey began in a two-seater buggy. The bride was so terrified that the horses would drop from the narrow mountain ledge into eternity that she clutched her husband's arm frequently until it was black and blue. At six o'clock on March 19, 1884, the newlyweds arrived home. The bride was so exhausted that she fell asleep only to be awakened by the sound of a mandolin being played. "For a moment I thought I had gone to heaven and was hearing the harps of angels."

The Smiths tried homesteading, then returned to their first love, fruit growing. Their orchards became famous, especially for the Grimes Golden apple imported from Jessie's hometown. After she was widowed she carried on the business, with her children aiding her in pruning, picking, and packing. She always recalled that first night of sweet music, her introduction to a Canadian shivaree. Her shivaree was a little different from that given most newlyweds on their first night home together, who had to endure a long night of clanging and clashing pots and pans, and numerous catcalls and whistles.

Another settler whose wife joined him was Alexander Graham who set out to find fame and fortune in the goldfields in 1886. In Vancouver he had been offered 60 acres of prime land but he lacked the $40 he needed to buy it. Instead, he went to the goldfields, then took up ranching with a partner in the Chilcotin from where he sent for his fiancee. Anna sailed from County Antrim in 1888. She had been trained as a teacher and as a soloist, talents that did not help her appreciate her first ride across the Fraser River in a flat-bottomed boat filled

The settlement of Nicola before 1915.   *A*

Duncan, Cowichan Valley area of Vancouver Island, after the area had been settled.   *C*

Riding was a pastime at Kamloops in early days.   *B*

Maple Bay area, Vancouver Island, in early days.   *D*

In the Okanagan, just about every new settler tried the difficult and temperamental art of fruit farming. This orchard is in full springtime bloom.   *E*

Big Creek Post Office where people used to enjoy meeting since picking up the mail was part of that rare social event that women could enjoy.   B

The faithful Chinese manservant who, when he no longer had employment with the CPR, became the trusted helper of many ranching families or worked as a cook in city homes.   A

Stampedes started in early days. Today the stampede at Anahim is known for its big star riders who arrive with their horses in the latest trailers.   C

Bella Coola in recent times; settled by families of Scandinavian origin.   D

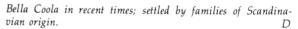

with sheep. Her fiance met her at Soda Creek, where he announced that they would have to take the wagon road back to Clinton, as the preacher was waiting to perform their marriage ceremony there.

When they arrived at Meldrum Creek, Anna noticed that saddle horses were waiting; dressed in high button boots and a long, voluminous dress, she had never sat on a horse in her life. Her husband must have wondered if she could accept the isolation around Alexis Creek, since his partner's wife had chosen to stay in Victoria. Other wives had been known to leave the area: everyone knew of the Cariboo cattle king whose wife had taken one look at the ranch, ignored the new log home and the imported piano, then taken the first stage out. Anna had spirit. If she couldn't be a soloist then she could sing as she chopped wood. She cooked on a woodstove, made candles from animal fat, was delighted when coal oil lanterns became available, and used the perforated lanterns to light the way to the stables. She forked hay alongside her husband, working in the meadows where they slept in a brush tent. She was 20 miles away from the nearest woman, but she coped with that too.

Everyone in the area trapped in winter to make some money to buy the annual or semi-annual supplies of flour, sugar, and tea. If the store owner was away, the goods were taken, and money left on the counter. A person's word was his bond. Anna learned Chinook so she could talk with the Indians whose husbands were ranching in the Chilcotin area, and together the women of both races would sip tea and chat. Chinese laborers sometimes came to her door, looking for work. One, Kim Nauie, joined the family as a cook because the Grahams had no work available for him forking hay or digging ditches: work for which the Chinese were famous. They would seam the ditches with clay and it was said the Chinese could make water run uphill.

The primitive life gradually changed as time went by: Anna acquired a piano, ran a post office and stopping house, accepted her husband's various ranching partnerships, and raised a family. She saw the first car come into the area as it spluttered its way down to the Gang Ranch in 1915. Her daughters rode horses, competed in gymkanas, and tried unsuccessfully to persuade her to allow them to ride steers. When visitors came, Alex Graham entertained by playing the violin or dancing the two-step, Anna played the piano and sang, her clear voice carrying in the crisp Chilcotin air.

While life was difficult for women who had arrived from Europe, the contrast between old and new ways was even greater for women from the Orient. Wong See was only ten when she accompanied a beloved grandmother to Victoria in 1888. She already had some education and could read and write Chinese, a rare talent for most Chinese females at that time. She continued to study when she attended the Chinese Language School opened in 1889 by her benefactor's son. When she was 16, Wong See met Lowe Dun Poy, who had come to Canada on the advice of his merchant father, a recent visitor to the country. The prospective bridegroom was a custom tailor and already had a large business so he employed a *muiyun,* or matchmaker, to see if he and the girl he liked would be compatible. The *muiyun* studied three generations of geneological charts, character traits, and birthdates, then decided they would make a suitable match. The ceremony was traditional; 10 days before the wedding, gifts of pork and cake

Chilcotin where Anna Graham went as a bride.   A

Lowe Wong See who came from China in 1888, settling in Victoria where she was the wife of Charlie Hope who hired an English tutor so he and the family would speak their new language correctly.   B

95

were sent to friends as a way of announcing the ceremony. After marriage, Wong See found she was not Lowe Wong See but Mrs. Charlie Hope. Her husband had anglicized his name; he also hired an English tutor so that they would learn to speak English correctly.

Wong See's life was a busy one; she cooked, sewed, and raised the family. The Hope children were expected to work in their father's business, learning the trade that would guarantee them work later in life. While other Chinese children studied at the Chinese Language School after public school, the Hope children went to the tailoring establishment where young Bessie learned that her first task was to sew 100 buttons onto a square of cloth. "My father drew 10 vertical lines with chalk, then 10 horizontal lines. I had to sew a button where the lines intersected. One hundred buttons—and he checked every one." Another tutor was hired to teach the children the Chinese language and customs in their spare time on weekends. Wong See and her husband converted to Christianity and attended the Presbyterian Church where they intermingled freely with all nationalities. Their lives were industrious and they concentrated their attention on the children, wanting them to have as much education as possible.

Women still were coming out to areas that were completely different from the settled cities they had known overseas. Nobody knows what happened to Mrs. "S" who gained preservation in the lines of an 18-year-old Osoyoos girl's diary, which recorded in 1907 that:

Mrs. "S" was rather quiet. She was 'starving for the sight of a flower.' She is rather small, dark hair, blue eyes, about forty, a rather pathetic little old maid who has lived all her life in a town surrounded by comfort and lady friends and flowers and parish duties . . . . And now, she has travelled out here to B.C. all alone (she has never been in a hotel by herself before), to marry a man she hadn't seen for years, and to live all alone on a wild ranch on a mountain, servantless and gardenless.

Maggie Cunningham adapted well enough. And if Thomas Barton had kept his sights on gold, he might well have made a fortune. The trouble was that the young miner, who had come from Quebec by way of Cape Horn and San Francisco in 1872, found himself staying around Mile 70 in the Cariboo in the 1890's. That was where Maggie, who had come from Scotland, was housekeeping for her brother Jack. There it was, a romance that couldn't be denied, so he gave up his dreams and built her a log house at Clinton. Soon he was running a hotel, an unsuccessful venture which he eventually exchanged for a road-working job.

Another chance of making a fortune stirred the Barton blood when the world's largest hydraulic mine opened near Quesnel. Maggie was willing to try the wilderness life, so Tom invested in the Bullion Mine, and the family of two adults and four children headed for Polly's Lake, where Tom took charge of the mine's water supplies.

By 1904, there were six little Bartons and no school nearby, so the family returned to Clinton, where Tom found work as a road superintendent, also clearing land. Maggie kept busy raising the children, of whom there were eventually nine. When the children were not going to school, they were feeding cows, chickens and pigs. "A typical Cariboo life," recalls one of the Barton girls, Molly Forbes, a former

Maggie and Tom Barton were well known Cariboo pioneers.

Vancouver tailoring store.   A

Glade community house with a supportive garden in the background.   B

Friendships were so important to pioneers: Mrs. Gibson on left and Mrs. J. D. Davies, Lone Butte, Cariboo friends, in 1924.   C

May Hardie on left in this Vancouver studio portrait. The Hardies were farming pioneers. Now Mrs. Leppington of 100 Mile House, she still recalls the days of the 1918 flu when she nursed members of the community and the days when the first street car drivers called out "All aboard."   A

While others lived in tents, these settled members of Esquimalt, near Victoria, enjoyed the annual Gorge Regatta. This picture taken in 1904.   B

Gulf Islanders were farming and living off the land and sea in 1908. This group, left to right, Martin Grainger, Mabel Grainger, Elizabeth Spalding, Beatrice Spalding with Eric Burton and Herbert Spalding in front. The occasion: a friendly get-together.   C

teacher and local historian who now lives in Lac La Hache. "When we weren't doing chores, we had a few other ways of spending time . . . housework, piano lessons, Sunday School . . . choir practice and games. If we didn't study hard, we knew that we wouldn't be going 'Outside,' boarding with other families in an area where we could obtain higher education. We'd be left making butter and scrubbing floors for the rest of our lives."

Three of the Barton girls became teachers, three entered the business world. One son died young, another was killed at Vimy Ridge. The third still has gold in his veins: he's a prospector today.

Some women went to new towns, others to townsites. Amelia Pillsbury arrived with her three children in Prince Rupert in 1907. She had come to the first house to be built in a tent-town that sat on muskeg. Even two years later, the local paper, *The Optimist*, reported that the place had been little more than a spot on the map until 1909.

The townsite actually had something less than Nature put upon it; even the ravens could scarcely find a roosting place within it. Today it has blocks of stores, roadways, sewers, waterworks and construction and houses scattered over a radius of two miles. It is a hive of industry.

As Amelia Hall, child of a well-known Boston inventor, she had known a secure and comfortable childhood in Massachusetts. Marriage to a civil engineer, Joel Pillsbury, meant moving around, something she cheerfully accepted. Her husband was employed as assistant harbor engineer of the townsite and dock area of the planned terminus of the Grand Trunk Railway. All the early work concentrated on the ferocious struggle of men, machines and dynamite versus rocks and forest. With some delays and financial hagglings, the glimmering steel tracks eased west so that the first train reached Prince Rupert in 1914, only four years after the town had grown enough to merit the status of city. Prince Rupert was a busy place and it soon became the largest port for halibut fishing anywhere in the world.

Housemoving in Vancouver in early days.

As the assistant engineer's wife, Amelia found she had to make visiting calls on families living in the nearby tents. Her daughter Katherine was with her on one visit and was startled by the bear-like rasping noise coming from behind the piano. One glance was enough—it proved to be the man of the house, hidden from sight by the piano where he was enjoying a deep sleep and snoring.

School was held in the Presbyterian Church, a leaking tent, so students were expected to take umbrellas along with their textbooks on rainy days. Childhood was a good time for the Pillsbury children, especially at Christmas, when all the single surveyors came to enjoy dinner, bringing presents with them for the children. Katherine recalls one Christmas when she received 25 dolls, all "Eaton's Beauty Dolls."

The life of May Leppington, formerly May Hardie, of 100 Mile House, is in contrast to that of the Pillsbury children. In 1912, the Hardie family was farming in the South Vancouver area. May remembers the large family house, and winning school prizes for songs like this:

Two little blue little shoes
Two little feet, where are they?
Come with the chatter, the laughter and patter
Of Baby who left them one day.

Winifred Grey and Rollo, 1939, Granville Street, Vancouver. Winifred and her sister, Mabel Higgs, came out in 1896 to visit their brother, then returned to the province to stay. On that first ride out, Winifred recorded "there were no closing doors on the coaches then so Mabel and I spent hours sitting on the steps, or in the open Observation Car, where we were duly hosed with dust and cinder." The train stopped at Hells Gate Canyon so passengers could view that "raging mad Fraser River."

She had Buster Brown, Mary Jane, and Tag dolls, and she learned how to make wigs for them from bits of her own hair whenever the dolls' hair was worn. She also learned how to dig out stumps and used a crosscut saw to cut wood. "'Show me what you can do,' my father would say," she recalls. "Well, I could split timber with an axe for a wedge; I could haul wood on the stoneboat, going through the fields to the house for what would be a city block; and I could work long hours too. I delivered milk and picked the farm fruit. Sometimes I still have dreams about the plum tree. I wake, startled, wondering did I pick all the fruit and deliver it all?".

May is Canadian, born in Vancouver. In 1914, all the young men she knew went off to World War I. In 1918, she nursed people sick with influenza, a skill that was useful later when she married at the beginning of the Depression.

"We had nothing. Who did? Just nothing. He was a longshoreman and they were striking right then. I soon found work. I was making 25 cents a day scrubbing and doing housework. Then he found work. We had the children, and I still worked. Soon I was making $1 a day."

Among the strong and resourceful women who made British Columbia their home were some who contributed greatly to community life here. Margaret Janet Hart can be numbered among them. A Nova Scotian, her family encouraged the women as well as the men to choose careers. Her sister, Lavinia McPhee, was one of Canada's first women physicians and hung out her shingle in Victoria for a brief time. Margaret achieved her own goals, studying at Dalhousie for her B.A. and M.A. degrees, teaching at Baddeck, and then becoming the first woman principal of the Nova Scotian Academy.

It was at Baddeck that she met Alexander Graham Bell, famous for his discovery of the telephone, among other inventions. He invited her to take her senior students to his laboratory where he demonstrated some of his ideas, including a new machine with which he X-rayed the teacher's hand. Young Dr. Edward Charles Hart was in the area practicing medicine at the time, and although Miss McPhee appeared to be busy organizing what was to be Canada's first Parent Teacher Association, he managed to persuade her that she should consider moving to the West Coast as his wife.

She followed him West in 1897, and their life in Victoria was an orderly one with enough time between child-raising and meal-supervising for the doctor's wife to pursue her own interests in English and history. When Dr. Hart left for Greece, where he superintended a medical unit, Margaret decided to rent their townhouse, and that country living on a 40-acre family farm at Albert Head would be good for the children. She found running a farm meant a busy time for everyone. Wong, the Chinese laborer, helped with the farm chores, while Minnine, the maid, obligingly took a pruning course, helped with housework, and sometimes chopped wood, once accidentally chopping off her own long braid of hair. Ellen, Edward and Lavina helped to feed the cattle and chickens, and they picked and packed loganberries. The lady farmer hoped to make a profit from her produce and did well at first, selling to neighbors. A disastrous arrangement with a wholesaler then produced problems but no profits. Despite these setbacks, Margaret Hart found time to become a school trustee at the local country school. She also worked hard to sell the paintings of artist Mary Riter Hamilton,

Margaret Janet Hart, M.A. She probably organized Canada's first Parent-Teacher Association in Nova Scotia, then made sure British Columbia history was recorded when she took up residence on Vancouver Island.

A

Main Street, Granville, 1885.　　B

The covered wagons leaving Ashcroft, May 3, 1913, with the Gilbert, Armishaw and Reid families planning to homestead in the Vanderhoof area.

C

Gastown, Vancouver, around 1884.

D

The fashionable city baby at turn of the century, Gladys Mason. A

Margaret and Olney Reid and the children. Note the lantern. B

Some pioneers brought their chinaware with them. C

who had gone to the smoking French battlefields to paint what she saw there.

When Dr. Hart returned to Canada in 1920, the family moved back into the city, and Margaret became involved in the University Women's Club, the Historical Association, and the Women's Canadian Club. She also helped organize the production of the first history of women written in British Columbia, *Pioneer Women of Vancouver Island*.

Florrie Evans, now a Vanderhoof resident, looks back to her pioneering days, begun in 1912, and considers them "all a wonderful adventure." She learned that single women could preempt land, something she did as soon as she arrived in the Nechako area. The petite woman was soon riding a horse along the area's trails; at that time, a single woman was news, and all the telegraph operators wired news about her to the Nechako Post Office and Telegraph Office where she rode one day with some community mail. Her arrival was graceful enough but when she started to alight the cinch under the horse slipped, the animal shot off in fright, and Florrie watched, horrified, as the mail bag broke away from the saddle horn, scattering coins and catalogue orders through the deep grass.

Cecil Lake Church—area homesteaded in 1930's and later. Even in the 1950's this country was still open to homesteaders.
A

Bill Evans, Florrie's future husband, had to ride to Vanderhoof to obtain the area's first wedding license. "Then he had to find a minister," recounts Florrie. "We knew there was one at Fraser Lake, so he set off there. It was a two-day ride, so he stopped at a cabin to ask directions, and accepted a bachelor's invitation to stay for a meal. The meal was bannock which he had hanging on the wall, just as though it was a picture. He took it down, broke off a piece, then put it back on the wall again. When Bill finally reached the minister's house, he found a young lady sitting on the couch was taking all the attention. The minister was far more interested in conducting his own love affair than hearing about ours, but he came to perform the ceremony, then went hurrying back."

The couple took an old scow to reach their home at Nechako Point. Florrie still held 160 acres of land she had preempted there, and Bill retained his land, so they lived at one property for six months, then moved across the river to the other for the next six months.

"The housewarming parties were fun. Someone played an instrument, usually an accordian. In winter there was a sleigh to gather up everyone in the area. We all had wraps, and warmed our feet on the small heater. We put heated stones in gunny sacks.

Grannie Caroline Purdy, aged 87, mother of Mrs. John Cadenhead, travelling to the Peace River and determined to stay on board no matter how low or turbulent the rivers were. 1912.
B

"Summers, well, there were mosquitoes and blackflies . . . but all you needed were a few essentials. All that work, clearing the land, working with your husband, why, it made you strong. You slept well, too, I can tell you."

Sleeping—or taking a nap—was what Granny was doing the day she and other women drifted downstream and found themselves temporarily grounded in shallow water. Grandmother Caroline Purdy, mother Harriet Cadenhead, and sister Elizabeth "Carrie" Cadenhead were moving with Douglas and Hassard Cadenhead from Edmonton to the Halfway River district, Peace River area, in 1912. The men had built two 50-foot long pointer boats that had six-inch running boards around the sides so that a navigator could make speedy stabs and pokes to ease difficult turns in lakes and rivers. Launching had been a complete success with only a few chickens lost to the wilds as the group reached the shallow lake. The men hired Indian helpers who used ropes to pull the boats upstream. The boat with the supplies and equipment was safe enough, but something went wrong with the rope pulling the women, and they were left drifting downstream. No drownings. Just a scare or two. Granny Purdy, secure in an armchair under a tent awning, was not at all perturbed. Later, when the boats reached another lake where a steamer was to give them a tow, the captain shouted out that the women should climb on board his boat. "If there's a wind in the narrows, they'll be swamped."

Granny was 87 years young and enjoying this voyage. "I've come all this way on one boat," she told the captain as she refused to leave her chair. "I'm not leaving it now."

She was riding a democrat when she first caught sight of the majestic Peace River as it ribboned its way through unsurveyed country. She didn't object to boarding the *Northland Call*, a new steamer which took them on one more lap of their journey. On this vessel, the passengers were put to work each evening, cutting fuel from the wooded shores to power the steamer's engines.

The settling experience was a good one for the Cadenheads, who lived in tents until their house was built. They broke the land using teams of horses and soon discovered that the stories of bumper crops were true. In 1918, when the terrible influenza epidemic ripped its destructive path through British Columbia, the Cadenhead home became an emergency hospital for the Beaver Indians of Halfway River area. Carrie Cadenhead rode on horseback, looking for Indians whose tracks in the snow might indicate that they were seeking her family's help, but most of the tracks were covered with fresh snow. Eventually she found six women and eight children still alive in their camp, and brought them back to the house. Night and day the Cadenheads nursed them—and they saved everyone.

Jenny Lawson Turnbull and her English Boer War Veteran husband had been living in New Zealand when they studied Canadian Government promotional literature and agreed to "sink their money into a Canadian ranch." The pamphlets described the land north of Prince George as if it were a Paradise. With their young daughter, Peggy, who had been born "in sterile, modern conditions" in a New Zealand hospital, they went first to Manitoba to live with a family who were to teach them the essentials of "Canadian farmin." Two years later, in 1925, with Jenny still dressed in semi-mourning out of deference to Grandpa Lawson's death, they headed for the paradise near Chilco, four miles or so from Vanderhoof, where they acquired 160 acres of land, 25 head of cattle and some chickens. Rainwater was collected from the roof to provide water for washing and drinking.

Jenny was typical of other women—she earned her pioneering medals by learning to make bread, butter, and jam, to go near the cows without trembling, to help deliver a neighbor's child—and faint afterwards. And those terrifying tracks that she had noted in a field on a rainy day did not belong to some mammoth after all, they were only the tracks of rabbits which had taken gigantic leaps. If she referred to the log house as a "hut", she also understood the flowery phrasing of the promotional literature which had failed to include some local information

After the land was cleared, there was the hay to consider for winter feed. This wagon proved its worth at Fort Steele, B.C.

about the blackflies and mosquitoes which harrassed everyone from break-up to freeze-up. She also learned that "sinking money into a ranch" was an excellent description of how some settlers' family funds disappeared.

The Cornwalls were famous for coyote hunting using hounds at Ashcroft. This photograph was taken in Victoria where Clement Cornwall served as Lieutenant Governor. A

Mrs. Caroline Purdy, Harriet Cadenhead, then 55, Douglas Cadenhead and party, proving that you can be pioneers at any age as they camped at Peace River Crossing to wait for the boat to take them on yet another lap of their journey.
B

Emma Stark trained at Nanaimo for her teaching career, then taught in a one-room school—a log cabin—in North Cedar district. Students who lived a long way from the area came to board with Emma. A

Moodyville, North Vancouver, where Superintendent Jessup was taken by canoe to inspect the school. B

CHAPTER SEVEN: RURAL TEACHING

26 August, 1891:

B.C. Express . . . one passenger on the stage. School teacher for Quesnelle.

In winter, at Kitsumkalum School, 90 miles east of Prince Rupert, some of the students would arrive by dogsled; after the steel was laid, they could come down the railway tracks on the speeder. In early summer at Masset, Queen Charlotte Islands, where the first school was located on a logfloat in a slough, students knew that their pens and papers would slide from desks as the tide fell. And in fall, in the Peace River Country, looking out of the windows of the log teacherage attached to the school, a teacher soon saw why the area was known as Bear Flat.

Early rural schools attracted more female than male teachers. The reason was simple enough: salaries were too small for a married man to support a family. A few single men did accept such postings but most considered other possibilities, such as the chance to pre-empt land or the chance of striking it rich in the mines. A woman was glad to be offered the job. Usually, but not always, she had some training for it; she had no objection to staying with local families—in fact, if she never had tasted isolation before, she preferred to board with a family— and she appreciated the challenge of teaching children from a variety of backgrounds. If she liked country life, well and good. If she loathed it, she tried to endure that first year; after all, no city school would consider hiring her until she had gained experience elsewhere.

A few women teachers were able to teach close to home. One was Emma Stark, whose descendents had known the full degradation of slavery in the southern United States but had purchased their freedom, worked in California, then joined the Negro exodus north to Vancouver Island and Salt Spring Island in 1859. Indian hostilities encouraged the family to move to Nanaimo where Emma completed her own education; she found herself teaching at the North Cedar School in 1874 where she taught for several years at the starting salary of just $40.00 a month.

The Public School Act was passed in 1872, a year after the first government of British Columbia was formed, and John Jessop was appointed as Superintendent of Education. Among his duties he was "to deliver, in each School District, at least once a year, a public lecture on some subject connected with the objects, principles and means of practical education and to do all in his power to persuade and animate parents, guardians, trustees and teachers to improve the character and efficiency of the Public Schools, and to secure the sound education of the young generally." On his inspection travels, he used whatever transportation was available, going by steamer, stage, horseback, and canoe to schools throughout the province. On the north shore of Burrard Inlet, he visited the school where teacher Miss Laura Haynes and

The stage on the Cariboo Road. Sometimes it was a wild journey for the passengers.

her students were smoked out of their building by the refuse burner of Moody and Co.'s mills. In his diary in the Provincial Archives of British Columbia, he noted:

. . . . Found 16 children in attendance—9 girls and 7 boys— school orderly and quiet—Classes merely beginning—reading and Spelling not good—But little Arithmetic and Geography— No grammar—Writing just commenced by 7 or 8 children. . . . No maps or blackboard . . . .

On the south shore of Burrard Inlet, he visited the school supplied by Captain Raymur, manager of the Hasting's Mill, noting:

. . . . School house large and comfortable, put up by the Firm and used as a church—Good stove in the building which Captain Raymur thinks ought to be used for school purposes—Desks required. About 25 children of school age in the district—the trustees, manager and parents anxious that Miss Sweney should be appointed teacher.

By 1873, Jessop and the Board of Education had prepared examinations to assess teachers' abilities. Two standards were applied, one for male teachers and one for women teachers. The examinations included topics such as *English Grammar, Bookkeeping Double Entry, Education and the Art of Teaching, History and English Literature, Vocal Music, Natural Philosophy, Mensuration, Animal and Vegetable Physiology,* and *Euclid.* For men, the averages were based on their marks in all subjects: for women, the averages were based on all except the mathematical subjects. It was not until 1877 that the ruling was changed to permit men and women to compete on an equal footing.

A woman teacher had to do a job that met with the approval of local school trustees and her personal life had to be circumspect or they were likely to report her to the school inspector. In early days, mail often took weeks to deliver and transportation was dependent on weather so a school inspector's arrival sometimes came as a complete surprise. At Spences Bridge in the 1890's, young teacher Miss Hopkins ran over to her neighbor, Jessie Ann Smith, complaining that a strange man appeared to be following her everywhere. What should she do? Mrs. Smith advised her to open the school as usual and promised to send her husband to the school to keep an eye on everything. No sooner had Miss Hopkins started the day's work than she glanced out of the window and saw the stranger marching up the school path. With the help of the larger children in the class, she pushed hard against the door. The stranger pushed from the other side. Harder and harder she and the children until finally they gave up and stepped back. The stranger staggered into the room and fell to the floor.

"I am Mr. Copperthwaite," he said slowly as he picked himself up. "The School Inspector."

If the complexities of travel meant that the teacher had no idea when an inspector would arrive, she herself had to be sure to arrive well before her appointment began. Sometimes the journey was a memorable one, as it was for Laura Blackwell and Jane Moore who took the four-horse stage from Ashcroft to the Cariboo in 1901, a wild ride with "someone perched shotgun guard on the hurricane deck." Jane taught at the 127 Mile School. Laura taught at Lac La Hache, boarding with Scottish settlers, George and Elizabeth Forbes.

Margaret R. Dallas, later Mrs. W. T. Slavin, who taught the children of such pioneer families as Todd, McLean, Gordon, Edwards and McQueen in the Kamloops region. She first taught in 1886 at schoolhouse situated one-quarter mile north of what is known as Rayleigh district.

It was Laura who fell in love with freighter Ben McNeil whose language, particularly when he was driving his team, shocked her pristine ears. She went away for the summer, but returned to teach a second year at the school and Ben proposed to her. She turned him down and left the area at the end of the school year with enough teaching experience to secure a city teaching job. She taught in Victoria, first at Sir James Douglas School, then at Central School. Ben appeared on the scene ten years later, a case of true love and little action. This time Laura actually waved her handkerchief at him. They started to talk and, this time, she accepted his proposal.

Rural teaching in her native Gulf Islands suited Mary Gyves in 1913, but by 1917 she wanted to see the rest of the province so she applied for a job in the Okanagan. Her journey included a horseback ride over the Hope-Princeton trail, and she stayed overnight in a cabin where two old prospectors made dinner for her before leaving her in sole possession of their home for the night. She taught at Otter Lake school, a few miles from Vernon, and lived at the famous O'Keefe ranch which was known for its beef and for the jewels which the owner's wife never had time to wear. In her spare time, Miss Gyves went riding for "miles and miles and miles."

Jessie Stott of Saanich was only 17 when she obtained her first teaching position at Redona Island in 1922. The school building was situated next to a fish reduction plant and she travelled there on the steamer with loggers and fishermen, arriving at low tide when the putrid smell of fish permeated everything. She thought herself fortunate to have a job however. "There were 199 applications for every teaching job in those days. She had expected to stay on the island but a plant official pointed out that, since she was the only woman on the island, she would not be able to use the company bunkhouse. Instead, she could stay with the family whose children she was to teach. "Here they come now," he said as a gasboat docked at the wharf. Jessie took a good look at the children, strung out along the wharf in front of the parents: there they were, her very first students. Two young Indian girls from Cape Mudge joined the family to make it feasible for a school to be opened. Each day, the teacher faithfully rowed the students to school until the fish reduction plant closed. "It seemed ridiculous to row to a deserted island so I taught from the house. Even when all the children had chicken pox."

Jessie later taught on Graham Island in the Queen Charlottes. One day she was enjoying a long walk on local beaches when a storm blew up. "There I was, a real apparition . . . sun glasses, and a scarf over my face to protect it from the sand that was blowing everywhere, a raincoat and boots . . .", when along came the cannery owner's son, Sam Simpson, driving the clamdigger's truck. The rest is history. On their ride back to the schoolhouse, they discovered they had much in common. He was completing an English Honors degree at University of British Columbia and they both liked editing poetry. It wasn't long before the teacher was Mrs. Simpson.

Famous O'Keefe Ranch today.   B

Teaching stood Jessie in good stead. When she and her husband returned from the coast to the Queen Charlottes to work in the canneries, she found work as a forelady which was "just like teaching. I showed the women how to work and checked on what they did." In 1967, because of the Simpson's experience, the Federal Government hired them

109

Mama and daughters, the Martin Beattie family who left Ireland in 1893 and taught in Kamloops . . . Elizabeth, Florence, Emily, Harriet, Minnie and Mabel pose thoughtfully. Elizabeth (or Lily as she sometimes was known) was a watercolor artist. She opened a select boarding school where such students as Lottie Bowron, gold commissioner's daughter, from Barkerville attended (Lottie went on to become secretary to Premier McBride and was first Rural Welfare Officer for rural women teachers). Florence Beattie taught at Shuswap, Emily at Campbell Creek, Harriet assisted Lily, Minnie served at matron for a private school, and Mabel taught at Enderby.
A

Interior view, temporary quarters, primary division, Phoenix Public School. Teacher Miss Rose Ella McGrade (1903-1910).
B

When Harriet Morrison of 100 Mile House was a Lone Butte youngster (Harriet Davies), the school was typical of others in the area. Note the tarpaper shack. Lone Butte was on the PGE tracks and not as lonely as it sounds.
C

to go to New Brunswick, Prince Edward Island, and the Gaspe Peninsula where they taught local people how to set up canneries, how to handle and pack deep sea crab, as well as designing the effective gear that would transport the crab live to the canneries.

Teaching jobs often led to unforeseen changes in the teachers' lives. Mabel Blake came to Vancouver in 1913, armed with an English teaching certificate, but had to wait until the following January before she found work at Minto on Vancouver Island. She had taught only a few days when a government replacement teacher arrived who had seniority over her. It was back to Vancouver on a storm-tossed ship with a group of drunken miners as fellow travellers. Another offer soon arrived, however, and she went off to Sand Creek School near Grand Forks, in the Kootenays. That Fall she found herself in yet another school, this time in a Swedish logging community of five families at Hilltop, situated some 2000 feet up from Fife, "a whistle stop on the Kettle River Railway." The schoolhouse was a square building with a large classroom in front, while the teacher's bedroom and kitchen were at the back. Mabel taught all grades, including one or two beginners who had to learn English first. The people were kind, giving her venison and firewood. "I was a greenhorn," she recalls from her North Vancouver home today. "One cold night I noticed some pieces of bark by the woodpile, and I fitted them around the inside of the heater, with the fire in the center."

At midnight she was awakened by a roaring noise and rushed into the schoolroom to find that the heater and the two lengths of stove pipe were red hot. Scared that the building would burst into flames any minute, she found there was nothing to do but watch the fire. "Fortunately, there was a tin sheet on the wall behind the heater."

At her next posting in Brideswell, she had to ride a horse to get to the school, going down a steep bank to a creek below, riding through the creek, then up another bank to the road. It was while teaching there that she met young Juliet Bell, a deaf student who changed her career. In order to help Juliet, Mabel decided to investigate what government programs were available for deaf children. She discovered that classes for the deaf were being held in Vancouver; by the following Fall, she had joined the staff at what was to become Jericho Hill School, British Columbia's famous school for the deaf and the blind. She became a vice-president in 1935, after taking time out for some specialized training in the United States. When she retired, after a career of 32 years at the school, the staff and students honored her by naming one of the buildings Blake Hall.

As Depression days came closer, teachers found conditions in rural areas harder to take. Community members were sometimes jealous of each other and counted the number of times the teacher visited each family. The teacher's behavior was discussed: she was expected to go to church, to set certain standards of politeness and to be neatly groomed. Sometimes, it was hard for her to board with a family where the mother was over-burdened with children, under-burdened with attention or money, and who soon resented the respect that the teacher commanded. "Boarding the teacher" became a competitive venture in a few communities where sometimes the living situation caused personal distress.

At the Normal School in Victoria, Dr. MacLaurin began giving "pep"

There is a bridge over the ravine today were Mabel Blake rode to the school at Bridesville. She taught at several Kootenay schools before devoting her career to teaching the deaf at Vancouver's Jericho Hill School. Riding was a skill that kept her and the horse in good shape. A

Mabel Blake today. Her teaching abilities and interest in the deaf led to a long and honored career at Jericho Hill School. B

111

Wearing the fashions of the day and posing in front of "the mechanical policeman" of Prince George, here are Pat Grimmond now Mrs. Keith Yorston of Prince George; Kaye Murray, now Mrs. George Warnock of Haney, Lauretta McCall, now Mrs. Holdridge of Victoria, and Louise McAllister of Vancouver.

talks to girls going to rural areas. His paternal advice was peppered with sound psychology: he warned the girls not to fall in love with the first men they met; that sometimes some of the male students would be almost the same age as the teacher; to understand that rural conditions would be very different from city life; and to expect loneliness and frustration.

Lauretta McCall was another pioneer teacher who struck off into the bush. "Mother was so upset when I left that she couldn't understand why I wanted to go off into the 'wilderness.'" While teaching at Bednesti School northwest of Prince George, Lauretta boarded with the Hoff family. "I had my own cabin to live in and ate my meals with the family. Mrs. Hoff always insisted that the teacher should have butter with her meals. That *was* a luxury. She had fixed up the cabin beautifully. There was a small heater, a lamp, and a bureau made from an old orange crate, then covered, and she had put up some pretty curtains."

To make a little money for essentials, the people in the area cut railroad ties, and the Hoff family kept a horse so that the logs could be pulled from the woods. The teacher was allowed to ride the animal when she wanted to go on visits. "I was glad of the chance to go out. I would ride to the Mud River dances. And I had a piano brought all the way from Prince George. This helped me through the long winter."

School was a four-mile walk for Lauretta and the Hoff children who were among her students. The teacher set a rule that the school would close only when the temperature sank dangerously below zero. "At forty below zero or so I used to wear breeches, boots, a coat, scarves, and a sort of helmet to try to keep out the cold," she recalls. "In winter, the lunches would freeze on our way to school." The sandwiches, often filled with bear meat, venison, and prairie chicken meat, had to be thawed around the woodstove before eating. During this season the grouse sandwiches would be blue from all the blueberries the birds had eaten.

"The year's big event for students was the arrival of books from the Victoria Open Shelf Library. The Big Day for teachers was the annual Teachers' Convention held in Prince George with teachers from as far away as Quesnel attending. These were the days when the British Columbia Teachers' Federation fees were just $5 a year. It was good to meet with other teachers to discuss problems, or just talk," Lauretta recalls. "We always had a guest speaker or two. It was a rare opportunity to unpack our trunks and put on all our finery. We women were wearing Princess Eugenie hats at that time."

Most rural teachers taught in a setting similar to that in which Telkwa's Margaret Swift taught in 1929 at Quick, now part of the Smithers district. She had a barrel heater in the middle of the school room, with a long stove pipe supported by wires leading to the chimney. The schoolhouse had a small porch for benches and coats, two wash basins with slop-pails underneath which forever overflowed, a pail of water and a dipper. Gas lamps were in vogue. Outside there was a well, woodshed, two privies, swings and a teeter-totter, plus a barn for the horses on which some children rode to school.

Inside the schoolroom basic equipment included maps of British Columbia, Canada, and the world; a globe, gelatin in a pan for duplicat-

*Frances Kirkham at Isle Pierre School.
Teachers looked forward to the Teacher's
Convention held once a year at Prince
George. At that, and at rural dances, they
could wear all the finery they had packed
away in the trunk.*   A

*Frances Kirkham and Lauretta McCall,
now Mrs. Holdridge of Victoria, getting
together to discuss their respective rural
schools at Isle Pierre and Bednesti. The
latter name was Indian and meant a
good stomachful of fish. Today, Mrs
Holdridge lectures at UVic and travels to
aid trainee teachers.*   B

*Only after she had a rural teaching job could a young teacher usually obtain a city job. Here
is Miss McKilligan, early member of staff at Boys' Central School, Victoria, B.C.*   C

Agnes Mathers first taught at Sandspit, Queen Charlotte Islands, and spent most of her teaching years on the islands. The Sandspit school was named after her. Here she is with her last class in 1969, grades five, six and seven. A

This was the Nithi River schoolhouse in 1931. Mrs. Grace Shepherd, then Miss Phillips, recalls that she ate "Chicken" all Fall—wild chicken or grouse, of course. B

The old schoolhouse at Walhachin where the grades varied from one to eight and where, at times, the teacher coped with up to 40 students. C

ing, drawing paper, foolscap, chalk, ink powder and pen nibs. In Depression days, bread wrappers sometimes served as drawing paper but store-bought bread became a luxury so teachers relied on local organizations such as the Women's Auxiliary to the Church or the Imperial Order of the Daughters of the Empire to help provide supplies.

Corporal punishment was the way teachers were expected to handle behavior problems. If problems were insurmountable, a teacher sought the advice of the local trustees. Janet MacGillivray, who had experience in several rural schools, was teaching at Bouchie Lake, near Quesnel, when she learned that in her area the trustees usually did the strapping. There was no way she wanted to permit that as she thought it fairer if she meted out punishments, which she did a few times.

The teacher was a celebrity in the community as Molly Barton, who taught at Lac La Hache in the Cariboo in 1920, discovered. Not only did she teach school, but she found herself serving as secretary for settlers who were having problems with the land department or had other matters that justified complaint. "Occasionally I was left in charge of the small post office to hand out the mail. And I played the organ for the monthly church service which was held in the big dining room of the 115 Mile House where I boarded. Sometimes I waited on table at the dinner hour when Mrs. McKinley had a crowd to feed and was hard-pressed."

Cariboo historian and former teacher Molly Forbes of Lac La Hache. She moved to Pitt Meadows but rancher Gilbert Forbes made innumerable visits to the coast and persuaded her to become a rancher's wife so it was back to the Cariboo again.

One attraction of becoming a teacher was the training period which was shorter than that needed for a nursing career and teachers could continue studies in the summer. Often, they were influenced by their own teachers, as Agnes Mathers of Sandspit, Moresby Island, Queen Charlotte Islands, was influenced by Marjorie Richards, the teacher who had taught her in 1917-1918. Agnes began teaching in 1929 at Four Mile, a community north of Hazelton, then went back to the Queen Charlotte Islands to teach, retiring there in 1969, when she was honored by having the Sandspit school named after her.

She and other teachers found the Christmas concert was a major production. A teacher's reputation for ingenuity and patience could fall sharply or rise meteorically because of that one event. Directors and players alike suffered from anxiety cramps, mothers sat frantically sewing costumes by the light of coal oil lamps, and fathers spent their time carting the cast back and forth to rehearsals. But not everyone could be relied upon to cooperate: one year the cold affected the chief prop, a Christmas tree that presented its own sad spectacle, when most of its branches snapped off in the cold as the tree was felled.

While a teacher's life sometimes could be difficult, particularly if she encountered a child with severe learning problems, she could sometimes forget everything and dance the night away to the fiddle and mouth organ music provided at country dances. Grace Shepherd, who taught in the Fraser Lake area, remembers the dances that often were held in the community halls or in the schools. "The men always wore suits and the girls wore party dresses, often long—never jeans. And there was the smell of coffee on the stove. Yesterday!"

Today, a teacher near retirement sometimes finds she is teaching the children of her first students, as Margaret Swift discovered at Quick, not so long ago, when a father introduced his son to her.

"Don't teachers ever die?" asked the boy.

Indian cemetery at Lillooet with its carefully carved headboard. During small pox epidemics many communities shrank in size.

CHAPTER EIGHT:

CRADLES
AND
COFFINS

I have been feeling unwell. I went to the store . . . and collapsed. Mrs. Eli Lequime attended me. It was Mountain Fever and I had a bad attack . . . . She did not know me; all she knew was that there was a young man lying ill in Knox's wagon-shed, and that was enough. Every day she walked through the fields from her place to Knox's ranch and brought me a supply of sagebrush tea.

Mrs. Lequime, Marie Louise Lequime, one of the Okanagan's first pioneers in the 1860's, had learned the value of her herbal medicines in her native France, using this knowledge and home-nursing skills to help others. When outsiders shot an Indian youth the family adopted in the 1880's, she carried out one of the area's first surgical operations, calmly probing the boy's numerous flesh wounds to remove pieces of bullets. The mountain fever she treated seems to be a lost disease these days although numerous travellers suffered from it then: Sophia Cameron, wife of Cariboo Cameron, died from it in the Cariboo gold-fields in the 1860's; Lady Sarah Crease had a touch of it when she rode the stagecoach to Quesnel in the 1880's. In Mrs. Cameron's case, her illness now is thought to have been caused by typhoid fever; the other cases of mountain fever experienced by people riding over newly cut trails probably were mild forms of malaria.

Whatever mountain fever was, it was only one of the diseases affecting settlers. Severe stomach aches that often led to death were believed to be incurable, too. Charles Ross, the Hudson's Bay Factor put in charge of the construction of Fort Victoria in 1843, suffered from agonizing stomach pains and died from what probably was appendicitis. No pioneer knew how to treat that ailment. Fortunately, settlers usually were healthy, they ate good, uncontaminated food; they breathed unpolluted air; and they had plenty of good exercise. However, an accident still meant that medical aid might urgently be required. Missionaries and pioneer nuns offered their skills but these were of little value to settlers in remote areas. Medical aid often was required immediately, as it was in the 1870's when a Cache Creek Boarding School student was bitten in the palm of her hand by a rattlesnake. Sarah Jones, matron at the school, and wife of the principal, both new arrivals to the Okanagan area, calmly bent down and sucked out the poison. On another occasion, when students at this school broke rules by swimming nude in the creek, principal John Thatcher Jones hurried to reprimand them while one frightened student fled over the hills, stepping right on to the piercing quills of a prickly pear cactus. Again, Sarah hurried to the rescue.

For childbirth, women relied on neighbors to help and sometimes hired a midwife who would stay during the confinement for a set fee. When Henry Moffat at Lansdowne House in the Cariboo went for a midwife in the 1890's, he had a three-day journey, starting with a boat

117

trip to Quesnel, after which he had to walk seven miles to the midwife's house to ask if she could attend his wife, wait while she packed, then return home with her to the stopping house and ranch he and Jennie operated on the Cariboo Road, south of Quesnel. The midwife had agreed to stay two weeks but when the Moffat baby still had not arrived at the end of that time, she refused to stay longer and left. Luckily, Jennie had some cousins nearby who rode over to help. At other times, the Moffats' babies arrived on schedule, as the family journal shows:

Wednesday, June 3, 1891:

Nellie Mason arrived here today on the stage to attend my wife during confinement. Lillooet Indians passed up on their way to Barkerville.

Tuesday, June 16, 1891:

Born this day at six o'clock in the evening in Lansdowne House by my wife a fine son weighing about ten lbs. and all well, thank God. Henry M.

Arrangements for Winifred Grey's delivery were typical of those planned by women in rural areas: on Christmas Day, 1901, Mrs. Grey's husband, Ralph, rowed her from their home to the Saturna Island wharf where she boarded a steamer that took her from the Gulf Islands to Sidney, Vancouver Island. There she caught a train to Victoria, and rode in a horse-drawn buggy from the station to the midwife's house. In the memoirs she left for the family, she described her experience:

Three weeks I waited, looking forward to bi-weekly letters from Ralph and writing to him. On the 15th of January, the midwife suggested an early morning walk would do me good. Fences came in handy.

Winifred Grey who "went out" from the Gulf Islands to have her fifth baby, leaving home on Christmas Day, 1901, and returning six weeks later.

She went into labor at ten that morning and still was in labor the following morning, "almost asleep in Jesus as we said in those days," she recorded. The visiting physician helped out and soon she had her baby girl, paying $25.00 for the doctor's fee. The midwife expected her to be walking around on the fourth day but she was far too weak, and rested in bed where pungent odors swept into the room from the adjacent livery stable. The letter she wrote to her husband to announce that all was well never did arrive so, frantic with worry, he had to row around to neighbors until he found someone who had received a letter saying that mother and daughter were well. When the new mother felt strong enough, she paid the midwife to accompany her in the horse and buggy to the station, then the train to Sidney, where she and the new child boarded the steamer for Saturna Island where Ralph Grey was waiting with his rowboat. Her confinement had meant that she had been away from the Gulf Islands for six weeks.

Interior and northern communities usually had a resident midwife, the wife of a settler who had an aptitude for nursing. In the Cariboo, Angelique Lyne was well known for her nursing abilities. She was five feet ten inches tall, with hazel eyes, that looked everyone straight in the eye. Her lustrous brown hair parted in the middle, and wound into a bun at the back for the day, or was plaited into two long braids when she went to bed. Daughter of Joseph Dussault, a former Hudson's Bay Company courier and his wife, Helene, the daughter of a Kamloops Indian Chief, she had been sent to the St. Joseph's Mission at Williams

Lake where the nuns had taught her. She had dreams of becoming a doctor but compromised by becoming a nursemaid for the children at the Dunlevy ranch. She married William Lyne in 1885. He ran a smithy where he shod oxen and mules. Soon they expanded into a ranch with a store that Angelique helped to run. She spoke fluent English, French, and Shuswap as well as the Chinook trading language. When local Indians were sick, they always hurried to Angelique, whose work became so well known that one physician who lived nine miles away at Soda Creek (a two-hour ride by team in those days) always called for her assistance at difficult births. She was capable of lancing infections and was calm and cool in an emergency. When she wasn't busy raising her own five children, cooking, washing, milking cows, gardening, making soap, canning or corning beef, making buckskin gloves and moccasins, sewing sheets, or herding sheep, she studied all the medical books she could find. Even in old age, people came to consult her.

Nancy Pearl Shaver who always helped others.   A

Nancy Pearl Shaver, affectionately known as "Granny", immigrated from Oregon to Merritt with her husband and three children early in 1918, then moved to the North Thompson area near Barriere. She delivered 50 babies in the Barriere, Louis Creek and Vavenby areas from 1919-1940, helped to clear a homestead, cope with a faltering marriage, and deal with the death of a beloved daughter. Her midwife skills were valued in nearby communities. On her own, she cared for her children.

Some midwives, among them Wilhelmina MacKenzie, received nursing training elsewhere. A Maritimer, determined to become a public health nurse, she went to the United States to study nursing, then she took her public health diploma at the University of British Columbia, becoming a public health nurse in Kamloops in 1921. Before long she married Roy Livingstone who was ranching, but who cut poles for cash to eke out the living costs on the homestead he had acquired. Wilhelmina carried on nursing as a volunteer community worker, travelling to people who needed her when necessary. The cost of any dressings or shots she would ask them to pay, but she gave her services free of charge. Her training enabled her to aid people hurt in industrial accidents both at a mill and a mine in nearby communities. When an epidemic of scarlet fever broke out in the community, she put on her starched nurse's apron, took plenty of disinfectant with her, and hurried out into the community; her husband was in total agreement with her plans to help others. He cared for the children and made cinnamon buns while she nursed others. When she had her own labor pains, her husband hitched up the team and rode five miles for help. It was too late; Wilhelmina had delivered her own child.

Gulf Islander Ellen Hawthorne (now Mrs. Stallybrass) was in her husband's cattle boat en route to the nearest hospital when Mary Ellen decided to be born.   B

As communities grew in size, small hospitals were built to serve local needs. By 1914, Gulf Islanders could use the small hospital established in Ganges, Salt Spring Island, although when Ellen Hawthorne set out from Mayne Island with her husband in the boat that he used for collecting sheep and lambs from all the islands, their daughter Mary Ellen decided to arrive before the boat docked.

In some areas, women without nursing experience found themselves called upon to assist at deliveries as Jenny Lawson Turnbull did when she became a "ranching wife" at Chilco near Vanderhoof in the 1920's. Her own memories of child delivery were vague since she had given birth to daughter Peggy in a New Zealand hospital, helped by a doctor, a nurse, and by considerable whiffs of chloroform. When a fellow set-

Wilhemina Livingstone, public health nurse at Kamloops who became community nurse in Little Fort and adjacent areas after marriage. Sometimes she escorted the sick on sixty mile train journey to Kamloops where the nearest hospital was situated. A

May Leppington, then May Hardie of South Vancouver, walked miles through the bush with a basket of medical supplies (homemade), when she helped people suffering from the 1918 influenza epidemic. B

The late Anne Young, Peace River nurse, shown with a quilt decorated with the names and birthdates of some 99 babies she delivered. C

tler, a new immigrant whose broken English was difficult to understand, came to the door for help, Jenny followed him to his home, assisted with the delivery of his wife's baby, and stayed around until the mother was rested and sitting up in bed with a cup of tea; *then* the new midwife fainted.

A community nurse often did not expect to be paid in the hungry Thirties but she was glad to accept fresh butter, eggs, or game. When one young English nurse arrived to run the Red Cross Outpost Hospital in Grandhaven, in the Spring of 1930, she rowed across the Peace River amid huge chunks of ice being carried downstream. Married to farmer Jim Young of Rose Prairie, Anne became a community nurse, going out to settlers in the district.

Once, when she was being driven in a sleigh to assist at a childbirth it seemed very cold, but bundled under rugs, a charcoal heater at her feet, she had no idea what the temperature was. The driver later confided that he had hoped the air wouldn't freeze the horses' lungs, as it was 70° below zero. She received a weaner pig as her fee that time; another time, she received a load of hay for her services, and once received two weaner pigs, since the family had not been able to give her any type of payment on her previous visit. Another Peace River Country woman, Mary Bennett, made her first ride on a saddle horse, travelling 75 miles to the Upper Halfway River area in 1932, where she spent three weeks with one rancher's wife, then a similar amount of time with another. She brought two children into the world, and took home a cow and a horse in payment for her services.

Trained nurses who married ranchers or farmers found plenty of occasions to practice their skills. Kathleen Telford of Alexis Creek, Chilcotin country, a graduate of St. Paul's Hospital, Vancouver, found herself back in home territory as a rancher's wife, often going on horseback to aid others. "Usually to fix broken bones," she says wryly at her Williams Lake home today. "And I seemed to be considered the local specialist for retained placenta cases."

Gertrude Stewart, another St. Paul's graduate, now a Kamloops resident, was living with her Provincial Policeman husband and one child at Agassiz in the Thirties when her second child arrived prematurely during a storm. "The whole house shook and there was little insulation . . . and there was the baby, could you believe it—one and a quarter pounds. That was all. The doctor said if she lived he would give me a medal. There was no oxygen for the baby, of course, so I put her in a shoebox stuffed with cotton wool. I had to put cotton wool under her ears, too, they were so thin they looked just like tissue paper, and I added just enough wood to the stove so the heat stayed fairly constant, then I put the shoebox with her in it, on the stove door. In two months she weighed two pounds. She's alive and kicking today, doing very well as an interior decorator.

Mrs. Stewart helped at clinics and always assisted when the local physician held his annual tonsil clinic—"There were always some 20 or 30 children who had to have their tonsils out."

When nursing assistance was not available, settlers had to make do as best they could, learning how to apply poultices, compresses, and splints until a patient could be driven by team or car the 50 miles—often more—to a doctor. Poultices of bread and goose grease made an

121

excellent liniment. It was a good idea to boil drinking water: "I'm convinced that's why we didn't suffer from typhoid fever when other families did," Peggy Russell of Fort St. James says today. Her mother, Jenny Turnbull, boiled everything on the Chilco ranch. "She scalded all utensils and set them out in the sun. And of course, it seems we were always drinking tea."

Herbal teas worked wonders, and still do. The sage tea that Mrs. Lequime used was probably served as a tonic. It's also excellent for easing a sore throat. Rosemary tea had a reputation for aiding migraine, strawberry leaves pressed against swollen gums decreased infection. The local women and the Indian women freely shared their knowledge of herbal medications. But neither herbal teas nor native medications could save numerous people from the 1918 'flu. It followed World War I, sweeping across the world as if mocking the loss of the many young men who had been killed; it brought further suffering to the women and children and aged. In cities, theatres and schools were closed. Hospitals were overcrowded and understaffed. What could anyone do?

"You kept them alive the best way you knew," May Leppington recalls. "It helped if you could get them to swallow some gruel." She and her mother nursed 'flu victims in South Vancouver with homemade concoctions of oils, lemons, brandy and castor oil. May recalls the night she was asked to help someone five miles away. She pushed through the bush carrying a lantern to reach her patient. "The family waited outside for me. I went in and saw that the fire was out, so the first thing to do was to light it. Then I gave the woman some brandy, a dose of castor oil, and then a hot lemon drink, packed her up with blankets, and let her sleep. She was on the mend within three days.

Young Winifred Francis of Ladner was a nurse in training at St. Paul's Hospital when her mother telephoned from Ladner to ask her to come to help the sick in the area. There were no nurses, no hospital, and only one overworked physician in the area. The student nurse and the doctor set up a makeshift hospital with the I.O.D.E. helping to provide supplies. When the local barber came to offer his assistance he was asked to knock down some of the building's walls so that bigger wards could be made.

Scandinavian pioneers, Hilda and Ole Larson were homesteading in the Cariboo when the flu struck. Ole was away on the traplines when his wife was taken sick. Before crawling weakly into bed, she managed to tell the children to pick and eat Saskatoon berries. Mrs. Larson was lucky: a passerby who heard her call for help sent his wife to do some home-nursing, then he hurried to locate Larson so that he would return to care for the children. The nurse rendered some animal fat, added turpentine, and soaked strips of wool in the mixture to make chest plasters. Mrs. Larson, who was in bed with her eyes closed, heard the woman tell her family that she thought the sick woman would not last very long unless her cough could be checked. There and then, determined not to leave her family, she decided that she would not give up.

During the wide-spread epidemic, emergency tent hospitals were set up in small towns with volunteers working all hour of the day and night. There was no antibiotic to help them in their efforts. Near Vanderhoof, an entire Mennonite community was affected, with whole families dying from the disease. In Merritt, the newly arrived Shaver family found they both had work in 1918: Mrs. Shaver nursed people in the community while her husband had the grim task of helping to bury those who were already dead and made handles for the hastily built coffins.

Later, when the family homesteaded in the North Thompson area, where Nancy Pearl Shaver became community midwife, she found there was nothing she could do to ease daughter Violet's severe stomach pains. The girl was sent to the Kamloops hospital.

The next news the family received was word of Violet's death. She had died from a ruptured appendix; all the home nursing and all the love in the world could not help an illness like that in the days before antibiotics.

Doukhobor cemetery at Brilliant, B.C.   *A*

Violet Shaver who had come up from Oregon to the Barriere district with her family. She died from something no home nursing could aid—a ruptured appendix.   *B*

When the Kuper Island church closed in the Gulf Islands, the Anglican burial grounds no longer could be used. The "C.V.H.S." stands for the Chemainus Valley Historical Society.   *C*

123

Three pans of gold, Barkerville, B.C.
A

Early days of Barkerville Dramatic Society.
B

The Bank of British Columbia, incorporated by Royal Charter, 1862—Here is the five dollar bill.
C

CHAPTER NINE:

They danced a'nicht in dresses light

Fra late until the early O!

But O, their hearts were as hard as flint

Which vexed the laddies sairly, O.

As chaste as china in a closet, or so the writers of the era would have
us believe, the Hurdy Gurdy girls were the second-best attraction of
the Cariboo in the 1860's. The first attraction was gold, of course, but
the girls drew men into the saloons and theatres where miners paid
50 cents for the privilege of dancing with them, a rate that soon soared
to a dollar per dance.

They were strong European girls, mostly German, who had been
brought out to the California goldfields first, paying back their passage costs at high interest rates to entrepreneurs who had foreseen
their popularity. They earned their name from the music they danced
to, the raucous kick-up-your-heels hurdy gurdy piano music of the day.
As dancers, they wouldn't have won any awards but they had stamina
and plenty of it. They spoke little English but this didn't seem to matter. They were tossed around, swung up and down, and sometimes
held upside down so their feet could "dance on the ceiling." They came
in all shapes and sizes and were known for their bizarre costumes,
usually a peculiarly unattractive outfit with a cotton skirt, silk blouse
and hats that reporters of the day described as resembling the top
knot of a turkey gobbler.

The first group of dancers to be brought to British Columbia came into
what was to be known as Barkerville in 1863, the year after Billy Barker
had dug deep into bedrock to find plenty of gold. The area was boom-
ing when the girls arrived. The syndicate that brought them to town had
ordered a piano from Victoria, which was shipped via Quesnel, then
carried in its crate by four men for the 59 mile journey to the goldfields.
The girls became so popular that their male supervisors had to ask
Madame Bendixon to supervise them. That redoubtable lady claimed to
be the only woman who had packed her own belongings on her back
from the mining town of Antler to Williams Creek, where she planned
to open a saloon. Already she was a well-built woman. Later she was
reported to have required two chairs before she could sit comfortably
in her saloon.

Miners cheerfully paid for the privilege of holding the girls in their
arms, or to stomp around "dancing." The women were so popular that
a second group was sent to the area in 1867. The *Cariboo Sentinel* made a
cryptic announcement of the group's arrival but described the dancers'
first ball in some detail in the March 16, 1867 edition:

Messrs. Adler and Barry's large saloon was crowded on Saturday night with the boys who had collected from every corner
of the creek, to have a peep at the "hurdies" who made their
debut . . . many of the boys were unable to resist the tempta-
tion of indulging in the "mazy" dance while their chums
crowded around them in a circle and applauded their efforts

*Organ in St. Saviour's Church, Barkerville. Early
pianos used in saloons were carried by men, not
horses, all the way from Quesnel.*

125

in a most demonstrative manner. So great was the noise at times that it was next to impossible for the leader of the orchestra to keep anything like regularity in the management of the dance...."

It was rumored that one of the girls indirectly caused the area's 1868 fire that burned Barkerville to the ground. She supposedly was ironing when a lonely miner insisted on kissing her, a gesture that either was so acceptable that she forgot about the hot iron, or else so disastrous that, in the ensuing struggle, someone knocked the stove-pipe out of place. Either way, the fire was started and it raced through town in an hour and 20 minutes, leaving only a couple of buildings standing.

Social events were attended by mining officials, businessmen and their wives, and always included the flamboyant Wellington Delaney Moses. Moses arrived in Victoria from the United States in 1858, made a disastrous marriage, then went on to the Fraser mining camps where he cut hair and sold his famous "Moses Hair Restorer". That concoction made triple claims of acting as a hair tonic, hair colorant, and cured headaches. How could it fail to be a popular item? Moses did well enough with it that he carried on to the Cariboo, opening a barbershop and haberdashery in the area to be known as Barkerville. His store served the town's elite, who bought their clothes there as well as anything they wanted from toys to umbrellas or medicines to watches. He sold mining shares on the side and loaned money to Dr. Chipps, the local surgeon, whose daughter bought her clothes from the Negro businessman. The Hurdy Gurdy girls shopped in his store, too, where one known as Gentle Annie ran up the following account on July 15, 1875:

Early view of Yale, B.C. showing the S.S. "R. P. Rithet", the sternwheeler operated by Captain Irving which was described as a "floating palace" when she made her maiden run in 1882.

Undershirt	$8.00
Hat	5.00
Lubin Extract	1.50
Cash Loan	3.00
2 Hankerchiefs	1.50
Stockings	1.00
Corset	3.50
	26.50
Ribbon	.50
	$27.00

By 1880, Madame Bendixon was heavier than ever and local children estimated she weighed several hundred pounds. Hurdy Gurdy girls and other saloon girls stayed until the cold weather arrived. Spring saw the snow melt, the return of the girls and such big social events as horseracing and elaborate Chinese funeral processions.

Wiggs O'Neill, who was seven that year, noted that there were innumerable town characters, including an Irishwoman who raised chickens behind her kitchen stove, "Old Norburg" who was paid in liquor for acting as chief mourner at elaborate Chinese funeral processions, and a policeman who loved a fight. Mrs. Charles O'Neill rode on horseback to make the rounds of mining camps where she collected donations for the Sisters of St. Ann who appeared occasionally seeking financial assistance for their hospitals.

Among the women in the area was a woman imported from China and described in the *Cariboo Sentinel* in August 10, 1872:

We understand that a Celestial Lady from the Flowery Kingdom changed hands during the week in Barkerville at the handsome figure of $700.00. It is said that the lady, who is a votary of the Cyprian Goddess, feels highly elated that her entrancing charms and wonderful fascinations should have realized such a satisfactory price. We recommend the subject to the consideration of the Grand Jury at the next Assizes.

Cariboo Cameron's first cabin, Barkerville. A

The "Creek area" was named Barkerville some six years after Billy Barker struck deep into the rich veins of glittering gold. A year after this he married a widow, Elizabeth Collyer, who helped him enjoy his money. Neither his marriage nor his fortune lasted long. He died penniless and had to be buried in a pauper's grave.

As the *British Colonist* pointed out in July, 1863, there were few "ladies" in that area. "There are about ten who have come up no doubt for reasons best explained in the book of Common Prayer." The newspaper described a recent banquet and advised its readers that another entertainment would be held soon: "*No cards* as paper is scarce, and the entertainers can't write and many of the invited can't read. Good reasons these."

The miners worked hard, as Alexander Allen, publisher of the *Cariboo Sentinel*, wrote to his mother to report:

March 8, 1868:

[Many] are now making their fortunes but it is also true that a far greater number rank as unfortunates . . . have to live in hovels . . . and this, too, in a climate where the mercury freezes. They often have to go to their laborious toil (pursued in holes where they are scantily drenched to the skin with water) with but scantily filled stomachs.

Cariboo Cameron and his partner, Robert Stevenson. Both men came from Upper Canada to the mining fields where they made a fortune. Cameron lost his through poor investments; Stevenson expanded his claims. B

Typhoid fever caused by a lack of sewage facilities ran through some camps and it probably was the cause of young Sophia Cameron's death. One of the few wives to accompany her husband to the mining area in 1862, she was staying in the Richfield area on Williams Creek while her husband John Cameron was digging for gold with his partner, Robert Stevenson. When she fell ill with "mountain fever," there was nothing anyone could do to help; Stevenson described her as "tall, beautiful and about 28 years of age" and he helped the grieving husband to find someone who could make a rough wooden casket encased in tin. Most of the miners had left for the winter and were living it up in Victoria, then a tent town with a small scattering of settled areas. Ninety miners attended Sophia's first funeral on an October day when the winds rose to 65 miles an hour and the temperature sank to 30° below zero. The coffin was then placed in state at the back of the mining cabin, while Cameron and his friends, all men from Upper Canada, began sinking shafts, staying with their work until they struck the rich bed of gold that ultimately became part of the Cameronton area. Their strike was made in December but they kept the news to themselves: Cameron was anxious by now to take his wife's body to Victoria for embalming.

General view of Quesnel, 1865.   A

The beautiful Sophia Cameron whose death and funerals promoted legends and gossip.   B

One of talented Sarah Crease's early sketches made at Fort
Yale in 1862 and depicting Indian Reserve.   C

Lady Sarah Crease in the garden at Pentrelew, Victoria. She
often travelled with her husband as he heard trials in courts
near mining towns.   D

Stevenson and the others in the group started out for Victoria at the end of January, 1863. They wore snowshoes and the late lady was in her coffin which was lashed to a toboggan. Blankets, a keg of rum, food, and 50 pounds of gold dust covered the top of the coffin. By the time the group had reached Antler and then Swift River, the temperature had sunk below zero. Occasionally the toboggan overturned and once did this on a hill when the keg of rum rolled away, striking a tree so that the bung was knocked out and the liquor drained away. By late that day, the men's situation was desperate: they had neither food nor matches and they no longer knew where they were. Stevenson volunteered to go ahead in an effort to locate a crossing at Keightley Creek; he was successful, so the group abandoned their toboggan and the coffin under the trees for the night, took the blankets and gold dust and hurried off to Keightley where there was a small roadhouse and store.

In the morning, they reclaimed the toboggan, and set off for Quesnelle Forks where they stayed in the hotel operated by the well known Mrs. Lawless, who had a reputation for drinking any man under the table and whose drinking habits sometimes led her to court where she always refused to reveal her identity. Some in the group elected to stay in the area, so Cameron paid $300 for a horse and he and Stevenson went on alone with the gold dust, blankets, new food supplies, the coffin, and the toboggan. Stevenson led the way, the horse pulled the toboggan, and Cameron plodded along behind. As they made their way through the Lac La Hache valley, they could see numerous snowgraves of Indians who had been killed by smallpox; most of the settlements appeared to be deserted with only one or two band members still alive. The tragic situation was duplicated at Lillooet and Douglas where there were more snow mounds covering the corpses who had been given this temporary burial until spring when the ground softened and permanent burials could be made.

Cameron and Stevenson arrived in Victoria on March 6 aboard the *Enterprise*, captained by William Mouat. Mrs. Cameron's frozen body was handed to an undertaker for embalming, and on March 8, a second funeral was held, with some 800 miners most of whom had wintered in Victoria, attending. The Late Lady, now preserved in alcohol, was given a temporary burial in the Quadra Street cemetery, and Stevenson and Cameron made their way back to their mining claims. They did very well and it was six months before they returned to Victoria, when Sophia was disinterred and placed in a new box. Her corpse, in its new coffin, was part of a shipment sent from the Colony of Vancouver Island via the Isthmus of Panama to Upper Canada. Cameron and Stevenson, both of whom made huge amounts of money, were returning home, too. A third funeral ceremony was held for Sophia Cameron in Cornwall, but when her relatives asked Cameron to open the coffin so they could view her body he refused to do so, an error which later brought about huge waves of gossip. The gossip increased, and after nine years Cameron was forced to face relatives who insisted that something was wrong: why was he so rich and why had he refused to show them that their Sophia was dead? The rumor made the rounds that he had sold her to an Indian chief and was living on the proceeds of the sale. Cameron had by now remarried, and had acquired a farm on the banks of the St. Lawrence, but this venture proved to be a disaster.

Forced to face local opinion, he finally opened the coffin and relatives agreed that what they saw did resemble Sophia. Now the ghost of his first wife was laid to rest, his farm was proving a disaster, and Cameron decided to head west with his new wife. They went to the Cariboo where Cameron expected to strike gold, but he was taken ill and died. By contrast, his partner, Stevenson, made excellent investments in the Fraser and Similkameen Valleys and was prosperous.

There still was enough crime in the mining camps to bring in stipendiary magistrates and visiting judges. Judges Cox, Brew, and the famous "Hanging" Judge Matthew Begbie frequently travelled to Cariboo towns. Occasionally, they meted out fines to the prostitutes who frequented saloons, as did Judge Crease who became Sir Henry Pering Pellew Crease, Attorney General for the Colony of British Columbia. For his July, 1875, judgment and lecture to "two women of the unfortunate class," he was mocked by the British Colonist. Lady Crease liked to accompany her husband at times, writing numerous letters back to her family in Victoria. She was a skilled artist, fascinated by natural history. She illustrated most of her letters, including the one she wrote from Quesnel on October 2, 1880:

Steamer leaves here for Soda Creek. There is not much to say of this place . . . the town looks much like others in the Cariboo, without so strong a Chinese appearance and without being propped up on logs. The Fraser is running past our window. Within a stone's throw on the other bank opposite are low hills, covered with scrub willow and cottonwood. Almost at right angles to the Fraser is the Quesnel, a swift river now very low . . . you must fancy Chinamen rocking for gold along its banks.

She forgot to mention that the Bank of British Columbia at Quesnel supplied plug tobacco free to customers who often spent hours around the spittoons discussing mining claims. The Chinese she described were mostly freemen who had come from California with other miners. Later, after the completion of the Canadian Pacific Railway, some of the Chinese who had worked for the railroad company headed north. They were placer miners mostly, working claims deserted by others but doing well enough. Their large community at Quesnelle Forks had impressive buildings with a Joss House that functioned also as a court house, employment bureau, spiritual sanctuary and funeral home.

Other mining communities were enjoying boomdays. In the Kootenays, Rossland was becoming an active town. Entertainment there in 1895 often consisted of mountain parties where Norwegian skiier Olaus Jeldness would ski down the slopes, right over any trains that happened to be waiting at the station. Rossland had its share of missionaries that year: Lieutenant Ziebarth and Ensign Woolem, two young Salvation Army lassies, were in the area to save souls; Anglican priest Father "Pat" visited the camps and trappers' cabins; and some Roman Catholic nuns arrived in 1896 to start a hospital. They started with a temporary building using packing cases as tables, there were seepages of water under everything, and there was no bank account. A store loaned the nuns a copper bath and each morning a volunteer bucket brigade of miners cheerfully filled the tub from a spring which flowed through the property. This gave the nuns fresh water. The women started their hospital in faith, hiring a contractor when they

Joss House, interior view, Chinatown, Victoria. Other such retreat and religious centres flourished in mining towns.   B

Chinese funerals were important and elaborate events Whether they were held in Quesnel, Barkerville or Vancouver. This one was held in Vancouver.   A

Tent town of miners in Victoria has melted into a respectable city in this picture where Empress Hotel is in final stage of construction.   C

Ikeda Mine, Queen Charlotte Islands.   D

Old Cornish Wheel At Bralorne, B.C.
Delina Litalien-Laventure Noel of Lillooet
joined her husband on pack train journey
in 1900 to Anderson Lake area. By 1902
she was superintendent of stamp mill and
top man in mining shafts. By 1909 she
took her own gold brick by stage to Van-
vouver assay office. Her claims for Lorne
Gold Mining & Milling were forerunners
to Bralorne Mine.   A

had collected some funds, and promising to pay him weekly. One Saturday night when no funds were available, the nuns went around all the hotels and saloons for money. They soon collected $500, which proved miners were generous men. Rossland had its notorious Red Light houses, the *Texas Steer*, being famous for its friendliness. It had two proprietors, Misses Watson and Harding, and "Six Ladies in Attendance." The "Saloon" printed a booklet with topical advice on the following subjects:

MONEY: Yes, we need thee, every hour we need thee. Should you call when the house is crowded, just put your money under the door, with your name and address, we will credit your account with same.

SOCIETY: Our society is select, and our friends chosen. Ladies applying for admission must come well recommended and without incumbrance.

POLITENESS: Ladies and gentlemen addressing each other in the parlour will please say "Mr. and Mrs. So and So." To address a person by their given names flavor too much of familiarity, which we try to avoid in the presence of strangers, besides it too much resembles a pink tea party.

In Nelson, girls from the Red Light district were hauled into court regularly. Once a month they faced the judge and it became accepted practice that a madam would be fined $40 for her role, the girls $10 each. Nelson's other life centered around its Opera House, where important guests were invited to sing. People came from nearby communities to attend performances, travelling by railway, although in winter a snow drift often delayed the train which was bringing the performer to town. Concerts often were held late at night because of this. International singers such as Dorothy Toye and Madame Melba sang in Nelson where the latter's presence raised the price of each ticket to $10.

One singer who always arrived on time was the soprano simply billed as Miss Irving. She had graced Victoria with her soprano voice early in 1875, then took her talents to the Cassiar mining area. She made $80 in Laketown where miners turned out en masse to hear the latest of popular music. However, one performance made its mark. Only a scattering of miners came to the second concert and the artist strode from the stage in a huff while the few miners in the audience hurried away to a local saloon. Laketown was not ready for opera.

On the other hand the Cassiar area provided another woman with plenty of success. Nellie Cashman, sometimes known as Nellie Pioche, probably because she had come from Pioche in the Utah mining district, opened a hotel there in 1870. To reach Cassiar, she travelled to Wrangell, Alaska, then took the route down the frozen Stikine to reach Cassiar. At Wrangell the United States Army were astonished to find a woman travelling alone on such a route and sent a corps after her on the trail. She was cooking a meal on a campfire and appeared to be enjoying herself so they returned to base camp. Nellie stayed single, although she had a strong maternal concern for everyone. She spent the harsh winters in Victoria and when she returned north each summer, she collected money for the city's St. Joseph's Hospital. In 1875, she saved the lives of a group of miners who were weak and suffering from the effects of scurvy. She took them medicine and made a brew from spruce boughs which saved their lives. After that, she always was known as the "Angel of Cassiar."

One of the few women entrepreneurs in the mining business was Alice Elizabeth Jowett, an English widow who left Bradford, Yorkshire, with four small children and sailed to British Columbia via Cape Horn in the 1880's. She was independent and optimistic, preferring to work for herself rather than for others. In England, she had learned the confectionary trade so she opened a confectionary store on Cordova Street in Vancouver, doing a good trade. The newspaper publicity and her customer's stories of mining successes in the Lardeau area whetted her own interest and business sense. She moved her family to Trout Lake, buying an old log lodge where she served meals and rented out rooms. Business was so good that she had the Windsor Hotel built at the lake's edge. The three-storey wooden building served local mining officials and miners and she used immaculately clean tablecloths of Irish linen and heavy silver cutlery. Her meals were good; she often served a traditional Yorkshire meal of roast beef, high-domed Yorkshire pudding and roast potatoes, all washed down by home-made port wine. To keep her hotel as one of the area's most popular attractions, she opened a games room and extended the bar, hiring a barman.

She believed in physical fitness and exercised at home with dumbbells. Outside she walked and rode horseback along trails that led past the miner's cabins. Talking to her customers, and seeing many of them at work on claims in the area, she gradually became more interested in prospecting, and staked some silver and gold claims. Becoming more knowledgeable, she ventured out to mining conventions. She continued to stake claims, one of which, a gold mine, sold for $20,000 some years later. Aged 92 in 1946, she eagerly accepted an opportunity to see how her properties looked from the air. When she was 100, she moved to a Kelowna rest home but she maintained a keen interest in mining ventures. Before she died in 1955, she claimed her nose had led her to gold and that she could smell a rich untapped bed of gold. Further, she said that neither courage nor a sense of adventure had made her an entrepreneur of her day: it simply was an abundance of energy. She liked to keep busy.

Getting the gold to the bank was a risky venture at the best for most miners. Robberies, crimes of violence, and fights had helped to create a new career for the shot-gun guard who rode the stage with a gun at the ready to handle highway robbers. Soon, there were other riders on the stage: women leaving the goldfields where they had been to dance, live in a Red Light District, or befriend a miner. Indian women, as well as the saloon girls of all nationalities, were noticed on the stage-coaches, all with a common characteristic: they were strangely fat around the stomach. These women were very quiet and snobbish for they carried a cache of gold dust under their gowns and under their chemises. They didn't dare speak to the men beside them for fear a confidence man might be on board. Holdups were common but no report had been made of anyone stripping women to see if they carried gold under their clothes. For their efforts, they gained a free ride "outside," and a generous commission—*after* they had deposited the miner's gold in the bank.

134

Mrs. Alice Jowett, taken June 22, 1947, who staked her claims around Trout Lake and adjacent areas, riding to them on horseback, claiming she could "smell out" the silver.   A

The circus comes to Nelson at the turn of the century. Pioneer Archie M. Johnson and his little daughter in the foreground.   B

Once a boom town with the mining day excitement now only a memory: Atlin, B.C.   C

Aboard the stage—in winter, of course, at Quesnel, B.C.   A

Old Fraser River Ferry at Quesnel,   B.C. circa 1909. Auguste Baker was ferryman.

   B

Clinton Hotel around 1868, showing oxen team, Clinton, B.C.   C

Riding the stage was an adventure at any time. The drivers were famous, handling the team with the dramatic actions of impassioned heroes or simply relying on skill and patience. Down steep grades, around curves, and along flat stretches of the road, the stage bowled, carrying passengers, mail, and freight. As the roads were built, they headed further north carrying an increasing number of women passengers, not gold carriers, but miners' wives who had been informed that strikes had been made, or that their husbands had given up mining, and had pre-empted some of that rich land alongside the Cariboo roads. There was the Lillooet-Clinton road via Pavilion Mountain, then the Yale to Clinton road, which joined the road from Lillooet, then edged beyond Soda Creek where steamers took the river route to Quesnel. Eventually, the roads extended to Quesnel, and finally into Williams Creek. Then the Canadian Pacific Railway ran its steel tracks into the dry belt area around Ashcroft.

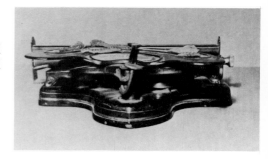

First typewriter in British Columbia. Mining meant papers and legal forms—and the typewriters proved necessary. A

Roadhouses varied in style and construction. Originally built for road-crews, the milehouses soon became stopping houses where freighters and stage drivers could rest, eat, drink, and sleep. The stage changed horses at some stops and roadhouse operators provided feed for the animals as well as hearty meals for the passengers. Some houses were notorious for their bed-bugs, while others were known for their bar.

When the Anglican Bishop Sillitoe went travelling, his wife often accompanied him and recorded her experiences. She described one stopping house where no other women were present:

I had been ushered into a large barroom, or at least what appeared to be one, with ten or twelve men lounging about. I was very tired, and making for the nearest chair, felt a great inclination to weep . . . to be left unprotected in the company of so many unknown men was terrifying. It soon became evident [that] they were equally [terrified] of me.

When her husband returned with his host after unharnessing the horses, the Sillitoes were ushered into superior accommodation: they spent the night in a one-room cabin with a mud floor.

Mule train at Hazelton, B.C.
B

Other travellers recorded their experiences. Martha O'Neill, a young girl leaving Barkerville with her brother and mother in the 1880's, remembered the shocking "Mrs. Marshall who smoked and cursed. This lady roadhouse proprietor, whose establishment was near Clinton, had a habit of kicking out her foot and scratching matches on the soles of her shoe. Horrors!". Kezia Pollard, who ran a stopping house on the Pollard Ranch in the Clinton area, was known for opposite qualities, of meekness and sweetness. South of Quesnel, there was Lansdowne House, popular with teamsters, where Henry Moffat had married Jennie Roddie on August 25, 1890. The couple kept a daybook and since Henry—sometimes known as Harry—was often away driving freight to Barkerville, Jennie's entries gave a view of a woman's life at the stopping house and ranch:

June 7, 1892:

China Boys stopped work today. Ditch is finished. Very heavy rain here tonight.

Alexander Bohanon Moffat started to creep tonight for the first time at 6 o'clock. . . .

I, Mrs. Moffat, had two little ducks come out today. Mother and ducks are doing well at Lansdowne.

June 28, 1892:

I, Mrs. Moffat, picked a little basket full of strawberries this morning. . . .

June 30, 1892:

No one passed today.

August 8, 1892:

Harry started up to Barkerville with load of potatoes today.

October 7, 1892:

Stage came here tonight with Judge Riely *(sic)*. Changed horses and went on to Soda.

December 14, 1892:

B.C. Express Company. To meal by Mr. Parker: $1.50. Mr. Tingley and Mr. Parker changed horses here last night.

December 23, 1893:

Mr. William Parker:
To staying overnight, bed and breakfast: $1.00.
Horse, hay, grain: $1.00.

January 2, 1894:

Mr. Middleton, Mr. Craig, Mr. Olson, Mr. McLeod, Johnn McInnes. All came here this morning and drunk wisky *(sic)* and ate cake so they could not see straight.

March 7, 1894:

B.C. Express Company:

To one meal by Mr. Parker: .50 cents.
Bishop and his wife went up as passengers.
Bob Orr has gone to Quesnelle. . . .

September 18, 1894:

Nan Sing: To one horse overnight: .75 cents.
Harry came home tonight. Brought back with him salt and sugar.

September 19, 1894:

Two Chinamen came here this morning to pick potatoes.
The Sisters called in on their way down; we gave them $1.00.

October 15, 1894:

Doctor Runnels and Family:
To staying overnight:

8 meals	$4.00
100 lbs. oats	2.50
3 horses hay	1.20
By cash	$7.70

Harry started off this morning for Barkverville.

Jennie was high spirited but her moods could rise and fall like the temperature. The family knew which mood she was in by the way she referred to them in the journal. Her husband was sometimes referred to as "Moffat," "Henry Moffat," or "Harry." He was Protestant while

Charlotte Kathleen O'Reilly, daughter of Peter O'Reilly, Magistrate and Golf Commissioner for the Colony of British Columbia. "Kit" O'Reilly led a life of picnics, banquets, balls and fashion and never saw how miserable the lives of some miners were. She dropped one fiancee, an English Lord, to date Explorer Scott, but he married someone else. Her gowns can be seen at Point Ellice House, Victoria.   *A*

The Moffat family at Lansdowne House in 1911. Famous Cariboo pioneers Harry and Jennie Moffat solved religious differences by raising the boys as Protestants and the girls as Roman Catholics. Lansdowne House is being restored by a fourth generation member of the family today.   *B*

Robert Dunsmuir, mine owner, whose tactics in strike-breaking caused controversy when he employed immigrant labor.
A

Mrs. Robert Dunsmuir whose husband promised her a castle and built one—Craigdarroch, in Victoria.
B

Fraser gold dredge.
C

she was Roman Catholic; they came to an agreement about the children: the boys would be raised as Protestants while the girls would become Roman Catholics. Jennie was busy raising a large family, preparing accounts, cooking for guests, but also found time to knit. She made a pair of gloves for her husband which had one finger noticeably shorter than the others. She cautioned him that he must never leave them anywhere as the entire world would see the flaw. One day it happened. He was at Boyd's Cottonwood House, talking horseflesh and freight, and he left his gloves behind. Jennie soon heard that teamsters, miners, and ministers had seen the two gloves displayed beside the prominent sign: Harry Moffat's gloves.

Son Roddie Moffat lives near the family ranch, now operated by the fourth generation of the family. He can remember the big boxstove enclosed by railings on which the freighters hung their wet clothes. The men sat chewing snoose as they "sewed on the poppers," the silk tassels on their whips. Every now and then a group would call to see who was going to a dance somewhere along the road. Men and women would go off on the stage, sometimes stopping to dance at all the other stopping houses on the way there and back. Among other customers, the Chinese "pigman" appeared each year, leading between 50 and 100 pigs all the way to Barkerville where he had an eagerly waiting group of patrons who wanted pork. Annually, he drove the pigs along the road, stopping at the roadhouses or ranches where he had made arrangements for feed. Young Roddie Moffat would sometimes take his own pigs down to the road which caused a scattering of pigs in all directions with a frustrated pigman waving his stick wildly until, eventually, all the pigs were sorted out and herded along the road once more.

As mining booms became less frequent, more and more people turned to the land, and as cars began to replace the reliable horses, roadhouses saw their business shrink. In their heyday each roadhouse had its own reputation: some for the food they provided, some for the liquor, and some for their hay beds where the bedbugs leapt around with lively appetites. They all had some things in common: from the stables there was the smell of dried hay and rich manure; from the kitchens there was the smell of roast meats or hot soup and from the meeting room the smell of musty-moist clothing drying near the potbellied stove.

Another woman who didn't get to the goldfields but whose husband's mining interests paid off. Mrs. J.H. Fletcher of Victoria.

The old Cape Beale Lighthouse, one of the earliest on the coast.   A

Helicopter pads are part of large lighthouse and wireless stations today.   B

CHAPTER TEN:

ISOLATION

Women settlers in rural areas often endured loneliness and sometimes isolation but they had an occasional chance to see other women, perhaps at a barn-raising event, a pie-social, or at a yearly, monthly or weekly visit to a store to pick up mail, to buy flour, sugar, and tea, and to stay for awhile to chat. The women on lighthouses or in the wilderness sometimes spent months without seeing another woman. They had to be self-sufficient, hardy, and able to deal with any situation that might arise.

Lighthouse living is still shaped by weather but the style of living has changed over the years. It's no longer necessary to live at the base of a building where the walls lean in. The light is now electric, operated by a switch. Union rulings and the complexities of equipment mean there is little repair work to be done. Lightkeepers today use radio telephone or telephone lines, and in an emergency they can summon a helicopter. Salaries now run from $8,000-$12,000, an amount not to be sniffed at as light and heat are usually free. In early days, if a keeper saved money, people were convinced he or she had been rum-running, a common enough occurrence then.

Lightkeepers and their wives needed courage, mechanical genius, self-reliance and plenty of inner peace in early days; if the latter was lacking they faced neuroses or alcoholism, sometimes both. Lightkeepers' wives often worked in close partnership with their husbands, often becoming assistants to them as did the wife of Emmanuel Cox, first keeper at Cape Beale in the 1880's. The Cape Beale light records showed what life was like:

October, 1886:

3   Indians here with mail bag. Paid him five dollars.

5   Rain running down east side of the Tower.

7   Glass broken.

8   *Hope* passed for Alberni at 8 of a.m.

9   *Hope* passed for Victoria 2 of p.m.

11   Glass broken.

18   Steamer *Douglas* passed here for Dodger's Cove at 10 of a.m.

February, 1887:

8   Plat *(sic)* glass in lantern frozen inside and outside.
Indian mail carrier here, he had to get 2 Indians to come here, the sea so bad, he broke his canoe going out. Had to let him have the Lighthouse boat.

25   Ship sighted at 4 . . . Gale commenced. Blowing with great violence all the time. The sheet iron on top of chimney wrecked. The brick loosed and portion of chimney burned.

Some lighthouse women were heroines, saving ships in distress and their owners. Minnie Paterson, wife of the Cape Beale lighthouse keeper 20 years after the Coxes served there, won fame for her heroism on two occasions in 1906. The first of these occurred early in the year when she went without sleep for some 70 hours, nursing the chilled survivors of the S.S. *Valencia* wreck. Later that year, Mrs. Paterson's courage and determination were demonstrated once again when she made her now famous journey through wet, gale-ridden forests to obtain aid for the barque *Coloma*; as a result of her heroic efforts, 38 of the barque's crewmen were saved from drowning. That day, howling winds already had brought down all the telephone lines connecting Cape Beale with Bamfield, and Bamfield with Victoria. As visibility diminished, Lighthouse Keeper Paterson could see the *Coloma* foundering in heavy seas. Peering through the fog and rain, Paterson noted that the barque's fore and mizzen masts had snapped off, leaving only the main mast around which the crew huddled while heavy seas washed over the vessel's decks. He could not leave his post to seek help, although he and his wife knew that the S.S. *Quadra* was near Bamfield, and that if she could be reached, she would be capable of attempting a rescue mission. Fearing for the *Coloma's* men, Mrs. Paterson, mother of five, volunteered to undertake the dangerous journey in search of aid, following the trail to Bamfield Creek.

She dressed in heavy clothing, choosing to wear her husband's slippers which were comfortable on her feet. She set out in a rip-roaring gale, carrying only a lantern to light the way through creeks, along the reaches of the shores, up cliffs, and along the corduroy trail where she slipped several times in the mud. Her journey lengthened because the gale had uprooted trees, making it necessary for her to try to find a way through the bush. It took her several hours to cover some nine or ten miles to the McKay homestead at Bamfield Creek. She was soaked through but in good spirits as she rapped on the McKay's door. McKay was out, repairing telephone lines but his wife Annie immediately set out with Minnie Paterson, the two women rowing out in a tiny boat in heavy seas towards the *Quadra*. A boat had just been lowered and officers were coming their way so they relayed the message, getting the assurance that the *Quadra* would go to aid the sinking ship. Mrs. Patterson stayed for tea and toast with her friend, then a couple of operators from the Bamfield Wireless Station accompanied her on part of the way home before she continued alone in the dark. She was cold and suffering from stomach cramps but she didn't dare stop for fear she would collapse. Press reporters who interviewed Mrs. Paterson later described her as a natural, quiet person, who wore her hair in braids. She didn't even consider that she had done anything outstanding.

Annie McKay, daughter of the lighthouse keeper Emmanuel Cox, formerly of the Cape Beale Lighthouse, knew all about isolation. On one occasion during her girlhood she helped her mother when a revolving mechanism of the light failed during her father's absence. All the Cox children and their mother took turns in the tower, turning the light's revolving mechanism by hand. They sent their friend, John Mack, with his Indian canoe on the two-day journey to Victoria for help. The *James Douglas* lighthouse tender brought back Mr. Cox, Mr. Mack, the Indian canoe together with a new revolving mechanism.

Point Atkinson Light.

Mr. McKay's sister, Mrs. Pattie Haslam, was working as a telegraph operator at Cape Beale when a full-rigged ship, the *Old Kensington* was becalmed and drifted dangerously close to rocks. Pattie wired Victoria for a tug but no company would come without a guarantee of $500.00. Pattie took it upon herself to guarantee that amount and the following day the tug arrived to tow the ship away from danger. Months later, the heroine received a package from China. The ship's captain thanked her for her action by sending a silk shawl, five pounds of Chinese tea, and a photograph of his ship under full sail.

The George Davies family was sent to Egg Island light in Queen Charlotte Sound in 1906 where the light then was situated on a small island linked to a larger island. They faced a unique situation there, since about every four years a huge sea washed in. Once it took out the hoisting shed, another time the oil shed. Long after the Davies had been transferred to another lighthouse, the new keepers looked out and saw the sea rising around them. They just had time to snatch up some supplies and wade across the flooded bridge to the other island. As they looked back they saw the entire lighthouse being swept away. Todays light is on high ground.

In 1910, the Davies family was sent to the West Coast's most harsh environment near the Scott chain of islands, Triangle Island which emerges from a chain of treacherous reefs and rocks in an area known for its fog, its terrible tides and moody winds. A light and wireless station were built there early in the 1900's; the tower sat on top of 700 feet of rock, overlooking the wild seas, flashing its warning to sailors who ventured along that terrible coast. When the family arrived to put the light into operation, they found that lifelines were strung from building to building. Sometimes they and the wireless operators had to crawl on hands and knees, hanging to the lifelines as they moved from one building to another ina strong wind. The lantern needed special bracing. On calm days, the children explored the bird sanctuary, where tufted puffins, exotic sea birds with white faces and large parrot shaped beak nested in burrows or the penguinlike murres nested on cliffs. The girls liked the sea lion rookeries, too. In the evenings they had their school lessons at home with one or other of the bachelors who operated the wireless station coming over to teach them Mathematics, English or History.

One woman, a widow, Mary Ann Croft, ran Discovery Island Light from 1901 until she retired in 1932. She was the daughter of a lighthouse keeper, Richard Brinn, and enjoyed the life; she had one assistant, a man who operated the fog alarm. Usually women worked in partnership with their lighthouse keeper husbands, chopping wood for those hungry old stoves, or cleaning the light itself. The light was treasured by most women; they enjoyed cleaning the prisms of cut glass. Among the numerous supplies the tender brought for lighthouse housekeeping were glass cloth, linen, flannelette and glycerine—the latter was smeared on the tower windows in bad weather so that the snow would slide off.

Pachena Light in the 1940's.

Water supplies came from an intricate piping system that gathered rainwater from the roof of adjacent or attached buildings, then filled the cistern. Buildings needed frequent upkeep and painting. Percy and Mary Pike who operated different lights on the coast for 48 years, re-

Mayne Island lighthouse which you can see from the ferries, one of the most attractively situated lights in the Gulf Islands.   *A*

Pachena supplies delivered in the forties when even lifeboats were painted "war-grey"; in this era, women on lighthouses often served as aircraft spotters.   *B*

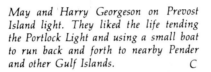

May and Harry Georgeson on Prevost Island light. They liked the life tending the Portlock Light and using a small boat to run back and forth to nearby Pender and other Gulf Islands.   *C*

member they had other tasks at Pine Island Light, off the north tip of Vancouver Island. Seas there sometimes brought in heavy logs that pounded against the steps, crushing them, necessitating their frequent replacement. Mrs. Pike liked the isolation of Pine Island, maintained a large garden and raised chickens. Life was peaceful with only minor mishaps but no major tragedies.

There were days when lighthouse keepers were shut off from the sea itself by dense fog or heavy rains but, despite the isolation, life was good. Fresh air and home-grown food were plentiful. Few women were ill and it was fortunate that they did stay physically fit since there were not many nurses to make the rounds of lighthouses. However one who did was Sue Patterson of Vancouver who braved high seas and a storm to go to the aid of a sick woman at a lighthouse at the turn of the century. In the 1920's, Red Cross Public Health nurses made annual visits to 10 lighthouses. After that, lighthouse personnel were expected to receive thorough medical checks during their longer vacations. A few children have been born "on lights" but most expectant mothers went to city hospitals to wait for the event. Schooling for young children was by correspondence with mother helping. May Georgeson hired a teacher briefly when she and her husband were on the East Point Light in the Gulf Islands. When they moved to another Gulf Island Light, the Portlock at Prevost Island, the assistant lighthouse keeper's wife taught the girls until she found out she was pregnant and wanted to move to a city. The Georgeson girls went off to school then, returning home at weekends and vacations.

The late forties when teenager Florence Georgeson fed one of two family goats on Prevost Light in the Gulf Islands.

Lighthouse keepers and wives are transferred from light to light. Many of them have spent time on Pachena Light and on Vancouver Island's west coast. This is a favorite station for some. Mona Patterson recalls how she would walk the trail to Bamfield where occasionally dances were held at the Cable Station. Once, walking home, she found herself facing a bear on the trail. "I was five miles from Bamfield and a good way from the light so I sat down on a log until the bear wandered away."

There were no oil tankers to worry early lighthouse keepers and families but even a small amount of ship's bunker oil did such violent damage to marine life that it was a cause for concern. The birds, the trees, and the beaches were as highly valued then as they are by today's lighthouse attendants. Darlene Tansky, who lives with her husband and children on the Pulteney Point Lightstation on Malcolm Island, says the area's quietness and the beauty are of great importance to her. She and her husband will be teaching their children by correspondence. The family travels six miles by boat to collect supplies and mail from Sointula, a journey that is dependent on the weather.

Supplies had to be brought in once a year for most families heading into wilderness areas. A former California socialite and actress who went with her Canadian husband to try homesteading in the Finlay Forks of the Peace River country sent a descriptive letter to a friend:

You ask what you could send that would be useful. Often I long for the touch of silk and velvet and satin and lace and bright colors-for the women's things that I left so completely behind me when I came into the woods. Find a good strong box and every time you come across any little pieces for cushion covers, or odds and ends about the house, or some shoes and dresses you can no longer use, just things too good to destroy but of which you have tired, pile them in and send them by freight via South Fort George. The trains are now running through and I will get them in the spring. What I cannot use I can always trade with the Indian girls for fur. Mark the box "Settler's Effects".

Lucille worked side by side with her husband with the only contention over their name: her dramatic interests caused her to change it from "Adams" to "Adems." Life in that area was harsh, with a land unwilling to be tamed easily. The Adems left for awhile, then in 1919 once again attempted to break the land, this time building and clearing land in the Peace River district of Gold Bar. Their dream of a large wheat crop did not materialize although they did build the house about which Lucille dreamed. Nonetheless, even with hours of work spent clearing the land, preparing for crops, and a non-cash living sustained by trading for goods with fur, they failed to produce more than a subsistence living and left the area.

A more successful venture was that of the Collier family of Meldrum Creek, some 45 miles northwest of Williams Lake, whose story of bringing back the beaver to the area was widely publicized in Eric Collier's *Three Against the Wilderness*. Lillian, now widowed, lives at Williams Lake today spending much of her time lecturing to schools about the work the family did with the beaver, and, as a member of the Trappers' Association, trying to locate a trap that will not inflict pain on animals. "The family trapped in order to survive," she said, her dark eyes flashing as she recalled the past. "But we ran our line as though it were a farm. We took only what we had to have."

It was a long time ago—50 years—when immigrant Eric Collier first stood outside that frontier trading post and saw Lillian "leading an unbelievably aged Indian woman by the hand." Lillian remembers she was wearing a white crepe blouse and a blue print skirt; her future husband described her face as having a magnetic quality and, since it was oval in shape, "as looking like the egg of a plover and freckled like one, too. The old woman, her Grandmother Lala, was the oldest human being I'd ever seen."

Lala persuaded the couple to give the land back to the beaver, the animals which had been "trapped out." It took 10 years of hard work just to prepare for such a venture; they had to study the past, to look to Nature for all clues, and to prepare the land. With the help of game officials, the beaver were brought into the area and released in the creeks. The Colliers went around to local ranchers and to Indians to persuade them to wait until the beaver increased their population before any trapping was done, informing them that, contrary to usual opinion, the beavers would maintain and provide irrigation systems that would nourish the dry land.

When numerous colonies of beaver were established, the Colliers and others trapped some. "They would have turned on each other and killed one another," Mrs. Collier explained. "And too many crowding each other out would have been disastrous if any had been diseased." As the beaver came back, so the other forgotten creatures returned. Moose came down to the water to drink. Otters groomed their fur by

Lucille Adems at the age of 86 at Finlay Forks, end of Kyllo riverboat run.

A dog team on beaver hunt in Peace River Country. A

"All's well", but it didn't endure, this house of Jack and Lucille Adems at Gold Bar, Peace River Country built early 1920's. B

Telegraph Creek, famous for its traplines, game guides and frozen river passes in winter. A

Settlers' cabins near Pouce Coupe, Peace River Country.
B

the creeks. Numerous varieties of ducks preened in the beaver-made marshes.

Trapping was a way of life for numerous pioneers in the Cariboo, Chilcotin and the Peace River country. Cash was an unknown commodity. "That'll be four coyotes and one weasel," meant that trade items were exchanged for furs valued at, say, $40. How else would pioneers have survived? Some women won't talk about it, while a few still weep over memories of animals dying in wretched agony. Trapping in North America is historical fact: in order to eat, pioneers and settlers had to trap. They trapped with the traps then available, some of which were humane and others which were not.

Bernhard Krebs, a trapper who came to Canada from the United States, settled in British Columbia. He went into the Peace River area in the 1920's, and described his life in a letter to his mother:

June 17, 1922

Dearest Mother,

As the mail is leaving here about the 22nd or 23rd, it is time I began my letter for you know I seldom finish a letter at one sitting.

This is Sunday and a most beautiful, warm day. It is about the middle of spring, according to our climatic conditions and the radishes are just getting to an edible size. The beans, peas, cress, spinach, lettuce, turnips and carrots are up too, but we need rain very badly. It has been a very unusual dry spring.

I am at present staying at Mr. Sherwood's place, tending the garden, the store, building a summer and mosquito-proof bedroom, improving the boat landing and doing jobs too numerous to mention, *but* taking loads of time to do them in.

Mr. Sherwood went to Edmonton leaving here the 10th of this month, while Mrs. Sherwood and daughter are staying here, so I am lucky in not having to cook for myself. At present we have a mining engineer, a Mr. Pendleton and his wife here as guests. They came down the Finlay River yesterday and intend staying a few days. They had their winter camp about seventy miles up the river. They are going out to Civilization now to procure their next winter's edibles, clothes, etc., for they intend coming back here in fall. There is very little travelling of woodsmen or tourists this summer.

Mother, what do you think of this? Mrs. Sherwood and Mrs. Pendleton have been in here since last fall and haven't seen each other, or any other white woman, or more than two dozen white men besides their husbands. Mrs. Sherwood comes from Boston, Mass., while Mrs. Pendleton hails from New York, yet they both like this desolate, lonely wilderness, having no hankering for city life.

June 19, 1922

The Pendleton's left here this afternoon. Just as they were leaving a boat and canoe came and landed at Government Island (which lies just across the river from here), and it proved to be three homesteaders and trappers besides one of King

George's right hand men, who holds or rather fills the postions of constable, game warden, fire warden, land inspector and numerous other offices. He comes in here every June and stays till fall and all he does is to sit on the island all summer. Although he has a canoe, he is afraid of water, so law-breakers are pretty safe around here. But woe be unto the man whom he catches stealing sheep. We all love him very much, just as we love a fire on a hot summer's day. One of the trappers came over and brought some news from *outside* (as we call civilization), also some eggs, apples and oranges.

Whenever one of us trappers go outside, we aim to bring in a few crates of eggs, some fresh fruit and some whiskey to divide with those that are in here. If anyone who reads this does not know what whiskey is, I will make it somewhat clear. It is a fluid, often enclosed in a glass bottle, earthen jug or wooden keg or barrel, which when taken internally, produces dizziness of the head and weakness of the knees. . . .

Had pretty fair trapping last winter and this spring as I caught 18 marten, 25 white weasel, 3 lynx, 9 mink and 22 beaver. Sold most of the hides during winter to a Hudson Bay fur buyer before the prices dropped.

July 5, 1924

Dear Mother,

I sent you a map of Northern B.C., so you may see our intended destination for this trip. We are trying to get to Bower Creek, which is a little ways below the long canyon on the Finlay River. That will be about 180 to 190 miles from Finlay Forks so please don't expect any mail until next year . . . .

Finlay Forks, B.C.

July 18, 1925

Dearest Mother,

Just a few lines to let you know that I am just as healthy as a young bear.

My partner and I came here from Prince George, landed last night and we are on our way up the Finlay River for another year of trapping and prospecting. We have our whole year's supply of grub and clothing with us. We are going up-river with a thirty-four foot long boat and have two marine engines to help us up. . . .

In 1928, the trapper had found himself a wife who was willing to "rough it." They set out from Prince George and Eileen Krebs kept a diary which shows what her life was like:

July 29, 1928:	Preparing to start down Crooked River.
30:	Started down river with Henry Fisher in our boat and Swiggum and Ostrom accompanying us with their boat and taking part of our load. . . .

Eileen Krebs outside the cabin where she made her home for several years from 1928 into the thirties.

Headquarters cabin and cache for Bernhard and Eileen Krebs at Finlay River and Bower Creek, Peace River Country.

Making their way via rivers, portaging when necessary, the Krebs used this boat to carry some supplies and to take them to their wilderness trapline.

The rugged coastline near Bamfield, west coast Vancouver Island.   A

The trading post at Fort Graham where the Krebs and other northern trappers took their furs for trade.   B

August 7, 1928:	Started up Finlay River. Had dinner with Mcdouglass (sic) at McKinnons. Camped at mouth of Ospeka River.
10:	
11:	Arrived at Deserters' Canyon.
12:	We took about 800 lbs at a time, taking our things through canyon with boat and engine.
November 8, 1928:	Bernhard and Brunlund left today for No. 1 cabin. I roasted chicken shot yesterday. Sewed on curtains.
	Gave shelves behind stove one coat of varnish. Cleaned all pots and pans thoroughly also stove with kerosene, sewed on cutains. Bernhard still absent.
25:	Did nothing much. Roasted goat ribs.
26:	Nothing much. Walked on snowshoes for the first time. Mended.
January 25, 1929:	Scrubbed other half of floor. Mended and did sundry things.
26:	Made batch of cookies. B. returned. Red fox and two weasel.
27:	Boiled cariboo tongue.
March 3, 1929:	Stayed at No. 1. B. sawed wood and I made steamed pudding.
4:	Returned to headquarters, 1 marten, 1 weasel.
22:	Mr. Melnyk and Mr. Robertson arrived . . . staying on McKinnon's, Finlay Forks. They reported the meeting of a strange man, who is now at the Indian camp.
April 20, 1929:	Embroidered. Sowed seeds in boxes. Japanese hop, nasturtiums, mignonette, wild flowers, mixed astors. Wrote letters. Numerous birds . . . also snowing.
May 7, 1929:	. . . about 15 ducks are at bend of river today.
11:	Saw moose across creek up hill—for short time.
12:	Saw four caribou early this morning across river at bend.
July 26, 1929:	Ironed. B. went up Irish Mountain, got two goats and varieties of flowers.
27:	B. dressed goats. Finished ironing. Preparing to go to Melnyks.
28:	Arrived at Melnyks about 7:30 p.m. Had dinner with them.

Checking the trap lines in Skeena River Canyon, near Hazelton.

29:	Moved into tent. Jack Fries boarding with us. Hudson's Bay freighters arrived.
August 1, 1929:	Freighters arrived with the last of the freight.
2:	Freighters left. Freis and Bernhard whipsawing lumber.
3:	Nothing much.
6:	Nothing much. Washed.
30:	Took Freiss up to canyon where he is going to work on Wilson's Cache. Baked batch of white and brown bread.
September 5, 1929:	B. and I picked raspberries. Four qts. canned and three pints of preserves.
24:	Two boats passed today going up Finlay. Believe them to be Wilson outfit. Baked bread and fish. Cinnamon rolls.
24:	I stayed at No. 1 cabin while B. went back to headquarters for another load.
29:	Washed all white clothes today and cleaned bathroom windows. Small snowstorm today.
October 30, 1929:	Swept ceiling and walls down. Cleaned windows inside. Not feeling very well. Lonesome.
November 3, 1929:	B. rendering grease out for soapmaking. Darned some.
9:	B. Returned: two martens, two foxes, eighteen squirrels.
11:	Nothing much. B. skinning.
15:	B. working on packsack.
November 27, 1929:	There was the biggest snowfall I've ever seen last night and the roof leaked so badly that I had to shovel the snow off this morning, that taking me two hours.
December 25, 1929:	Celebrated Christmas very well. Fries here too. Had Cariboo heart roasted with dressing, creamed potatoes, carrots, corn, gravy, apple salad, cranberry relish and sauce, pudding and sauce, Xmas cale, tutti fruitti cake, apple pies, macaroons and ice cream.
April 3, 1930:	B. left today for cabin no. 3 at Lake way. Thawing a little. Bare around buildings now.
4:	Heard wolves howl about 4:30 a.m. for short time. Thought I heard a robin sing this morning, but seems too early for these birds.

June 6, 1930:   Arrived at MacLeod's Lake . . . sold
                  beaver, fox, wolverine and fisher for
                  $400.00. Visited.

Trapper's cabin near Churchill Mountain, B.C.

Sister Mary Gertrude, Sister of St. Ann, who was first superintendent and instructress of nurses at St. Joseph's Hospital, Victoria. (Hospital now is Victoria General Hospital.) She recorded: "I am not trying to make the nurse a close competitor of the doctor. On the other hand I find it unjust to find fault with the nurse because she knows somewhat of the doctor's business. It is the duty of the physician and teacher to fortify the nurse with knowledge. This we must faithfully do, even at the terrible risk of teaching her a few facts more than absolutely necessary." A

St. Ann's Academy, circa 1871, Victoria, B.C. B

Classroom in St. Ann's Academy, circa 1906. C

CHAPTER ELEVEN:

SERVING OTHERS

Human nature out of tune longs to be soothed and comforted.
Sister Mary Gertrude, Sister of St. Ann
(1873-1914)

The four nuns chosen to go west were all Sisters of the Roman Catholic Order of St. Ann in Lachine, Quebec. Sisters Mary Lumena (Virgine Brasseur), Mary Sacred Heart (Salone Valois), Mary Angele (Angele Gauthier), and Mary Conception (Mary Lane), travelled by train to New York, by boat down the Atlantic coast, by train across the Isthmus of Panama, by boat to San Francisco, and then to Victoria on board the *Sea Bird* where they were jostled by other passengers. Some 1700 rowdy miners were on board, jammed elbow to elbow against each other, an astonishing number to be crowded on one sailing vessel.

When they arrived in June, 1859, Sister Mary Angele wrote that they were surprised to see some 200 wooden buildings under construction as well as "thousands of tents for the miners making preparations for the gold at Yale, on the Fraser." The Sisters' accommodation was humble, just a wooden building, 30 by 18 feet, without a nearby well. On the first night a woman brought them some coal, wood and water. "Our first act of charity," Sister Mary Angele recorded, "and not our last." Early the next morning, they arose to go to Bishop Demer's house to "scrub our consciences which had not received attention for a fortnight." They returned home to open their school to the first eight students.

Teachers by day and nurses by night, they met a need so great that other members of their order were sent to aid the sick. In 1859, 22-year-old Sister Mary Providence arrived to organize the founding of convents and hospitals throughout the area. Nuns who followed went on fundraising expeditions through the Cariboo mining towns or sent down to Oregon for nurses training.

The other missionaries who came west also found nursing skills were essential. The Oblate priests aided the sick and so did women missionaries who came later. In the 1890's, Elizabeth Emsley Long was sent to that "remote area" of Fort Simpson, to the Wesleyan Methodist School where she not only had to cook, sew, play the organ, but to teach and nurse the sick. Caroline Knox, who married fellow Wesleyan Methodist Charles Montgomery Tate, found herself in the isolated areas of Bella Bella, Rivers Inlet, and Burrard Inlet, among people whose culture she failed to understand. She often had to care for the sick and later helped her husband organize the Coqualeetza Indian Residential School, which became a hospital. Her journals, the property of the Provincial Archives of British Columbia, note that she was at a West Coast location from 1897-1898, where she noted:

Tremendous noise in the village tonight. The wolf dance is abroad tonight, the screams of the trumpets, the yells of the women and the banging of the drums, making a perfect pandemonium more like as though the inmates of a lunatic asylum had been let loose than anything else. The devil is doing all he

St. Ann's Academy in recent years. The building now is used for government and business offices.

159

can to upset our work, and weaken those who have just started out as Christians.

November 30:

Moved into an Indian house in the midst of the village. Not very pleasant as other houses crowd around us . . . the large room must be used as bedsitting and dining room here, also the Indians who come need counsel, medicine . . . . We miss good drinking water and would very much like to find a place where we could have a good walk. The village is about a quarter of a mile long and the walk is along the uneven tottering sidewalk in front of the houses. When the tide is out there is the sand beach but it extends no further than the village and is soft and muddy in places.

Missionaries took it upon themselves to aid the Indians and the indigent but it soon became obvious that hospitals were needed. Anglican clergyman Edward Cridge, who later became Bishop, formed a committee in 1858 which was responsible for opening a hospital. Soon a larger building for Europeans and Indians was opened on the Songhees Reserve. In 1859 collections were taken at Christ Church, Victoria, for the Royal Hospital and on February 13, "Hospital Sunday" was held for the hospital. In 1868 Mrs. Cridge, with the Female Aid Association, established a female ward on Victoria's Pandora Avenue, an event sparked by the number of sick women arriving in the colony; among them two passengers from the *Robert Lowe*, one of the brideships, who died shortly after arriving. A year later, the Royal Hospital amalgamated with the women's ward, while the old Reserve building was used for the mentally ill. It wasn't long before there was a demand for more beds so that a larger building was needed to serve as a general hospital. A vocal group of citizens protested that the proposed site at Cadboro Bay Road and Mount Tolmie (as the roads then were known), was not close enough to the city. Others "without horse and carriage" supported the proposal of building on a 20 acre site. Given the new name of Provincial Royal Jubilee Hospital to honor Queen Victoria's approaching 1888 Jubilee, the hospital opened in 1890. It became the first western hospital to establish a school of nursing, with the first graduate, Marie De Bou (Mrs. W. H. Bullock-Webster) graduating in 1892. At first the hospital was lighted with coal oil, and sometimes the Matron and Head Nurse had to sit up all night as there were no extra nurses available to care for special cases.

By 1875, the Roman Catholic Sisters of the Order of St. Ann had opened their 35-bed St. Joseph Hospital in Victoria. In a March 27 journal of that year, the Sisters recorded that their first patient was "a poor paralytic." Other entries showed their extracurricular activities:

In preparation for the home manufacture of the hospital mattresses, all hands are at work picking the wool from off the sheepskins. 36 were plucked today. 75 still remain to be done. The work is repugnant to touch and smell but the motive is proof against the objection.

65 among us, including sisters, orphans and even boarders sat courageously before the task of picking some 200 and 50 lbs of wool, while 2 sisters made up mattresses. Our fun was spoiled by excessive heat.

Bells, Holy Rosary, Vancouver, B.C.
A

Mrs. Edward Cridge, wife of Bishop Cridge, whose work helped the sick and needy. *B*

A male attendant was hired and several women trainees came to work. When the School of Nursing opened in 1900, Sister Mary Gertrude gave lectures on chemistry, anatomy and communicable diseases and cautioned the trainees that they should not wear ribbons or flowers on uniforms, that they should enter a patient's room smiling, and shake any dusters from windows.

As immigration to British Columbia increased, trained nurses from abroad arrived. Irish-trained Nurse Devine worked in Vancouver, saying she never could keep her red flannel petticoats since she was always "taking off her own to wrap around the newborn." In the early 1900's, her sister, a Mrs. Reid, opened Vancouver's first private nursing hospital where operations took place on a kitchen table; sea sponges were used as swabs and took "days to sterilize."

Nurse Patterson was known for her care of millworkers at Hastings Mill and made one heroic mission with two Indians in their canoe to brave heavy seas in order to reach a sick wife of a lighthouse keeper. The Crickmay sisters also were well known nurses. They arrived from England with their widowed father and five brothers in the 1880's. Elizabeth Crickmay, who trained at London's Guy's Hospital, was hired as assistant matron at Vancouver General Hospital in 1888. The hospital was a small wooden building that had replaced the tent hospital organized by CPR Surgeon J. Lefevre, who aided sick and injured railroad workers. The illnesses of the day were white plague (tuberculosis) and typhoid as well as numerous wounds caused by frequent violent fights in an unsettled population of 5,000. Typhoid decreased as a better sewage system was organized. Nurses had to work a 12 hour day.

Male assistants were often hired by early hospitals, a practice the Royal Columbian Hospital followed when it opened its doors in 1862. It was 1901 before amalgamation with a maternity hosptial took place. The maternity building, sponsored by the Women's Christian Temperance Union, later by the Local Council of Women, was an eight-bedroom home. St. Mary's Hospital, New Westminster, St. Paul's Hospital and St. Luke's Hospital were opened in Vancouver by this time. When St. Paul's Hospital opened its Nursing School in 1909, students were promised that they would learn "the management of helpless and convalescent patients and the diet of the sick, the best method of friction to the body and extremities, prevention and treatment of bed sores, bed-making, changing clothes, making poultices and applications of formentations and cups, leeches and bandaging; and the dressing of wounds, burns, blisters and sores of all kinds."

At St. Paul's, the Sisters of Providence checked students' work closely, although the girls always knew when the Superintendent of Nurses was coming near wards in 1912 since the petite Sister Mary Alphonsus had a characteristic perky walk that caused her beads to rattle. The Roman Catholic hospitals opened training schools to women of all races although some hospitals turned down applications from Oriental employees in early years. By 1932, the Vancouver General Hospital had revoked their 1920 decision and began to accept Oriental trainees but they complied with Canadian Government overall policies concerning Japanese in 1942 and asked three Japanese students to leave; one girl only had two months left before she graduated.

Graduate nurses, 1902-03, Provincial Royal Jubilee Hospital, Victoria.   A

Miss J. F. MacKenzie (1914-1927), the eighth Director of the School of Nursing, Royal Jubilee Hospital, Victoria.   B

The late Margaret Rankin who graduated in 1903 from the Royal Jubilee School of Nursing.   C

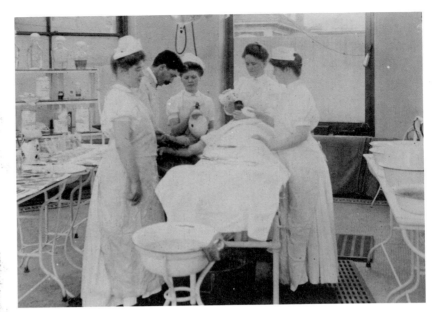

The operating theatre of Victoria's Royal
Jubilee Hospital, about 1902.   A

Class of 1908, St. Joseph's Hospital,
Victoria. The hospital is known as Victoria
General Hospital.   B

Patients and nurses, St. Joseph's Hospital, 1900.   C

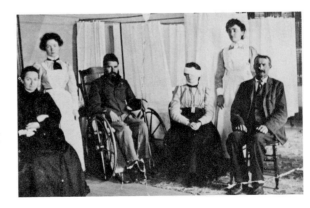

None of the hospitals could have survived without the aid of auxiliaries. The Royal Inland Hospital, which had opened in 1885 as the Kamloops Hospital, was aided by the Ladies Auxiliary in 1899 when 34 women met to discuss hospital matters and fund raising. Since then, "there have been strawberry festivals, teas, musicales, benefit concerts, tag days, raffles, fashion shows, rummage shows," says present auxiliary member Margaret Shumka," in fact, almost anything that would swell the treasury has been tried." In 1930 the Chinese community arranged a day-long dramatic presentation to raise hospital funds. In 1899, when meetings were held in the home of Dr. Proctor, the good doctor "thanked the ladies for their purchase of a water bed to be used in the 7-bed hospital which was looked after by matron Eleanor Potter, a Toronto General Hospital nursing graduate and Nurse Baker." The auxiliary members deplored the tremendous cost of hospitalization at that time which was $1.62 per day.

Nurses had some difficulties persuading others that they were qualified to handle numerous duties. Some physicians regarded them as aides; while others saw nurses as competitors. It took time before the balance of theory and practice was reached and nurses could fulfill the role for which they had been trained. They had to fight for better pay. Married women were expected to leave their work but were recalled during and after the Second World War. Before that time, they had a better chance of obtaining work in small communities where trained nurses were in short supply. When there was no nurse available, a physician sometimes trained an apt student.

The late Grace Bloomfield in 1925, Fort St. James.

The late Grace Bloomfield of Fort St. James was among these students. Mrs. Bloomfield, a trained musician, was one of five settlers in the Fort St. James area where the Indian population spent summers on reserve land, catching and smoking their winter supply of fish, then spent much of the late fall and winter on traplines. It was a two day journey from Vanderhoof to Fort St. James in the 1920's with the physician using a horse and buggy in summer and horse and sleigh on runners in winter. He rested at a stopping house at Dog Creek and at a trapper's cabin. Mrs. Bloomfield was strong in spirit but she had taken one look at the bleak homestead her husband had chosen north of Vanderhoof, then persuaded him to accept the job he had been offered at the Indian Residential School, then in Fort St. James. The family spent two days getting to the area with the girls Pat and Evelyn herding cattle ahead of the wagon. Mrs.Bloomfield learned everything the doctor could teach her, often doing minor operations and going out by dogteam in winter and boat in summer. She went to isolated regions around Stuart Lake and further north. Dr. Stone's daughter, Mrs. L. Calvert of Prince George recalls he was often paid in butter and hay. "Mother put her foot down at accepting live animals." The nurse he trained passed examinations so successfully that she was paid by the Department of Indian Affairs, receiving $88 a month, working for 25 years. Daughter Pat Liversidge of Vancouver recalls that "Mother went out in all weather no matter how cold it was—and it was cold. She wore the warmest clothes she had and moccasin rubbers."

When Kathleen Patterson graduated from Winnipeg General in 1932 she couldn't find a local nursing position. She did hear of one in British Columbia's remote northwest coast region of Bella Coola. She applied and was hired by the United Church 35 bed hospital there. She arrived

Matron Eleanor Potter of Royal Inland Hospital, Kamloops (1890's).

after a rough December voyage by Union boat. The community was made up of resident Indians and incoming Norwegian settlers, mostly fishermen and there was one road that led to a few outlying farms. Hours were long but her salary rose from $35 to the grand sum of $50 a month all found. In August, 1933, she participated in a travelling clinic in which a doctor, two other nurses, and the local policeman went to visit Indian encampments checking general health. They lived in tents, ate moose and grouse and found the work exciting. The young nurse recorded her memories of nursing in an isolated community as giving "total experience. A nurse learns to pull teeth, deliver babies and colts, give anaesthetics, is ready to assist the doctor with anything from a breast amputation to calsomining the ceiling, is introduced to the business of undertaking with all its grimness and to the art of comforting the bereaved, is destined to the kitchen on the cook's day off and to the laundry when the laundress has the 'flu. She is exalted to Medical Advisor for perhaps weeks when the doctor is saving a life over and beyond mountain ranges and sweeps the floors, or does gardening when the janitor has a pain."

On one occasion she went with the doctor to answer the anguished call of a rancher. It was February, so she wore her "fleece-lined lingerie." The doctor and nurse took a variety of sleighs and horses along a 40 mile "road." When there was still sixty miles to go, they mounted horses. "Not an easy job when you're wearing two set of fleece-lined underwear, heavy breeches, three sweaters, heavy macintosh, six pairs of stockings, two pairs of moccasins and rubbers." They rode all day and slept in the loft offered by a hospitable trapper. The next day they began climbing the steep trails, changing horses partway, and passing moose and deer. They arrive in the moonlight and since the rancher's wife seemed a little improved, they had a few hours sleep, then made preparations for the necessary operation. "We nailed boards to the table for stirrups, a blanket hung between the anaesthetist and stove and the sterile table set. With the help of the governess as "circulating nurse," the operation was performed. They left two days later when the patient's health was improving. Instead of sleeping in a cabin. they chose to sleep on the snow in sleeping bags. "I wouldn't have missed three years of it for anything," she says now.

Tiny communities relied on their nurses and the occasional visits of doctors until hospitals became an urgent need. "It took a united community effort," recalls Catherine Monks who raised funds for the Tofino hospital. "It was Depression time. No grants. No Social Security. All it took was everyone working to save quarters, dimes, and even less. If a woman purchased a new dress, you heard mutterings of "doesn't she know we need a new hospital! Oh, the absurd ways we had of making money—but it was all for one end—our hospital." Japanese, Indian and white loggers and fishermen cleared the forest for a very first hospital building. The community grew, with fishing villages linked by roads, then industry came to the area, and a larger hospital was needed which meant another drive. The Indians of Ahousat, 15 miles north of Tofino donated $2,500 from the sale of timber rights. In the Bulkley River Valley, where the townsite of Smithers was founded in 1913, settlers suffered from common ailments: "ruptured appendix, influenza, hay fever, and from wrists fractured by the back firing of those new Model T Fords." When Dr. Hankin arrived to open his practice,

1975 class of graduates, receiving their nursing pin from the current Director of the School of Nursing, Miss M. Irving. Third in front, seated, is Mary Richmond, now Director of Health Education Services and an advisory member of University of Victoria's School of Nursing to open 1976.   *A*

Vancouver General Hospital Nursing Graduates of 1901-1905.   *B*

Medical Superintendent, Dr. A. M. Robertson, reclining on lawn of Vancouver General Hospital in early 1900's. He is surrounded by twenty nurses, including Lady Superintendent, Miss Margaret Clendinning.   *C*

University of British Columbia Public Health Nursing graduates 1920-21: top row, Miss Thom, Kier Hardy; 2nd row, Miss Buckley, Hornby, Peters, Ehlers, MacKay and Snelgrove; 3rd row, Miss MacKenzie, Whitaker, Frazee, Harmon, Cuddy and Hamlin; 4th row, Miss Griffin, Munslow, Hughes, McLaren, Lewis and Lancaster.   *D*

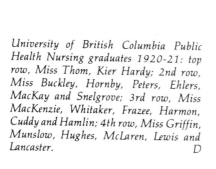

Bella Coola General Hospital, 1930, when the only roads ran only as far as local ranches. A

Nursing staff Bella Coola General Hospital, 1934. Kathleen Patterson (now Mrs. Drummond) third in row. B

The four Victorian Order of Nurses pioneers who took the Klondike Trail in 1898, going through British Columbia with Faith Fenton (Toronto Globe reporter) and receiving huge amounts of publicity fed by Toronto Globe reporter Faith Fenton (on right). C

Process on welcoming Lord and Lady Aberdeen, Kamloops, B.C., 1894. On this visit, Lady Aberdeen, head of the National Council of Women, sparked women's groups into action and heard of need for community nurses which led to formation of Canadian Victorian Order of Nurses. D

an abandoned two-storey building was transformed into a 15-bed hospital with three nurses, a cook and an engineer who fuelled stoves and killed rats. However, financial problems plagued the venture, provoking an appeal to the Sisters of St. Ann who took over the hospital in 1933.

In Burns Lake, the Northern Interior settlement mushroomed from a tent town occupied by miners who had returned from the Klondike and by construction workers who had completed railwork. Settlers' Land Grants at the end of World War I brought homesteaders. In 1919, the Women's Missionary of the Presbyterian Church opened a tiny log hospital at the side of Francois Lake with Mary Kennedy as matron. A second small hospital was opened at Prosser's Point, but by 1924, the hospital had moved to Burns Lake while a deaconess-nurse still travelled to remote areas. Pioneer women aided the hospital: Marion Gerow undertook fund drives and oversaw hospital housekeeping, Hughena Linton canned preserves to supplement supplies and others raised funds. Today, the hosptial overlooks the land. It has everything except a blood bank, although the local telephone exchange has a list of donors who can be called in emergencies.

Old Hazelton Hospital, in days when many northern hospitals had one door for Indian patients and one for settlers—a policy that now has changed.

Outpost hospitals were opened as early as 1898 by the Victorian Order of Nurses who staffed a Vernon hospital, then founded others at Revelstoke, Kaslo, Arrowhead, Rock Bay, Fernie, Quesnel, Barkerville, Ashcroft, Ganges and Windermere, the latter being the last of the cottage hospitals, built in 1917. The Order had been founded in 1897 by Lady Aberdeen, president of the National Council of Women and wife of the Governor General of Canada (1894-1898), who was given the idea by Vancouver's Mrs. James Macauley and Mrs. Duncan Gain. Catcalls and jeers from the critics greeted news of the formation of the Canadian Order which was based on the English Institute of Queen's Nurses. The negative response hastily reversed itself when four V.O.N. volunteers went to the Klondike in 1898 accompanied by Faith Fenton of the *Toronto Globe*. They travelled up the Stikine River and Telegraph Creek, then over a mountain pass above Teslin Lake to the Cassiar Mountain on their way to the Upper Yukon River area. The journey was highly publicized and stories noted they went "from bog to mountain, their mules mired in swamps while they marched on with miners giving them bannock, dried apples and coffee."

In Vancouver, Nurse Maud Hill visited settlers' homes in 1901, travelling by British Columbia Electric, which gave the V.O.N. free tickets on street cars. Supported by auxiliaries which collected funds, Nurse Hill soon was joined by others. In 1907 the V.O.N. had branches in North and South Vancouver. By 1912, a small training school had opened on Venables Street in an area frequented by Chinese who "were ready to pay for service." Annie Colhoun made history for the Burnaby branch, travelling a 32 square mile territory by bike, tram and on foot. By 1918 the minutes of a V.O.N. board meeting recorded the influenza epidemic:

478 cases, 2,196 visits, only 8 deaths. In many cases the whole family was found to be ill, sometimes 10 in number; then it was a case of lighting fires, supplying clean bedding, etc., feeding and general nursing care. The New Year finds us with the influenza still raging, help of all kinds almost unable to be obtained, people dying for want of nursing care. The hospitals so crowded that but for the Victorian Order many more lives would have been lost.

In 1920, a District Superintendent recorded:

We are face to face with the problem of transportation for our nurses (13); an automobile is badly needed as our nurses spend too much energy and good valuable time in walking between cases . . . we have purchased a cycle for the nurse in Collingwood and a motor scooter for the North Burnaby nurse.

Patients were expected to pay a small fee for service "to maintain self-respect", although some could not afford even that in Depression days. Retired V.O.N. Nurse Flora McDonald of Burnaby recalls that police worked side by side with nurses, taking messages and escorting them on bad roads to emergency cases.

Audrey Price, a graduate of Victoria's Royal Jubilee Hospital, who nursed at a Powell River Hospital then took courses in different areas, worked for the V.O.N. and took her public health diploma from the University of British Columbia before she finished her career at the V.O.N.'s North Vancouver branch. She recalls that "the rewards were seeing the patients in their home and being able to give help that obviously was needed. It was bedside nursing at its best. We were proud of our work—it came first in our lives, too. It gave women a real sense of accomplishment." She remembers the new mothers and their babies particularly and says she expected to work long hours with only every other weekend off. Ethel Janzow, former administrator of Victoria V.O.N., valued the work "for the breadth of knowledge that was required and for the sense of responsibility it inspired, as well as the feeling of independence." When the Victoria branch closed in 1974 at the time the provincial government inaugurated a Visiting Nurses program, she compiled a history of the branch which includes items familiar to auxiliaries and nurses at other branches:

1911: Funds were sparse and hard to come by . . . the group was dealt a blow when the most successful collector resigned before the end of the year.

1913: The two nurses were kept busy and did excellent work with Child Welfare. There were 2,096 visits made to 322 patients.

1919: The Tag Day netted $1,500 for which a Ford Coupe was bought.

1920: There were now four nurses. The head nurse was paid $80 a month and the other nurses $70 and board and lodging was supplied. The charge per visit was 75 cents.

1936: 23 home confinements.

1941: Population increased by 2,000 in four years. There was an advent of larger numbers of infants and young children. 56 Home Nursing classes were given.

1944: British war brides had problems with Canadian foods and marketing and required orientation.

1950: Parentcraft classes were started.

1963: A male nurse and a licensed practical nurse were added to the staff. The charge per visit was $3.

1971: Paramedical examinations are now being done for several insurance companies.

Celebrations of opening of convalescent home at Duncan, B.C., around 1910.   A

Hospital, Queen Charlotte City, 1909.   B

Alice Ravenhill promoted crafts, collected Indian myths and was an advisor on Home Economics, lecturing and writing on this.
A

National Council of Jewish Women: Well Baby Clinic Committee, 1936.
B

Olive Garrood with high school Junior Red Cross girls whom she trained while a public health nurse.
C

1972: The Victorian Home Care Project came under the sponsorship of the government. A V.O.N. nurse is co-ordinator.

Public Health Nursing had become a concern as far back as 1866 when the Colony of Vancouver Island united with the Colony of British Columbia. The Legislative Council of British Columbia initiated "an Ordinance for promoting public health in the colony in case of epidemics." When British Columbians became Canadians after Confederation in 1871, this ordinance became part of the provincial statutes just in time to prevent a typhoid fever epidemic from spreading though mining camps in the Kootenays where sewage systems mainly were "pit and pail" arrangements. Tent hospitals were set up with a doctor and nurse in attendance. Alice Ravenhill who had studied for an English Home Nursing Diploma with the National Health Society, as well as studying Home Economics, began setting up home cleanliness and care programs for the Department of Agriculture in 1911.

In 1936 a Women's Institute member at Hazelmere, Mrs. R. E. Kocher, fought for a municipal public health system geared to include dental inspection in schools. She won a long fight, with such clinics opening in 1937. Public Health nurses had been working for two decades by then, with four Public Health nurses on Vancouver Island in 1917. By 1919, Ethel John was organizing a University of British Columbia nursing program which gave a degree and which later added a one year diploma course for public health nursing.

When Australian-born public health nurse Olive Garrood arrived in the province in 1926 she was sent to the Kootenays "walking for miles to go into rural schools to lecture." In 1929 she worked in Kamloops. "I walked miles there, too," she recalls. "All of us worked hard in different areas. We weighed babies, examined dressings and tried to teach good nutrition. I talked about anatomy in schools even though the children laughed at my drawings on the blackboard. I could hold their attention but I never could draw. A public health nurse considered herself a nurse-educator."

It was no problem to find married nurses eager to return to nursing who would preside at clinics. "Nursing was a way of life, a total commitment. In the evenings I spoke to different groups and taught the St. Johns' Ambulance Society members. Paid? Of course not. I wouldn't have taken money for that."

There were Red Cross Public Health nurses, too, sponsored by the British Columbia Division of the Canadian Red Cross Society organized in 1919. In 1920 nurses visited lighthouses as well as rural districts. Eight nurses were posted to rural areas with transportation provided— sometimes a car, while horses were provided in two districts. Anna Stabler was the first supervisor of this program in 1921. Lack of funds forced a limitation of the service for a time but by 1925 attention turned to educational work and Outpost Hospitals were established, particularly in areas of the Peace River district where settlement rose in the Thirties. Nancy Dunn established a service aiding 12 districts and in 1934 was awarded the MBE for her work. In 1935 the *Peace River Block News* reported that Miss Dunn would supervise a new health unit in which free dental and medical services would be given to needy school children and pre-school children.

Hospitals were established elsewhere, too, including the Kyuquot hos-

Red Cross Nurse Miss Claxton of Peace River District Outpost Hospital, with friend Mrs. Crawford. (1930-40).

Pioneering nurse cum social worker Kate McRae with social worker Florence Skitch at Nanaimo, 1948. A

Social worker in Cranbrook Government Office in 1940's: Back row, Eric Winch, Florence Skitch; front row, Oliver Wall (Cranbrook), Sophie Birch (Fernie) and Bessie Snider (then supervisor for the Kootenays). B

pital on the west coast of Vancouver Island, where Kyuquot trollers transported building materials free of charge in the midst of their fishing season. A six-bed hospital at McBride, on the CN line between Prince George and the Alberta border, dealt with one serious railroad speeder accident among other emergencies. Plane service and hospitals in nearby areas eliminated the need for some hospitals but others administered by the Canadian Red Cross Society and by the provincial government since 1973 are open today. Lillian Hiltz, Director of Family Health of the Vancouver branch, points out that "any emergency one can imagine has no doubt been coped with at one time or another at the Outposts."

Nursing has undergone numerous changes as methods of treatment changed and drugs have aided patients suffering from diabetes or from tuberculosis. Patients have become more ambulatory as rehabilitation and physiotherapy procedures developed. Dr. Edith Green, a pioneer librarian who switched to nursing and found "tremendous outlets within this profession," points out that today many patients are life or death emergencies—acute cases needing urgent aid. As one of the organizers of a nursing school in Alexandria, Egypt, under the auspices of the World Health Organization, a lecturer and organizer of American nursing schools, she sees a time when "team nursing is the way to give the best aid. Pressures are tremendous and medical technology is constantly changing. A team of specialists working together can use the latest diagnostic and treatment procedures. Each person on the team can specialize in specific areas."

One area in which nurses dealt is the work of social workers today— counselling and community care. Many early nurses, such as Kate Mc-Rae, who served an area from Prince Rupert-Nanaimo, became interested in their patients' problems and worked as Child Care advisors. The University of British Columbia has a full degree program these days but in Depression days it was offering a one-year diploma course. Florence Skitch tried a business career but took the course to see what she could do to help others. Sent to The Kootenays, she found the work exciting and challenging: "all that responsibility. You had to hope that you had made the right decision. And it helped to be a good mechanic on those roads." Jean Bennest had a B.A. when she returned to school at the beginning of World War II "to quit being a social member of society and to become a social worker." Working first in the North Vancouver Family Service Agency she moved to the Okanagan where she is now Director of Human Resources, Penticton, trying "to free social workers to develop and function independently but to draw on others in the office and department for support and consultation." She believes that British Columbia must adjust to changing economics and social needs without losing sight of the basic concept that we all respond and grow in wisdom and strength, through nurture and encouragement, through struggle and praise—and through the warmth that comes from our association with each other."

Jean Bennest, Director of the Department of Human Resources, Penticton.   A

Lillian G. Hiltz, R.N. Director of Family Health, Canadian Red Cross Society, Vancouver. She returned from a three-month stint with Canadian Red Cross Medical team in Bangladesh in 1972 to supervise six provincial Outpost hospitals, care in home courses, sick room equipment loan service and a home-makers service.   B

Mother Cecelia Mary, Anglican nun famous for her administration of the Good Animal Shelter Foundation, Mill Bay, to care for abandoned and stray animals.   C

Modern missionaries Fletcher and Eleanor Bennett of Prince Rupert who travel extensively in their small plane to spread the word of the Baha'i faith.   D

Hannah took this superb portrait of her husband. Note the composition.   A

Richard Maynard took his wife's portrait. She had taught him the art of studio photography although they ventured into field work, too, travelling, extensively throughout the province.   B

Mrs. Maynard travelled with her husband by stage and steamer, taking photographs. Here is the S.S. "Charlotte" at Quesnel in 1897.   C

CHAPTER TWELVE:

SHOOTING
STARS

There was Mama, keeping a firm grip on Simon's shoulder so he would not move, and trying not to smile at Father's stern expression. The reason Father was holding his head so high was because that starched high collar scratched his chin. And just look at Samantha, practically weeping because she had to stand on that "poor dead polar bear." Just a few more minutes . . . everyone still. There! Mrs. Maynard was almost hidden by black cloth, working behind the huge black box, the camera, which had extendible bellows by which it was focused. Hannah Hatherly had married Richard Maynard in 1852 in the County of Cornwall, England. A sailor who had apprenticed first as a leathermaker and shoemaker, he had dreams of success in Canada. The couple soon left for that new country, taking up residence in Bowmanville, Ontario. By 1859, the news of gold strikes had carried there and Maynard travelled west, while Hannah stayed at home, filling her time by studying photography under the tutelage of a portrait photographer. When her husband returned home in early 1861, reporting that prospects seemed excellent in Victoria, she assembled equipment, including glass plates and a camera, and planned to start a photographic studio out west.

Richard Maynard with Captain C. N. Chittenden with whom he "explored" the Queen Charlotte Islands.

The Maynards sailed down the east coast, travelled across the Isthmus of Panama, then sailed up the west coast to reach Victoria, the city she later described as a "city of tents, gullies and swamps." The city's inhabitants were mostly miners, some with plenty of money to throw around. Navy ships were frequent arrivals also, with officers deciding to pose for posterity. Before Hannah knew it, the studio she had opened adjacent to her husband's shoestore was doing so well that her husband decided that he, too, would learn the business. She taught him and soon they were photographing government and mining officials, leading citizens, visitors and miners: "I think I can say with confidence that we photographed everybody in town at one time or another," she told *The Colonist* in 1912. Together, the Maynards travelled by stage coach, sternwheeler and canoe through the province, taking pictures of early towns and scenery. Many of these photographs were credited to Mr. Maynard as it didn't occur to people that his wife was just as skilled a photographer as he. While Maynard went off on frequent exploration trips, including one stint to photograph seal hunting in the Bering Sea during international seal fisheries controversies, Hannah carried on as usual, raising a family, and taking portraits in her studio. She used the wet plate process, making daguerrotypes.

While Hannah was "shooting" for posterity, other women were becoming interested in photography and several of Kamloops' early photographers were women: Mina Gale opened a studio in 1891; in 1899 Mary Spencer, known for her fine cloud effects, opened a studio running it for ten years before she sold it to Mrs. L. M. Walker.

By that time, Mattie Gunterman had been in the province for 14 years.

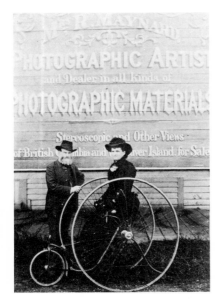

Hannah Maynard really was a photographic artist as her advertising proclaimed. Here she poses with her husband and those bicycles of the day.

Mattie Gunterman in center of this picture she took by using string or piece of hose to "trip" the shutter.

Born Madeleine Werner in Wisconsin, she had married candymaker Bill Gunterman in Seattle. With their young son Henry, and a pack-horse named Nellie, they had come north in 1896, walking the old fur trails, and finally settling at Beaton in the Upper Arrow Lake. Mattie had learned her photographic skills from an uncle and she had numerous chances to practice them as she worked as a cook in mining camps, and hunted and trapped with her husband. She liked to take a canoe out on the lake, to ride horseback, and to dance the Spanish Waltz or French Minuet. When she died her glass plates were stashed away in a shed, stored in an apple crate in which rats had excreted and nested. Her son Henry who had become a trapper, showed them to Roy D'Altroy, Curator of Historical Photography, Vancouver Public Library when he made a tour of the Lardeau Valley area before the area was flooded by the Hugh Keenleyside Dam. The 200 plates, some in good condition and others which had to be restored, provide a rich heritage of joyful scenes showing people at work and at play. Her fine sense of composition showed in such pictures as children seated on different levels of swings, and her puckish sense of humor was sometimes disguised by a pose of mock severity. This was particularly evident in one picture in which she stood with enormous homemade snowshoes on her feet, dressed in a fashionable hat, a jacket and a long skirt, holding a gun and a dead duck. To make such pictures she placed the camera on a tripod, tripping the shutter by pulling a string or by stepping on a bulb at the end of a long piece of hose.

While Mattie used her camera in the mining camps, another star was making appearances: E. Pauline Johnson had begun to read her poems to miners. She gave a reading in Cranbrook in 1899. She also read in Kuskincook, a typical mining community, with a scattering of matchbox houses and 18 saloons. Her fees were donated to a proposed church. Born in 1861 at "Chiefswood" on an Ontario Mohawk Reserve, she was daughter of George Henry Johnson, Six Nations Chief and English immigrant Emily Howells. Both sides of the family were against the marriage, which proved to be happy until Johnson was killed as the result of a beating he reputedly received from white ruffians. Pauline sometimes used her Indian name, "Tekahionwake," which meant "smoke haze of Indian summer," although there was nothing vapor-like about her performances. She was a born actress and knew exactly how to rivet attention upon herself as she appeared in costumes of buckskin with ermine skins and a large necklace of bearclaws. Her father had been a member of the Wolf Clan but wolfskins were not part of the luggage packed in her saratoga trunk. Her dark curly hair, her magnetic grey-green eyes and the dramatic stance captivated audiences which considered her exotic. They seemed to have enjoyed the poetry, too, which was often studded with romantic or spine-chilling allusions to paddles, feathers, fir trees, scalpings and war.

She had a few poems published in the early 1890's, read her work to an appreciative group of the Canadian Society of Authors in Toronto in 1891, and then had her first book of verse, *The White Wampum* published in late 1894. It included "The Song My Paddle Sings," a poem which made her famous and led to a visit to England where she was an instant success despite lack of critical acclaim. By the turn of the century she had struck up a friendship with another performer, a man often referred to as "McRaye", who was 14 years her junior and who also recited poems. By 1903 they were touring the Cariboo areas and she met Premier McBride, who was out stumping to aid a local candidate for a Lillooet by-election. She read in McKinley's bar room at Lac La Hache where whites gained entrance to the performance for $1.00; Indians paid 50 cents.

She continued to read and write poetry with allusions to Indian life, something of which her family in Ontario disapproved since they felt she was exploiting her background. She came into contact with numerous Cariboo characters such as the stage driver Buckskin Billy Halton, who took her and McRaye from Ashcroft to Barkerville where they entertained for two nights and made $700.00. In all, she made 19 trips back and forth across the Rockies and sometimes crossed the border to recite. She settled in Vancouver in 1909, living on Howe Street, near Stanley Park where she spent a lot of her time. Already cancer had snaked through her body but she tried to ignore it.

She frequently visited Chief Joe Capilano of the Squamish Band to discuss legends. A chance opportunity led to the first publication of her legends in the *Vancouver Province*. Another writer, Isabel Maclean who wrote as "Alexandra" encouraged the editor to pay her $7.00 for each legend. Members of women's groups, including the Vancouver Women's Press Club, helped to have the legends published in book form in 1911. They were an instant success. A collection of poetry, *Flint and Feather*, was also selling well. Cancer had riddled her body but not her spirit and whenever McRaye visited her, he pinned royalty cheques on her pillow. After she died in 1913 her ashes were placed within sight and sound of Siwash Rock in Stanley Park, the place where she had wanted to be buried. She had not wanted a memorial but her will was not found until years later and, by that time, the Women's Canadian Club had erected the memorial in her honor at Third Beach.

A paddle, a buckskin dress, and a saratoga trunk symbolize Pauline Johnson's life but other articles conjure up the image of Emily Carr. People described her cluttered rooms full of cedar mats, weavings, frisky squirrels turning cartwheels in cages, griffon dogs panting under chairs, pottery, and bowls of sword ferns. The stock characters, such as Susie the Rat who slept on the family bible, and who could be tucked inside a purse; Woo, the monkey who almost died from eating paint, the cat that had kittens in a hat, the caravan, the houseboat, the gasboats, the canoes, the Indian villages, the trees, all are part of Emily and her canvases. Moody, taciturn, beaming, determined Emily was born in Victoria on December 13, 1871. She and her talent combined to have the full force of a thunderbolt that touches some shaman's pool in coastal woods, ruffles water, extends shorelines, brushes the salal, then races up that high fir that towers in the city. ("No, I prefer not to paint sunsets," said Emily. "On canvas, they look like broken eggs.") Touching lives then, today she lives on in stage plays, documentaries, dramas, books; a ballet has been written in her honor. Her canvases, photographed, catalogued, have won audiences that failed to come when her work was exhibited in Vancouver. A few friends appreciated her talent, including Dr. Charles Newcombe and his son. Once a Chinese vegetable peddler standing at the door saw her work and asked if he could bring his friends to see it; for an entire weekend, she held an impromptu exhibition for them.

Her first commissioned drawing was made when, as a young girl, she

Pauline Johnson in 1904 who knew how to use a stage presence and interesting clothing to gain full audience attention.

A daughter of the province, born in Victoria in 1871, Emily Carr died in 1945 after her genius finally was recognized.

177

Totems at Kitwanga where Emily Carr did so much painting, and sketching.

One of Emily's paintings. Her subtle use of color is not evident with black and white photography although the boldness of her style picks up the dimensions of primeval forest and Indian culture.   A

Emily Carr's Ucluelet sketch of three Indian girls.   B

sketched her father with his patrician face and long white beard. She received 50 cents and an order for four more drawings. She was "Milly" to close friends; some spelled this "Millie." Her childhood provided material for the *Book of Small* which she wrote: she was the youngest of nine children, of whom only three girls survived. Both parents died while she was a teenager.

There was enough money for her to take formal training at the San Francisco School of Art where she studied under Mark Hopkins. Later she gave lessons in Victoria, then made a trip to the West Coast, to Ucluelet where the normity of woods and the inner peace of the Indian people touched her and affirmed her own wish to paint the "real Canada." Later she went to England and then to France where her acceptance of the Fauve and then post-impressionist style of painting led to a new feeling of painting as she felt and saw the world around her. For all her efforts—she had acclaim in France—she failed to attract students in Vancouver and was forced to return to Victoria to live as a landlady, taking in boarders and raising over 300 bobtailed sheepdogs in order to survive. Her brushes were put away; her bitterness grew and sometimes her sense of rejection flowed out in anger in the boarding house. When at last she could return to her beloved woods and villages, she began to experience the first sense of inner peace she had felt in years; in tune with the people who sensed her clear spirit, in tune with their woods, in tune with herself, at last she began to smile and laugh a lot, fulfilling an Indian name given to her on the West Coast—"Klee Wyck: Laughing One."

Her brush strokes were bold; feeling and technique combined to produce the work that still elicited response elsewhere. When anthropologist Marius Barbeau heard of her through the Indians he met on his visits to the West, he informed Eric Brown, Director of the National Art Gallery in Ottawa. Brown had no idea of her abilities but asked for canvases. Immediately he saw her genius and selected 17 canvases. It was 1927, and she was 56 when her talents were recognized. Franklin Carmichael, Lawren Harris, A. Y. Jackson, Frank Johnston, Arthur Lismer, J. E. H. MacDonald, Tom Thompson and Frederick H. Varley, the Group of Seven, knew that at last the West had an artist to note. "Confidence sprang to my work," she said later. At home attitudes still remained lukewarm but she continued to work. Encouraged by Lawren Harris to note down some of her experiences, she took creative writing classes at Victoria College, winning a prize for her short story, "The Hully-Up Letter." She also took a correspondence course in writing although her first manuscript was rejected by publishers, but refusing to accept rejection she sent her manuscript to former Victoria High School teacher Ira Dilworth, a Canadian Broadcasting Corporation employee, who became her "Dear Eye," editing her stories. It was June, 1939, when she wrote to artist Nan Lawson Cheney in Vancouver about the acceptance of scripts by C.B.C. The letter is now preserved in UBC's Special Collections Library:

Just heard from Ira Dilworth. Dr. Sedgewick has consented to be reader of my Indian stories over the air, date as yet unknown; says Dr. Sedgewick enthusiastically agreed to do so. Won't it be funny to hear one's thoughts spouted out of nowhere. Thinking aloud.

She was still recovering for a heart attack suffered two years earlier

The house where Emily Carr was born, now used as an art gallery. She once tried to start a drop-in gallery for art enthusiasts and artists but few people came.

Dr. George Clutesi, given an honorary degree by University of Victoria for his contributions to literature. A member of the Tse-shaht Band, West Coast, Vancouver Island, he was a young man when Emily Carr considered him her protege, leaving him some of her brushes and canvases.

and was painting less. Her writing grew into several books, some of which were found in manuscript form in the trunk she bequeathed to Dilworth when she died in March, 1945. They include *The Book of Small, Growing Pains, Heart of a Peacock, House of All Sorts, Klee Wyck* and her diaries, *Hundreds and Thousands. Klee Wyck* netted her the Governor General's Award in 1941.

Once Emily said: "I tell you it is better to be a street sweeper or a char or a boarding house keeper than to lower your standards. These may spoil your temper, but they cannot dwarf your soul." In 1971, the Federal Post Office chose her painting "Big Raven" to issue a commemorative stamp in her honor. Vancouver Art Gallery curator, Doris Shadbolt stated that it meant that "thousands of people in Canada or all over the world will see her vision which was reproduced 27 million times."

Old ladies still mutter about her eccentricities, others stand awed before her work . . thunderbolt Emily Carr touched us all because she dared to remain true to herself.

Gitksan people always have been aware of their rights. They turned away others but allowed Emily Carr to paint their villages, totem poles and forest. They could see through to her spirit of sincerity. This year, Vancouver born actress Margaret Martin won praise for her portrayal of Emily in the Canadian Broadcasting Corporation film documentary. With producer Nancy Ryley, a cameraman and assistant, she travelled to locations to retrace the artist's life. During filming she sometimes "felt Emily take over. I was using a dry brush and a dry palette but I could feel the paint actually flow under the brush." Playing Emily in a stage production in Victoria, where she lives with her husband and children, she dutifully sipped coffee each night of the performance as part of a scene of Emily with her suitor. On the last night she decided to ask for real coffee "not that cold ucky drink." "My, but you don't drink that do you?" asked a horrified props lady. "It's poster paint." Margaret felt Emily would have appreciated that, "having the paint inside and out." Acting is a longtime love for this actress who was encouraged by her aunt, Anne VandenBoer in Delta and by Victoria director Peter Mannering. As well as standard productions, she toured the province's schools for Bastion Theatre performing plays for schoolchildren. She has received six awards for her acting, she's played in CBC's "The Beachcombers," and had a bit role in the film "Harry In Your Pocket." "None of this would have been possible without the complete co-operation of my husband," she says. "I've always considered myself liberated." One of her most precious theatrical memories came when she was acting in a summer children's production in Bastion Square. A man, rather shabbily dressed, began talking of his former life as a circus clown, of his bout with alcoholism, and of the now quiet life he led. At the next show two hours later in another square, Centennial Square, he reappeared. "This time he was dressed up in a suit. He gave me a gift he had treasured for years, something he called a mitty bag—a crocheted tube with a silver ring at each end. Apparently, actors at the turn of the century carried this containing their money over their belt. I wanted to thank him but he slipped away."

Margaret Martin *is* Emily Carr, the critics said in September. Emily inspired "Klee Wyck: A Ballet for Emily" which was commissioned by the Vancouver Art Gallery under a $25,000 grant from the Secretary of State to commemorate International Women's Year in 1975. Vancouver's Anna Wyman choreographed the ballet while Ann Mortifee wrote the score. Ann Mortifee, composer and singer, first won national recognition when she appeared as a balladeer in George Ryga's "The Ecstacy of Rita Joe" in 1969. She had the chance to become a New York star and was signed to a contract in that city after playing Off Broadway in the all-Canadian revue, "Love and Maple Syrup." She loathed "the games in the theatre business. They really wanted to make me a star. I just wanted to sing my songs. I'm home and I'm glad."

Famous artist Emily Carr inspired two British Columbians to produce "Klee Wyck: A Ballet for Emily", a work commissioned by the Vancouver Art Gallery to commemorate International Women's Year. Anne Mortifee (above), the composer and singer who won acclaim as a balladeer in George Ryga's "The Ecstacy of Rita Joe," wrote the score.   A

Award-winning actress Margaret Martin IS Emily Carr in the Canadian Broadcasting Corporation's drama-documentary on the artist's life. During filming, she sometimes felt "Emily take over. I was using a dry brush and dry palette but I could feel the paint actually flow under the brush."   B

General view of Vancouver from south, 1890.
A

May Day, 1906, in New Westminster.
B

Mary Ellen Smith, first woman member of the Provincial Legislative Assembly and first woman Minister. In an article in "The Champion" she said that women's place in the house was neither more than or less than a man's since many household pursuits were being carried out by machines.　C

CHAPTER THIRTEEN: SPEAKING OUT

It took years of lobbying and organizing—and then more effort—but at last on April 5, 1917, the Amendment to the Elections Act granted women the right to have their names on the register of voters for electoral districts "and to vote at any election of members, to serve in the Legislative Assembly upon the same terms, in the same manner and subject to the same conditions as men." Even then, many women were overlooked: East Indian and Oriental women did not obtain their right to vote in provincial elections until 1947, native Indian women had to wait until the 1952 Provincial Election before they could vote although they received their rights in 1949.

The first political party to bring the matter of women's suffrage to its members was the Provincial Progressive Party, a short-lived entity, which discussed women's rights at a 1903 Kamloops convention. Women fighting for suffrage came from all walks of life. Some were well known, such as Susie Lane Clark or Mary Norton (the latter helped to bring about the Workmen's Compensation Act of 1918), while others, like Minnie Cummins, who arrived in "that wretched little hole" of Greenwood in 1905, organized women's teas and socials as well as a Votes for Women Campaign. The large women's groups such as the Women's Christian Temperance Union, the Local Council of Women, and the Political Equality League, worked hard to raise public awareness.

The Political Equality League was formed first in Victoria, then in Vancouver in 1910, but groups united to form the British Columbia Political Equality League, later known as the BCPEL. Members stated their goals in the first edition of *The Champion*, dated August 12, 1912: they wished to achieve suffrage, to publicize the inefficiency of provincial laws affecting women and children, and to establish "political, social and industrial rights for men and women." Organizing secretary Dorothy Davis toured the province receiving encouraging support from Okanagan people. Mrs. Lashley Hall, Vancouver president, also travelled the province, giving speeches such as one delivered in Revelstoke, in which she pointed out that "women did not wish to antagonize men but to cooperate with them." On Valentine's Day, the *Vancouver Province* reported that 60 suffragettes were to present 10,000 signatures demanding the government for the right to vote. In 1916, suffragettes carrying "Votes for Women" banners were marching to the Legislature, rerouted by police through Victoria's Red Light district. Pioneer librarian Dr. Margaret Clay, school trustee Margaret Jenkins and suffragette Dorothy Cameron were among them.

When victory was announced, women began to consider that next step—supporting a woman who would run for political office. In January, 1918, the first woman to gain a seat in the Provincial Legislature, Mary Ellen Smith, won a by-election caused by the death of her husband, Ralph Smith, Minister of Finance for the Liberals. Elected as an Independent, she made her maiden speech on March 1, 1918, saying: "I have faith in the intelligence, honor and integrity of every member of this House. Not only do I come to ask for legislation in the best interests of women and children, but also legislation for the protection of the best interests of all people of this province." Joining the Liberal ranks, she steered important bills such as the Deserted Wives Maintenance Act, Equal Guardianship Act, and the Mothers' Pension Act, and helped establish a Boys' Industrial School. In 1921 she declined Premier John Oliver's offer that she become Speaker of the Legislative Assembly, believing she could achieve more as an elected Member; she did accept the position of Minister Without Portfolio but resigned later that year, saying: "I have been in the unfortunate position of having to assume the responsibility of acts of the government without being in a position to criticize or advise . . . ." Re-elected in 1924, she served until 1928 when the Progressive Conservatives under Dr. S. F. Tolmie swept into power.

Vancouver's Helena Gutteridge had been spending her time organizing women laundry and garment workers. "They were timid and easy to please, an easy mark for unscrupulous employers," she recalled in a March, 1957, *Pacific Tribune* article. "Their low wages, long hours, and miserable working conditions became a threat to everything the unions had won." She obtained union endorsement of proposals while UBC University Women's Group drew up proposed regulations for working hours: as a result, the Minimum Wage Act for Women and Girls was passed in 1918. Section three of the Act stated that one of three board members must be a woman: Helen Gregory MacGill was appointed. She and Emma Stanton had been among the first women to obtain Trinity College degrees in the 1890's: Helen had studied for her M.A. too. A journalist, she became chairman of the UBC University Women's Club Committee for Better Laws for Women and Children, in her research finding that many laws were based in antiquity. At her own expense, she wrote and published: *Daughters, Wives and Mothers in B.C.: Some Laws Concerning Them, 1912.* A former Progressive Conservative, she joined the Liberals in time to back the Equal Guardianship Act of 1917, the year in which she was appointed British Columbia's first woman provincial judge, working in the juvenile courts until 1928. Ten years later, the University of British Columbia awarded her an Honorary Doctor of Law Degree.

Women lawyers across Canada fought to change the British Columbia Law Society's Statutes which made no provision for women like Hilda Cartwright to practice. Mabel Penery French, another lawyer who wanted to start her own practice, refused to accept defeat and took her case to Vancouver lawyers, Russell, Russell and Hannington, but they met defeat in the Court of Appeal. She and Mrs. J. W. deB. Farris, president of University of Victoria Women's Club made strenuous appeals to the provincial government. The result was Bill 45, passed on February 12, 1912: "An Act to remove the disability of women so far as relates to the study and practise of law in this province." On April 1, 1912, lawyer French and 19 male lawyers were called to the Bar. Early women lawyers included New Westminster's Janet Silley, Vancouver's Winnifred McKay, Pat Rennie, E. Seaton and Jean Whiteside. Hilda Cartwright was accepted when she wrote exams in 1923.

Judge Helen Gregory MacGill. She maintained B.C. laws dated into antiquity, saying the mores of 1660 were reflected in a Guardianship Act originating from the reign of Charles the Second. Among other interests she helped see the first Women's Building established in Canada—built in Vancouver. A

While Mrs. James Dunsmuir (Laura Surles) enjoyed the duties of being a Premier's wife in 1900, others were living in poverty. In 1906 as Lieutenant-Governor's wife, she entertained lavishly. B

Anne Sutherland who practised from 1920 to 1968 was one of Vancouver's best known lawyers. Judges said she "ran her own legal aid service for the poor."

Women physicians were rare at this time, but Maritimer Lavinia McPhee hung out her shingle in a Victoria office in the 1890's; three women were practising medicine when Dr. Elizabeth Anderson arrived on the mainland at the turn of the century, and in 1907, the first school doctor appointed was Dr. Georgina Crawford who inspected some 8,000 Vancouver school children annually. In later years, Vancouver Island's Dr. Frances Oldham Kelsey who studied pharmacology at McGill and studied medicine after marriage and between child-raising in the United States, was awarded that country's highest civilian award, when she refused to permit the use to Thalidomide, a tranquillizing drug, which Europeans prescribed to pregnant women; many of the women bore babies with deformed hands and with rudimentary fingers on a stub below their shoulders.

Early Chinese family, Kamloops. A

As women fought to practice their professions in early years, cars were beginning to replace the buggy. An airplane was exhibited in Vancouver in 1910. By 1913 the Local Council of Women in that city was training women in parliamentary procedure: they asked the Canadian Pacific Railway for matrons on trains (the company said conductors could handle all situations), and they voted against allowing educated Oriental women to join them to discuss the plight of young Oriental immigrant women. They were not in favor of 'Hindu' women immigrating unless they came to join their husbands. They were concerned about noise and smoke pollution. Unemployment was on the increase with a quiet but worried crowd meeting to discuss this on Vancouver's Powell Street where they were dispersed into "a struggling mass of frightened humanity" when the mayor sent police to break up the crowd.

When Canada declared war on Germany, August 5, 1914, enlistment was high. Among women signing for overseas duty were Margaret Moss of Cowichan, organizer of that district's Red Cross Society; Arminella Cunningham of Shawnigan Lake, who joined the Eighth Serbian Army, and Julia Henshaw, botanist, ecologist, mountaineer and journalist, who performed ambulance and encruitment duty, bringing back numerous awards to Vancouver. Women organized Red Cross Societies; the Imperial Order of the Daughters of the Empire undertook to care for "widows, orphans, sailors and airmen, in time of peace, or under sickness, accident or reverse of fortune." Women's Institutes made jam, knitted garments, packed tobacco, sold patriotic buttons and raised funds for overseas hospitals.

A woman "made it" in music—Barbara Farrow became a member of the Kamloops Orchestra in 1898. B

Gwen Goldsmid who arrived in Canada on the last boat west in 1917 was hired by the *Vancouver Province* to cover work being done by women on farms and orchards. Her stories picked up the day's war theme as this July 10 story did:

Strange battle cry . . . B.C. Varsity girls have joined the trousered battalions and sixty-one of them help to harvest the fruit crops of Vancouver Island . . . through the long forenoon, they can be seen in their regulation uniforms, squatting in the trenches between the rows of berries, trenches that in the case of Gordon Head ranches, are covered with straw to protect the berries from the fine dustlike soil of the district.

Hiking was allowed and these women marched over the Kamloops hills when boots were a good protection against rattlesnakes and cactus.   *A*

Our special outings—a Nicola tennis tournament. The ladies watched.   *B*

No day care centres existed for children then—they waited in the canneries as these Japanese children did.   *.C*

Mother works at the filling children while these little Indian children wait for her to finish work.   *D*

Gwen Goldsmid, now Gwen Cash, cover-ed orchard and farm stories during World War I and since then has written two books, "A 100,000 Miles from Ottawa", and "I Like B.C."

By Fall, she was married to Bruce Cash, living in Officer's Quarters, and supervising an Alien Camp at Vernon which housed German immigrants whose allegiance to Canada was suspect.

During the war women were recruited for farmwork and some English women were brought to the Fraser Valley farms where Mission girls boycotted the men, forming a Sweethearts Union saying that if they dropped local girls in fruitpicking season, there would be no winter dates available. Women replaced men in all types of work which previously had been male preserves: city offices, insurance companies and banks used women as stenographers, typists and clerks. Imperial Oil used women as gas jockeys at Vancouver gas stations, while at some canneries women inhaled toxic fumes as they varnished cans with a lacquer that burned ungloved hands.

Alien's Camp, Vernon, B.C.   A

After the war, the dreadful influenza epidemic swept through the country. Women worked as hospital volunteers; nurses set up tent hospitals in small towns. After the epidemic, unemployment was still high. Vangie MacLachlan, a Women's Institute co-ordinator, started a Buy B.C. Products campaign, while Institutes were promoting wool crafts among settlers. It was an era of increasing hard times, but there were also gay times with fox trot, May Day Queens, flappers, and pro and con arguments over liquor sales. In 1927, Girl Guides won praise for their smart appearance and drill and the first Dominion Day Camp in Canada was held in Victoria. A later Guider was famed alpinist Phyllis Munday of North Vanouver who climbed Mount Waddington in 1926.

The Soldiers' Settlement Board enabled veterans to homestead but farm costs were high. The fall of the stock market in 1929 threw everyone into the Depression. Rural families used ingenuity to provide school clothing, transforming flour sacks into school clothes. Ellen Georgeson, now Mrs. Stallybrass of Galiano Island, then a widow with two children and an aged grandfather to support, took in washing, "miles and miles of washing," daughter Mary Backlund recalls. "The soap came in hard cakes so it had to be carefully shaved and used sparingly. Bleaching was done on the grass, pretty successfully, too." Martha Philips grew berries and daffodils at Brander "but what did it matter if the berries were as big as thimbles? Who could buy them? We were all growing daffodils and we all had chickens and eggs, and eggs, and eggs." She and her husband moved to New Westminster but could find no work. "He was too proud to take relief." She found a job scrubbing floors. Mennonite families also moved into the province, farming in Yarrow and Sardis, southwest Chilliwack, finding that farming would not support everyone so some asked for relief. By 1931 more families had arrived at Abbotsford, where public health nurse Evelyn Maguire reported families had inaugurated a medical plan, paying $10 yearly for physicians' fees with doctors calling weekly at ministers' houses to learn who was sick. In Maillardville where the mill closed, the Catholic priest led new French-Canadian communicants through the streets, stopping to pray outside homes where altars graced porches. Marie Lizee tried to stretch a family paycheque when her husband brought home $15 for twelve days work a month. She found work grading peas at a cannery, taking a hunk of bread smeared with lard for lunch, occasionally adding a dill pickle as a luxury. At Agassiz, Gertrude Stewart made soup for the people her provincial policeman

Ellen Georgeson, now Mrs. Stallybrass, fed the family and worked hard, too, during Depression Days.

B

Viola Carr Wood recalls days in cannery as well as one attempt to become a beachcomber, selling logs. In later years she became women's editor of a weekly but returned to that teenage base, the Queen Charlottes. A

Bindo Beadall becomes Bindo Lalari at this Victoria Temple ceremony in the 1950's. All the people shown are her relatives who originally came from the Punjab area.

B

husband "peeled from the trains" on frosty days. Women rode the rods, too.

In the Cariboo, "steers were selling for four cents a pound," Molly Forbes of Lac La Hache recalls. "We boarded some city teachers who wanted a taste of ranching life. My husband built some cabins to rent out." Lee and Margaret Moxley homesteaded at Moose Heights, north of Quesnel, clearing land and building cabins. They had no running water, no electricity and little cash: the children liked the freedom of country life. In the Chilcotin, a weary couple with a lean packhorse knocked at Anna Straube French's door offering to pay for a meal; she fed them free of charge then returned to forking hay. Near Vanderhoof, pregnant Peggy Russell, her husband and small child, went mining in local creeks. Everything they had was carried in backpacks. "No roads, of course. Just trails. When we were lucky we found as much as $2 a day but it more often was 50 cents. We were young and healthy," she recalls. "No money for those misery makers, booze and tobacco. And we'd have been insulted if anyone called us poor." The Queen Charlotte canneries remained open, but the humpbacks were running late one year; then they came in, hundreds and hundreds of them, and the more they packed at the Simpson cannery, the more they lost— prices had dropped overnight. At one cannery, Viola Carr was living with a girlfriend in a tarpaper shack, going in a truck to dig clams for three hours before working "on the lines," with hands going like lightning to slit clam necks and livers. Sometimes soaked through from digging in rain, they just had time to make their baloney and tomato stew with supplies bought from a cannery commissary, when the whistle blew calling them to the lines. Sometimes they made 25 cents an hour.

Relief camps dotted the province. Many occupants were young men, others had faced war only to return to personal defeat. A mass rally of mothers formed in Stanley Park to draw attention to the men's plight. Hobo jungles sprung up everywhere. In Prince Rupert, people were forbidden to cut down trees for needed firewood. Local Council of Women groups asked for relief for women, but were told there were scarcely enough funds to aid unemployed married men. Somehow, Dr. Helen Gordon Stewart who drove miles through Fraser Valley roads, persuaded residents to support a library with their taxes.

New Canadians arriving then, particularly groups of East Indians, cut wood and sold it door to door. Later, many proved excellent businessmen, owning mills in Lake Cowichan, Vancouver Island. The transition for East Indian women was hard: "Some had lived in villages cooking out of doors. They had to get used to stoves and indoor plumbing," says Victoria-born Bindo Lalari, a school secretary whose parents came from the Punjab. "Modesty was another matter. They were shocked when they had to undress before male physicians at clinics or hospitals." Temples were built, children went to public schools, women who had relied on relatives as interpreters shyly began speaking for themselves as they ventured into the communities. Swimming pools turned away Chinese; ballrooms sometimes turned away Blacks, and native Indian families had a hard time finding a room in city hotels.

University life attracted women whose families could afford to send them to school: Prince Rupert's first student to enter the University of British Columbia in the late Twenties was Katherine Pillsbury who

Imperial Oil hired these efficient women to serve gas at their Vancouver stations. Note the uniform which proved a suitable one for the work that women proved they could handle well.
A

Hilda Leighton started the first four Guide companies in Victoria under the auspicies of the I.O.D.E. in 1915. In 1916 when the Duke of Connaught, Governor General, made his first western tour, everyone was "amazed by the fine drill and appearance of the Girl Guides."
B

Apple picking in the Okanagan orchards.
C

Women replaced male stenographers in offices such as this one of the D. E. Brown and Company, Estate Investment and General Brokers, Vancouver, B.C.

D

189

Machinery was doing the work earlier women had done by hand at this cannery in the 1940's. *A*

Interior view of B.C. cannery. *B*

Yukon Southern Airways, amalgamated in 1942, becoming Canadian Pacific Airlines. Stewardess is Jewell Butler, serving Jessie MacLean. *C*

Priscilla Dean, actress, at Pathfinders Exhibition at Willows Beach Park, Victoria, 1919. *D*

took her B.A., then went to Boston to study Home Economics. After doing field work, she returned home to marry Hugh Keenleyside, a student she had met across a UBC debating table where he had won the "Resolve: Life in the Elizabethan Age was preferrable to that of today." As the diplomat's wife, she lived in Ottawa, Tokyo, Mexico City and New York, joining international women's groups and heading the United Nations' Women's Guild. Other women pioneered in the sciences: Edith Berkeley taught zoology at UBC in 1916, then continued a lifetime research into polychaete at Nanaimo Biological Station. Her daughter, Alfreda Needler, studied at UBC in the late Twenties, then went to Toronto for her Ph.D., spending her research on British Columbia material—shrimps; her daughter Mary Needler Arai is a zoologist at the University of Calgary today. Other University of British Columbia graduates were Dr. Gertrude Smith, who researched salamanders, and taught zoology at the university, Dr. Mildred Campbell and Dr. Verna Lucas, and Dr. Josephine Hart, who attended Victoria College, UBC, then the University of Toronto, and who still continues her research on crabs, contributing her articles to international scientific journals.

Other women studied agriculture; several studied dairy science and horticulture by the time Joan McTaggart-Cowan took a double major in botany and plant nutrition in 1938. She was one of a five-person team sent by UBC Extension Department to encourage people to learn and use what was available on their farms. "A Depression days program," she recalls, "in which we lectured to anyone between 16-26 in winter months."

Some new careers for women were unfolding. Vancouver widow Hilda Publicover became Canada's first woman lifeboat expert, passing exams and joining the crew of the S.S. *Prince Rupert* as stewardess. Pat Eccleston, now Mrs. John Maxwell, of West Vancouver, was chosen as the province's first air stewardess in 1938. A graduate of St. Paul's Hospital, Vancouver, she had done enough post-graduate work to hold key supervisory positions and was "dared" to try for the position advertised by the fledging Trans-Canada Air Lines. "I put in my application at the last moment and three days later, I was astonished to hear that I was hired." Stewardesses studied aerodynamics and meteorology in those days to serve on the infant line, which inaugurated its first run between Vancouver and Seattle, a 50-minute journey in which the tiny Lockheed Electra ten seater flew some 2,000 feet above the Strait of Georgia and Puget Sound. Paseengers wanted assurance and having a nurse on board gave them confidence. The tiny planes had to be loaded carefully; every time the stewardess moved up and down the aisle with lunchboxes the pilot had to trim the aircraft. Women also learned to fly, among them Tosa Trascolini, a legal secretary for Angelo De Branca in Vancouver. Lessons "were $20.00 an hour and I was making $60.00 a month in 1929 so I sometimes could only afford part of a lesson." After she told her family what she was doing, they decided it was time she learned to drive the family car. Today, she lives in California with an airstrip on her property and her own plane, which she bought for $1,500 years back. With Margaret Fane, Betsy Flaherty, Alma Gilbert, Hollie Moore, Jean Pike and Elaine Roberge, she became one of the "Flying Seven", forming Canada's first women's aeronautical club, at an all-day flying event in which each woman flew in

Pat Eccleston, now Mrs. John Maxwell, who was the province's first stewardess. There was a sense of comaraderie in early days of flights says this stewardess who flew with Lucille Gardner of Winnipeg and later trained other stewardesses. Passenger planes were 10-seater Lockheed Electra, then 14-passenger Lodestar, 20-seater North Star, then the 90-seater Super Constellation.

Betty Wadsworth at controls of her Stinson Voyager. She covers most fly-ins in province, reporting and doing photography for aviation magazines as well as doing volunteer work for a provincial search and rescue team.

Japanese evacuation cabins at Lillooet, B.C., in use until 1950. Of 23,000 Japanese in the province, 2,400 were naturalized Canadians and 13,400 were born here. B

relay succession. Their flights attracted women who wanted to learn flight theory and parachute packing. In 1940, the group dropped one million pamphlets on Vancouver in a fund-raising campaign "to buy our boys more planes."

Betty Wadsworth, aviation photographer-reporter learned to fly in 1958, winning the Page Trophy for the highest marks in ground school and flight theory, when she competed with 53 men. "When I was a little girl I saw Captain Ted Dobbin barnstorming in his Gypsy Moth," she recalls. "He came to Kaslo for the Cherry Festival, flying over the new road from Kaslo to Nelson." She bought her plane, a Stinson Voyageur in 1960. In the Seventies, she was elected British Columbia Director of the Canadian Owners' and Pilots' Association, and was re-elected for a new term; she also become the first woman Air Service Chief in charge of a Provincial Emergency program, a resource service for air and sea rescue. Soon after the Japanese bombardment of Pearl Habor, the Japanese also shelled Estevan Point lighthouse and wireless station. On Canada's West Coast fear became panic. The Provincial Chapter of the I.O.D.E. sent out thousands of petitions together with envelopes to be mailed to British Columbia members of the Federal Government asking that all Japanese, irrespective of sex or place of birth be removed to the Interior. Japanese who had worked as berry-pickers, produce growers and fishermen, were sent to Alberta and Manitoba beet farms; 11,600 went to camps in British Columbia's Interior. At Steveston, local women were recruited to replace cannery workers, packing salmon under supervision of the army. When Victoria City Council, backed by numerous groups, considered sending out a referendum suggesting all Japanese be returned to their homeland, Greenwood Municipal Council wrote deploring such action. They had 1200 Japanese interned in that town, they wrote, "and they were law-abiding under very difficult conditions. The children were excellent students." In later years, a Salt Spring family, the Iwasakis, sued the Federal Government for the low price received in compulsory sale of Gulf Island waterfront property but lost the case, while artist Shizuye Takashima published her experiences *A Child in Prison Camp* in 1970.

Canada entered war with Germany in September, 1939. German-Canadians were fingerprinted. The local policeman arrived on the Queen Charlotte farm of Hedvig Lubow Ross to take away the gun she used to scare bears from calves. She received the printed card that said she was an Enemy Alien. "It hurt," she recalls. A widow with two young sons, her neighbors helped her with haying; later at election time, she was asked to be Deputy Returning Officer.

From 1940-1944 the provincial women's workforce doubled from 30,000 to 60,000. New Westminster's Ivy Leatherdale replaced a man packing cottage cheese in Fraser Valley Milk Producer's Vancouver plant, working a 49-hour, six-day week at first. "I don't remember what I was paid then but I know it was a lot better than my first job—I had worked in a laundry for 13 years at $13.50 a week, six days a week." After 33 years of dairy work she retired when she was making $5.33 an hour on a 36-hour week. Mills hired women to replace men at war. Marie Bailey Forslund worked on the greenchain at Honeymoon Bay in Lake Cowichan, taking lumber, grading and stencilling it. Paid fifty cents an hour, she travelled down the railway tracks on a speeder. Made timekeeper, she found men were paid more the women.

Early Japanese pioneer family: the Uyenobe family, of Victoria. A

Japanese women had proved efficient workers in canneries such as this one. Their removal from Steveston meant other women had to work under a wartime emergency program to fill their place. B

Popular Salt Spring family, the Murakami family, who were sent to different sites in B.C., Alberta and Ontario. They were released in 1945. C

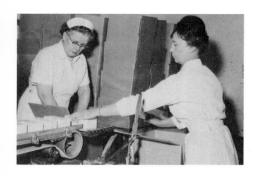

Ivy Leatherdale and Lily Scott packing butter. When war started, there was a demand for cottage cheese which was not rationed and Mrs. Leatherdale (with cap) packed this for Fraser Valley Milk Producers' Vancouver plant. A

Wartime work packing in the canneries. B

Some women went to war: Kamloops-born Norah Vicars, worked as dietician on the *Letitia*, one of two Red Cross Hospital ships plying the Atlantic, while Rossie Hughes Crowe of Victoria was one of 13 nursing sisters on the *Letitia's* sister ship, the *Lady Nelson*. Mary Patricia Leith, a Victoria Royal Jubilee nursing graduate who served in Northern Europe, used her war credits to put herself through medical school. Vancouver's Molly Lamb Bobak spent the war years as a war artist; while Victoria's Myfanwy Pavelic made $10,000 for the Red Cross by crossing the country to make portraits.

Women musicians found work in orchestras or teaching. Concert pianist Dr. Ida Halpern had been laughed at in 1939 when she told immigration authorities that she planned to collect British Columbia's native Indian music. She did just that, although her first attempts were discouraging. Later C.Mudge Chief Billy Assu offered her 100 songs; of which she took down 88. When a record was cut, royalties were turned over to Indian people and she continued to collect this music, once travelling with writer and artist Mildred Valley Thornton who was painting portraits of Indian Chiefs. In 1965, she returned to the University of British Columbia where she had taught 20 years and prepared a unique course in ethnomusicology. Vancouver's Jean Coulthard composed choral works, chamber music and works for cello, piano, solo instruments and voice, winning world recognition. "In this age of scientific development, I feel that human values remain the same . . . unless music is able to reach the heart in some way, it loses its compelling power to minister to human welfare." Barbara Pentland, who came West in 1949, continued to write orchestral works; her String Quartet No. 2 was chosen for performance at an International Musical Festival in Stockholm in 1956. She and poet Dorothy Livesay worked together to produce"The Lake Chamber Opera in One Act." Today her major interests is in producing music for students.

In the 1940's, women made their names on the political front. Nancy Hodges, a Liberal, gained a seat in the Legislature on her second try in 1941, accepting the role of Speaker of the House in 1949—a role she later described as that "of glorified referee." A columnist for the Victoria *Daily times*, she led in party decisions of coalition between Conservatives and Liberals in 1941, continuing to write her "One Woman's Day" column in which she discussed what she did, ruffling many feathers when she wrote that nurses did not need more training than they then received in order to function as bedside nurses. She lost her seat in 1953 when she was beaten by Social Credit Lydia Arsens who had brought up the matter of reusing garbage, foreseeing the current development of recycling centres. Mrs. Hodges was made a Senator later that year.

Four other women were in the House when she first took her seat, Tilly Jean Rolston, a Progressive Conservative who switched to Social Credit, became Minister of Education, and CCFers Dorothy Steeves, Laura Jamieson and Grace MacInnis. Dorothy Steeves was first woman socialist elected to the British Columbia Legislative Assembly, serving from 1934-1945. Born in Amsterdam of Irish-Dutch descent, she had a degree of Doctor of Laws when she came to Canada with the Canadian she had met and married during World War I. Interested in women's rights, she fought for a minimum wage "for that most exploited class of workers, the domestic servants," sparked the idea of credit unions, and

Women and machinery replaced the men of the Okanagan who had gone to war at this fruit packing station.   A

Some women lived on float houses, planted gardens and taught the children not to fall overboard. Here is a float camp at Nimpkish Lake, Vancouver Island.   B

Barbara Pentland, composer. Influenced by the Austrian musician, Anton Webern, she sometimes performs her own piano works in public.   C

Jean Coulthard, Vancouver-born composer who began musical training with her mother, Mrs. Walter Coulthard, who was an early exponent of the then radical music of Ravel. Jean Coulthard's music for orchestra has received international recognition.   D

Nancy Hodges, newspaper columnist and Speaker of the Provincial Legislature. She served as a Member of the Senate from 1953-65.   E

195

This portrait of Linda William taken by Juli Porter in Burnaby in 1930's.

Juli Williams Porter. As a child she used to watch famous artist Alan Brooks draw and paint his bird pictures at Kelvin, the Mount Tolmie family home.

Peggy Muenter, well known Vancouver Island potter.

was known for her stand concerning Canada's World War II effort which she felt should be fought through industrial as well as military outlets. Laura Jamieson served in the Legislative Assembly from 1939-1945 and from 1952-1953; active in earlier suffragette activities, she was named Judge of the Juvenile Court for Burnaby in 1929. She helped to found the Women's International League for Peace and Freedom. She also became an alderman on Vancouver City Council from 1948-1950.

Grace MacInnis served from 1941-1945 in the Provincial House and from 1965-1974 in the Federal House. She gained political expertise from working as an aide to her father, J. S. Woodsworth, former Laborite who founded the CCF (Cooperative Commonwealth Federation) party which became the New Democratic Party in 1961. Her husband Angus was a well-known member of the Party, holding a six-term Federal seat. Throughout her career, she was known for her concern for the poor and for consumers. In 1966, she proposed that the Adult Occupation Training Act should be amended to include any woman "who had been engaged in domestic service of her home for a period of not less than three years." She showed genuine altruistic concern as a member of a committee of the Department of Energy, Mines and Resources which was dealing with Bill C-144, the Canada Water Act; she suggested that rather than rejecting suggestions on the grounds or wording or technicalities, the idea should be studied to see if it contained any logic. "Let the government rewrite it, and bring it in as their own amendment. We don't care who gets the credit. The important thing is that this bill be as good as we can make it." Earlier, she had pointed out that it was unethical for the Science Council of Canada to have a chairman who at that time was a vice-president of a company making phosphates. She was British Columbia's first woman Member of Parliament.

Arts were an expanding outlet for women in the Fifties and Sixties: in small communities, markets proved available for weavers, potters and painters. Juli Porter of Maple Bay ran a photographic studio in Duncan which brought parents with small children who appreciated her child studies: "Others still were using the old slow camera. I acquired a press camera and took children 'on the fly' with lots of shots and a fast aperture." An artist, too, she opened a gallery to show local work and was amazed how well it sold; in one summer she sold 40 local paintings and 200 pieces of pottery. Much of the pottery had been made by Peggy Muenter, now of Lantzville, who liked playing with clay as a child and studied to perfect the art later: "Today form is more important to me than surface decoration, although I am working to bring the two together," she says. Another potter making a name for herself is Carol Southward who ran a Salt Spring studio before she opened a studio near Mill Bay.

Some of British Columbia's artists have begun to collect national acclaim. Sculptor Elza Mayhew selected sculpture rather than other art forms, making a commitment to this medium when she took drawings cast in sand to an iron foundry where they were cast in iron as reliefs; masks were made by the same method. She bagan making cement sculptures, then bronze ones. A recent commission was "Column of the Sea" which stands at Confederation Centre at Charlottetown, Prince Edward Island. "Sculpture is a language to learn over the years;

Elza Mayhew, sculptor: drawing by artist Myfanwy Pavelic.   B

197

it is only when a sculptor ceases to translate that he can achieve any firm expression." Pat Martin Bates, a printmaker, began winning awards and continue studies of this ancient art: her prints utilize different shapes, mandalas, squares and rectangles with tiny pin-pricked perforations. Some prints make sculptural cubes. "A rectangle is a door, something we can get past through," she has said, explaining her work, "circles are the first thing a child draws and the dot is the universe of God. A square is a window." Audrey Capel Doray, Sherry Grauer and Evelyn Roth were making a name for themselves in Vancouver art circles in the Sixties and early Seventies: in 1969, UBC and UVIC graduate Carole Sabiston took her young son to Spain for a year to see "if I really had the dedication and ability to work on my collages and wall hangings full time." Her unique fabric collages and wall hangings are often multi-dimensional; she uses leather, lace, silk and other materials for textural contrasts, arranging and setting these within a deep frame and using different sizes of work. The experiment paid off—she now has enough commissions from architects and galleries to do this work full time in her Victoria home.

Joan Mason Hurley, playright, has written numerous productions for stage and radio. She has been honored for her contributions to drama in British Columbia.

In small towns, married middle-aged women say they want more to do. They've helped with all the auxiliaries, Little League and the school and now they're not trained to do much else. Besides, they're in their forties. It's a good age for others. Joan Mason Hurley, playwright, returned to the University of Victoria for a B.A., then went to UBC for a M.A. in Creative Writing, producing plays that recently won her a trophy for her contribution to drama in the province. Since her first play, "Immolation" was produced at Vancouver Little Theatre in 1967, she's written many more for radio and stage. In 1975, her drama-documentary "Our Own Particular Jane" honoring the bicentenniary of distant ancestor, Jane Austen, was presented at UVIC's Phoenix Theatre and on CBC radio. Before she went back to school, she did some writing but most of her time was spent in running Shawnigan Beach Hotel with her husband, raising a family and typing business letters. She says facetiously that a lot of people reach the age of 40 and face a triple choice: "to find a new house, a new husband, or a new hobby. Husbands mellow and get better as they age like good cheese; real estate was high priced, so I found a hobby." In more serious tones she points out that she had to get down to do what she always wanted to do, her family gave full and complete encouragement and the opportunities were there.

Women in sports brought home awards to British Columbia in the Sixties. Swimmer Elaine Tanner of Vancouver won the United States Championship in the 100-yard backstroke and butterfly in 1966, also setting a world record of 2:33.3 for the 220 yard medley at July British Columbia championships. She won four gold medals and three silver medals at the British Commonwealth Games and brought back two silver medals and one bronze medal after her 1968 Olympic performances. Nancy Greene of Rossland who learned to ski on that city's Red Mountain slopes, in 1967, zigzagged at breakneck speed to win the slalom and giant slalom, brought the World Cup home in 1967; she also won a silver and gold medal in 1968 Olympics and the World Cup, too, before turning professional skiier. Karen Magnussen of North Vancouver was Canadian Skating Champion in 1968, placing second in 1969. She won the World Championship in 1971, and again in 1973,

Carole Sabiston, known for her unique multi-dimensional collages and wallhangings.   A

Pat Martin Bates, printmaker, whose travels throughout Turkey and Iraq focused her attention on the intricacy of mosaic and mosques. In this work, "The Heart of Rumi Nets a Spinning Dance", she pays homage to her favorite 12th Century Persian poet.   B

Nancy Greene used to say, "Why come second when you can come first." She was known as the Tiger of the Slopes by sportswriters.   C

Karen Magnussen wanted to be a snowflake in a winter carnival but went a lot further as a skating champion.   D

Joni Graham with partner Don Phillips won Canadian Dance (Skating) Championships in 1966, 1967 and 1968. A

Small towns, big towns—sports events got a big boost in the fifties. Catherine Cauldwell of Quesnel became known as a sprinter. B

before turning professional skater. Community sports attracted more women although North Vancouver's Evelyn Roberts, now Mrs. Allyn, beat them to it in the Forties when she managed and sponsored a 45-boy soccer team, Heywood Hornets, who won local championships on the North Shore. Elected to the North Shore Junior Commission she said that some people did not think she would last long as a manager and the team's winning record helped. "Women had their place then, and it certainly wasn't on the soccer field but I found it a wonderful and rewarding challenge."

Women became more involved in civic politics: Marianne Linnell was well known for her long stint as a Vancouver alderman, while Ethel Ogle of Mission, Carrie Cates of North Vancouver, Carrie Gray of Prince George and Frances Elford of Oak Bay became mayors. Serving in Oak Bay, a municipality of Victoria, Mrs. Elford's appetite for civic politics was whetted when she joined the Association of Women Electors, studying reasons for apathy among women voters. Encouraged to run for office by group member Columnist Elizabeth Forbes, she gained an aldermanic seat in 1963, was re-elected in 1965 and 1967, then became mayor in 1969-1973. "It was satisfying to see a library and Senior Citizen's Centre established—and on land I and others had voted to purchase for future purposes earlier." She helped save a park from developers and found her 60-hour work week, which included meetings and reading reports, "thoroughly rewarding, an excellent arena for women, although I believe civic politics must be non-partisan." Only three women held civic positions when she entered office in 1964 while 30 held positions in 1972. Kay Grouhel, Ladysmith mayor, became first woman president of the Union of B.C. Municipalities.

In 1971 Helen Beirnes, who grew up in Penticton, became Canada's first woman president of a Chamber of Commerce in a metropolitan area. She had worked as a fashion model in Paris and Rome before opening a charm and modelling school in Victoria, in 1950. Active on numerous Chamber committees over a ten year period, she used her presidency to promote the "idea of visitor industry rather than smoke and noise polluting industries"; she sent business people into schools to "give business careers a boost" and helped start Victoria Days, a week long festival of events and sports that utilize an early Victorian era theme.

In 1972 when the New Democratic Party ousted the Social Credit's 20 year reign, Pat Jordan, Socred member for North Okanagan, retained the seat she had won in 1966 and 1969; she made a strong stand against Bill 42, the controversial land bill, seeing it as a "fabian flag, hoisted on a Marxian pole, draped around the bodies of our farmers and laying on our land forever." Earlier she had proposed an ingenious solution to deal with Indian Land claims when she suggested paying the native Indian population a yearly grant equal to the amount of interest had they sold British Columbia to the white man at his price, then invested the earnings. Five NDP women were elected as MLAs: Karen Sandford, Daisy Webster, Phyllis Young, now Minister of Consumer Affairs, Eileen Dailly, Minister of Education, and Rosemary Brown. Eileen Dailly was elected to the Legislature first in 1966 and again in 1969; as Minister of Education she immediately banned the use of the strap in schools, saying "if we want to reduce acts of violence in our world and in our community, we must eliminate acts of

Logging communities often had active women's groups such as the Youbou Women's Auxiliary, Vancouver Island, July 12, 1944: front row l-r, Mrs. H. Avison, Mrs. W. H. Gold, Mrs. A. N. Johnson, Mrs. J. Beeson, Mrs. A. Bourdages, Mrs. G. A. MacKay; second row, Mrs. M. Leschasin, Mrs. C. A. Plowright, Mrs. G. Leask, Mrs. J. Howden, Miss E. I. Young (secretary), Mrs. H. Hanson (president), Mrs. R. T. Lynn (vice-president), Mrs. F. Seed (treasurer)' Mrs. J. Brooks; third row, Mrs. H. M. Russell, Mrs. A. Thommassen, Mrs. W. Tyler, Mrs. N. Habart, Mrs. J. Harness, Mrs. J. W. Whittaker, Mrs. Lal Booth, Mrs. R. Salter.

A

Frances Elford, former mayor of Oak Bay who found the position full of interest. Her family supported her efforts.   B

Pat Jordan, well known member of the Social Credit Party who was first elected to the Legislature in B.C.   D

Canada's first president of a Chamber of Commerce in a metropolitan area, Helen Beirnes (Mrs. C. Watling), in Victorian Days dress.   C

Minister of Consumer Services, Phyllis Young. Under her supervision, the Trade Practises Act, the first law of its kind in Canada, has been put into effect. A

Eileen Dailly, Minister of Education.
B

Rosemary Brown. When someone asked what was left if you took away her race and sex, she calmly replied, "a socialist." C

Simma Holt, Member of Parliament and former Vancouver Sun reporter author. "Terror in the Name of God" was one of her books and discussed the Doukhobor radical Sons of Freedom sect. D

Frances Fleming, first woman superintendent of schools. E

violence in our schools." With Bill 173 she introduced controversial bargaining rights for teachers and trustees which meant local bargaining instead of regional bargaining. She also created the position of Director of Indian Education and in September, 1975 Jacqueline Leo, a member of the Kyuquot Band through marriage, became the second person to hold this position. Frances Fleming, former teacher and school superintendent of Quesnel School District became the first woman superintendent of schools. Rosemary Brown, social worker, lecturer and former ombudswoman for Vancouver Status of Women, has become known for her appeal for a ministry to deal with women's affairs. She still wishes to see more women given positions of responsibilities. "Sixty percent of welfare recipients are women and therefore women should have more say in the decisions concerning them," she has said. Three of the bills she promoted are Bill 75, Vancouver Charter Amendment Act in which no warrant can be issued to remove single parents, senior citizens, low income families or unemployed from housing unless alternative accommodation has been found; Bill 17, the Tenants' Collective Bargaining Rights Act, enabling tenants to form a Block Tenants Association with legal rights to bargain with a landlord, and the Affirmative Action Plan Act which promotes employment and educational equality for all. In 1975 she ran for national presidency of the NDP, coming second to Ed Broadbent. As a child, growing up in Jamaica, she watched her grandmother fight for suffrage and still reiterates what she said in earlier speeches: "women in politics can achieve equality, improve the caliber and level of politics and improve the quality and reality of life for all people."

The British Columbia daughter who became a Prime Minister's wife: Margaret Trudeau.

It is in cities and big towns that elderly women seem lonely. "Am I to be discarded because I'm nearly 70? I can see hear, smell and talk. Surely I can do something?" a retired teacher asks. Another woman, moved to a city to be with relatives she rarely sees, sits in her room because "my feet are bad. I can't walk much. I'm thinking of going back home. At least I'll have friends there." Dealing with these problems is one of Liz Bristowe's duties. As Provincial Director of Special Care, Adults Division for the Department of Human Resources, she says that the elderly "must be given choices of lifestyles. We must give them the ability to make a choice whether it is to go to a Rest Home or to stay in their home place in which case we can arrange to take the services they need to them. Home-nursing, meals on wheels, enable the elderly to be independent. And we must stop labelling people, segregating them because of age or because they are of this age or need that." She herself faced an overwhelmingly insecure future at the age of forty when she was widowed, left with five children ranging in age from eight to 18, little money and an incomplete education. "I had no idea of what I wanted to do or what I would do. I probably was a potential welfare case." Going back to school was the solution she chose and in the third year of university she decided to train as a counselling psychologist, which meant a long stint of studies to materialize in a Ph.D. degree. "There *were* scholarships, grants and loans available— as there are for others. Age no longer is a deterrent to choosing a career."

Problems of the elderly are the vital concern of Liz Bristowe, Provincial Director of Special Care, Adults Division for the Department of Human Resources. The elderly must be given a choice of lifestyle, she maintains, ". . . we must stop labelling people, segregating them because of age. . . ." B

Two British Columbia women, both Liberals, Simma Holt, Vancouver Kingsway, and Iona Campagnola, Skeena, became Members of Parliament in 1974. Former reporter Holt has spoken for a stricter control

Gene Errington, Provincial Co-ordinator for Status of Women during International Women's Year. Travelling throughout the province in 1975 she reported on women's need and her work will continue in future years.   A

concerning drug abuse among the young. Mrs. Campagnola, parliamentary secretary to the Minister of Indian Affairs, has made her concerns the Indian people, freight rates and ocean transportation and amenities for "the little, distant places." In Terrace, speaking to a women's group, she said she had set steps to political goals by joining the Prince Rupert garden club where she learned "how to write a newsletter, and to run a meeting a lot about flowers and more about people." She also served on city council. "Pry open that first painful door, move into the political system at every level, so we can alter the futures for our daughters," she told women.

Kathleen Ruff became Director of the Human Rights branch of the Department of Labor in 1973. Her staff investigate complaints, then try to reach a settlement; if this fails, a Board of Enquiry is held. The Provincial Human Rights Code now guarantees equal rights for all in employment, tenancy, property ownership, membership in unions and employers' associations. In International Women's Year, former social worker and Status of Women ombudswoman Gene Errington was named Provincial Co-ordinator, Status of Women, seeking to investigate needs of women and report these back to the Government for action. "It is in the northern areas where women particularly feel isolated," she says. "Women have little opportunities for work and few day care centres." She sees a solution in building communities where secondary industries support the central industry, larger centres perhaps where people commute from outlying districts and where women can find work. Heavy equipment, now mechanized, means that 'brute strength' no longer is valid.

Looking at achievements of women in this province, it seems women accepted the right to vote as a victory but few continued to work to change laws affecting them. We still have poor women in this province, women who need work and women with children who need housing. We need more people to advise women of the opportunities that are available to them; elderly women suffer a sense of isolation and need to have their talents utilized by communities. In universities and in several community colleges such as Cariboo College, Kamloops, active women's programs are unfolding and are proving successful. We must look at the history of the women of this province, for then we can know and shape our future.

Pat Carney, UBC graduate, won acclaim for her business columns in the Vancouver Province in the 1960's. In 1975 her writings on northern economic situations appear in the Vancouver Sun.   B

The Champion

A Monthly Magazine *Published by*

The Political Equality League (Victoria Branch)

75c. a Year, Postage Paid

Single Copies 5c.

" The Woman's Cause is Man's."

| Vol. I. | SEPTEMBER, 1912 | No. 2 |

POLITICAL EQUALITY LEAGUE

Victoria Branch.

President, Mrs. Gordon Grant.
Hon. Treasurer, Mrs. Baer.
Organizing Secretary,
        Miss Dorothy Davis.
Recording Secretary,
        Miss McDonald.
Office,
    Room 2, 647 Fort Street, Victoria.

1. This Society adopts as the fundamental principle of its Constitution the establishment of the Political, Social and Industrial Rights of Women and Men.

It recognizes as indispensable the possession by Women of the Parliamentary Vote on the same terms as it is or as it may be granted to men.

It demands from the Government immediate legislation to secure this.

The further aim of the Society is to take active means to remedy existing evils and to bring to the knowledge of the public the inefficiency of some of the laws of British Columbia especially as they affect women and children.

2. The objects and aims of the Society as set forward above, need very little explanation. We intend to expose in every way possible to us, the dual standard existing for men and women, to demonstrate the evil resulting therefrom, and to force public recognition to the direct connection between this dual standard and the political disability of women.

We stand to emphasize the fact that **causes** of individual cases of injustice can only be satisfactorily and finally dealt with by legislation in which women have a direct share.

3. Regarding the enfranchisement of women as essential to the attainment of equality between the sexes, we are necessarily working primarily for Woman Suffrage, and the principal item on our programme is therefore the demand for a Government Measure giving the Parliamentary Vote to Women on the same terms as it is or may be given to men.

EDITORIALS

The Premier in his speech at Goldstream last month made the following remarks:

"In British Columbia woman suffrage is by no means a live issue. The women of British Columbia are quite content to allow the men of the country to settle the various public policies that arise from time to time, and to busy themselves with the domestic duties which appertain to their sex. But I must admit, having said so much, that a great part has been played by the women of British Columbia in the useful works associated with the provincial charities—hospitals and various other channels of usefulness—and that today they are in a position which gives

Nancy Apsassin with friend, Harvey, in 1951 when Nancy, a Beaver Indian woman was seventy. She had been a good friend to settlers such as Barbett and Sadie Dopp, teaching local women how to dry berries. A

Down by the river, the remains of the old Fort St. John Mission. B

Halfway River area, Branding and Cutting Day, 1960's. C

CHAPTER FOURTEEN:

REFLECTIONS IN INTERNATIONAL WOMEN'S YEAR

It's International Women's Year, 1975, and I'm looking for the thread through the labyrinth of women's history in this province. The Provincial Archives, some museums and university libraries' Special Collections Divisions have some material but other places, such as Nanaimo, report that their museum has no material on pioneer women at all. The only way to find out what life was like-and is like-for B.C. women is to start asking questions. This also leads to my travelling.

One Sunday in May, I am sitting on Teresa Cheeky's bed in a Prince George hospital. We talk for awhile before cowboy music drowns the conversation and the music lifts me back to the Peace River District, an area that Mrs. Cheeky, a Beaver Indian, knows so well. . . .

Living at Fort St. John for two years in the early Sixties, it surprised me how the summer dust painted everything grey. It was Fall when there was a last surge of life, when leaves turned red and silver and cinnamon-colored and black bears appeared on the flats seeking berries, while the silent blue Peace uncoiled through mauve foothills before the winter snow and ice mantled the countryside.

Mrs. Cheeky tells me she once lived in a moosehide tent, and used to make pemmican. Today she no longer needs to do either. She lives in a modern house with a stove. She still likes fresh fish.

The trout, Dolly Varden and Rainbow, bit the moment the lines dimpled the water whenever the Kyllo Brothers took people out in their riverboat. They read water the way others read blood samples or count stars. Rapids they could handle without a qualm. The countryside dominated others: a Russian agricultural settlement failed although the people made periodic visits back. Nicholas Ignatieff was immortalized by that bronze capped stone in the river; trappers died of starvation, a few killed themselves or each other; prospectors found only fool's gold near Mount Selwyn but Alexander Mackenzie portaged that awesome Peace River canyon on his epic 1793 search for the route to the Pacific Ocean.

Ma Murray, famous for her headlines, former editor and publisher of the Alaska Highway News, Fort St. John, B.C.

Mrs. Cheeky informs me that when she was a young woman, she sometimes made squirrel stew. It sure was good.

The cowboy music stops at last. Mrs. Cheeky clutches my arm. "My coat," she says urgently. Her dark eyes scan my face. "Why they take my coat?" It takes time to seek answers. The coat is down the hallway. I tell her it is to be given to her when she leaves. Yes, of course, she is leaving. Soon . . . when her leg heals. "Ahhhhhhh . . ." the relief floods her face. We sit like old friends, clasping hands.

One evening the bus from Quesnel takes me to the Moffat ranch where I am to stay overnight, guests of Kate and Harry Moffat. Harry was as much a part of Cariboo history as wild horses, rodeos, and the train

The writer, Jan Gould, talking with Granny Peterson at Ruby Lake, near Prince George, summer, 1975.   A

Mary Jane Wood taken outside Forbidden Plateau Lodge which she and her husband sold in 1944, moving to Campbell River where they instigated plans to bring electricity to the area.   B

that still screeches through the dark soft night. Kate married Henry in 1948, they took over the ranch when his father retired in 1950. Now Harry tries a new career, selling farm machinery at Quesnel. Their son runs the ranch, also restoring Landsdowne House, the famous Moffat stopping house for stage and freighters in the 1890's. His fiancee, a veterinary surgeon, plans to open an animal clinic nearby. Kate answers all my questions. "Yes, I've cooked for threshing crews, we hired a man in summer and took in a city boy. Paid the boy. Running water? We always had that, and hydro came in 1959. Before that it was gas, coal oil lights, gas washer and sad irons. What I really liked were the weeks in the meadow, haying." She has chased cows on horseback, hauled bales of hay, worked on the potato planter, helped with branding and calving, maintained a garden, and raised a family. Most ranchers' wives have done all this.

On Galiano Island, Jean Lockwood "reached that age of middle- life when I decided to do what I wanted to do- start a newspaper." Her *Gulf Islander* utilized one other employee and five who came to fold and staple the paper once a week in a renovated chickenhouse. 500 free copies grew to 1,500 subsribers paying $2.50 per year in the 1960's. She blasted government for neglecting island roads, local people for not approving school improvement bylaws and was scolded by RCMP for printing homemade wine recipes. When business costs rose in 1968 she 'retired', selling the paper to Salt Spring's *Driftwood* and started to research local history. One campaign produced a $30,000 trust fund to build a 15-mile powerline to 15 houses and a cuple of lighthouses straggled out on the end of North Galiano which B.C. Hydro had declined to service. Loggers and fishermen cleared land then work parites were organized with the campaign manager dolling out $1.00 or $2.00 per hour depending on duties. Schoolchildren peeled logs donated by timber companies. "And on the day before Christmas Eve, 1966, the lights went on." The Gulf Islands have received their share of publicity: Poet Phyllis Webb produced poetry in her Salt Spring Tepee, Vancouver novelist Audrey Thomas used the Islands as background for books.

On the islands and in small towns, elderly women seem at peace with themselves, content in their environment. One day I go to visit Mary Jane Wood, at Alder Point near Courtenay on Vancouver Island. With her late husband, Clinton, and one of her sons, she became the first woman to climb Mount Albert Edward, the highest mountain in the Forbidden Plateau area. The beauty of a lake washing against Castle Mountain struck old dreams and they named it Moat Lake, then made the decision to live in the area, building the famous Forbidden Plateau Lodge and cabins. "We started with nothing—made cedar shakes from the yellow cedar trees. I cooked on an old stove—it had been abandoned there by a logging camp. A marvellous stove. I used to put an umbrella up if it rained while I stood there cooking." A lively octogenarian now, she found a new interest when she became too old to ride or hike, writing articles for outdoor magazines and newspapers.

Elderly native Indians still hold that special position in family life, one that is revered. Dr. Barbara Efrat, Curator of Linguistics for the Provincial Museum, shows me the books produced by Indian artists and writers in summer, coloring books with numerals and names given

Familiar Cariboo and Chilcotin sight : the Russell fence.
A

Jean Lockwood when the lights went on, 1966, north end of Galiano Island. *B*

Left to right: Mabel Dennis, Mary Jane Dick and Bernice Touchie put on tape hte languages of Robert Sport, left, grandfather of Mabel Dennis and Joshua Edgar, granduncle of Bernice Touchie. *C*

Bridge to village of Kiskegas, north of Kispiox. A

Susan Musgrave, British Columbia poet, seen here with the children's book she recently wrote. B

Bessie Tang, standing to right, with other workers making masks and lanterns for Chinese celebrations. C

Quesnel-born artist Nita Forrest now of Victoria. Portrait-painting by Victoria's Myfanwy Pavelic. D

in specific Indian languages. Leafing through the Tsimshian book produced by Ray Wesley, I see he has dedicated it to Tsimshian Grannies, including his own grandmother, Georgina Scott of Port Simpson, "for it is through them that we have learned pride for our past and the courage of the future." Dr. Efrat works closely with the University of Victoria which now offers a one-year Diploma Program in native languages.

I have numerous notes: Victoria Status of Women have a $32,000 grant to produce the Museum Exhibit concerning important women: they choose 15 women to portray different eras of our "Hidden Heritage" and invite surviving members of the "Flying Seven" and mountaineer Phyllis Munday to opening events. On Cortez Island, Sylvia Holland sent out questionnaires concerning Women's Spirituality. Living on the island in a small dome in a rain forest with no power, a wood stove for cooking, no chain saw, well water and trees, she and her husband did crafts and research. "An exploratory study, oriented to feminist women—exploration that has only just begun," she says. "So far, responses have expressed a synergetic interaction between their feminism and their spirituality: a realization of their unique potential as persons, a desire to achieve wholeness, to learn balance and not to develop one aspect of their being to the neglect of other facets; a dependence on their own sense of God as the ultimate authority in their lives, and a concept of a 'God' not limited by sexual form."

Suddenly Grace Gainer comes to mind, the frail and tiny former teacher of rural districts near Kamloops. My friend, Jo Fitzsimmons takes time from her life to track down Mrs. Gainer's address since she is 95 and some people do not know she still is alive. "I must dig deep into my mind to answer you," says this woman, who has been described as a former student as a "Holy Tartar." I wait for the artifacts of her past. We talk for awhile. Later, I see her marching down the hallway with her stick: her back is straight, her face is framed by a cockade of white hair and she has the strong beaklike nose of a proud eagle. Others tell me in shocked voices that she has dared to defy the resident authorities by scattering bird crumbs on her veranda, something no one else would dare to do. "All that learning, all those intellectual theories I had when I left Oxford University and came out to this country to live, well, that was how I began my life. I spent my life here, the real learning part of my life. And what I learned was something so simple that it's hard to know it. Love is the important knowledge, that's what I learned. Love makes us all equal."

Dr. Barbara Efrat, Curator of Linguistics, Provincial Museum .   *A*

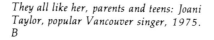
They all like her, parents and teens: Joani Taylor, popular Vancouver singer, 1975.
B

HOW TO READ A PHOTOGRAPH

As an archivist charged with the keeping of visual materials, it has always amused me how a researcher will spend days in meticulous study, tracing records, sifting through letters, pouring over diaries, and analyzing documents, line by line and word by word. Then, almost as an afterthought, he will come to me murmuring a request for photographs.

What both authors and readers of illustrated writings so frequently fail to recognize is the literal truth in the old adage, "One picture speaks ten thousand words". Often, I might add, ten thousand times more subtly, more eloquently, and more truthfully than the text it means to illustrate. A picture is an historical document in its own right. Like every other historical document it is meant to be read, all ten thousand words of it, with at least the same care and attention to detail as a letter, a diary, a manuscript, or a book.

What can a photograph tell us that the written word cannot? To illustrate what it is possible to learn from photographs, let me choose a simple example. The interpretations that follow are highly personal ones—my own—others are possible, indeed, invited. I mean only to suggest the techniques that can be employed. Look closely, if you will, at the two photographs which follow. Both are family portraits not untypical of the kind that have come down to us from the last century, and very likely similar to many found in most family collections. On the face of it, there is nothing very remarkable about either of these pictures. They are standard group portraits. Now look more closely at the first picture. What does this picture tell us?

When I first saw this photograph, I had no background information at all about its content, who these people were, or what relationships existed between them, apart from the reasonable assumption that this was a family. All the same, it is possible to know a great deal about these people. Their clothing tells me that this picture was taken either in the late nineteenth or early twentieth centuries. Though well-dressed, the plainness and lack of ostentation in attire and background leads me to believe that the family was comfortable, but not affluent, perhaps working or lower middle class. It is a large group. There are more children here than we are likely to find in today's population-conscious families, revealing an older, traditional attitude towards family size. We will see, if we look carefully, that there are two sets of twins in this picture, the four girls at the "corners" of the group identically dressed. The overall impression is a pleasing one, everyone appears to be relaxed and at ease, pleasant if not actually smiling.

The strongest impression I have from this family group as a whole is its special kind of solidarity. The degree of supportive and protective cohesion in this group is remarkable. Mark especially the placement of bodies and hands, how every member in this family is linked to every other by touch. Note, too, how many supportive/protective groupings can be seen—older children and parents on the edges around younger, more vulnerable children in the centres, or, one adult in the midst of every group of children. No one central figure stands out to dominate the group, however; an equality is suggested, emanating from an order in which every member has his special place, drawing support and strength from the unity of the whole. Evidently, this is a very close-knit family.

I later learned that this is the family of Michael Manson, pioneer, Cortez Island trader, and eventually (1909) member of the British Columbia Legislature until his death in 1932. His papers are held in the Provincial Archives in Victoria. Michael Manson eloped with his bride, Jane Renwick, of Nanaimo, who had been abused and beaten by her father. The couple made their way by Indian canoe to Victoria where they were married in 1878. The early years of their marriage were trying and heart-rending ones for the Mansons; they lost their first-born from illness in 1881, then, in 1890, tragedy struck again when diptheria claimed four children within a month. Only one child, Margaret, survived—the young woman in the photograph. Seven children were born in later years, including the two sets of twins, and this is the family we see in the portrait, taken about 1906. Reading Manson's own words and the accounts of those who knew the family, we gather that the Mansons were, as the photo confirms, a close, loving, and devoted family.

It is immediately obvious to us that the family depicted in the second portrait presents a stark contrast to the Mansons. Lifestyle, attitudes, and their interpersonal relationships caught in this image bespeak an altogether dissimilar family dynamic at work. A number of differences can be readily observed. For instance, the group is smaller, only half as many children. Whereas elaborate trappings are missing from the Mansons' simple backdrop and plain dress, the clothing here is fashionable and well-tailored, the background is ornate and crammed with detail, and the pose itself has been characteristically formalized as in a painting. The Manson picture could conceivably been taken by Uncle John in the parlour, but this second portrait is unmistakably the work of a professional. All of this suggests affluence.

From beneath the surface more profound differences arise. There is no group-feeling, no contact between family members in this photo that I can detect, physical or otherwise. The impressions created, particularly by the men, are those of uncompromising individuality, and might we also say, detachment? Although this family no doubt exhibits a solidarity of its own ("solidity" seems the more appropriate expression), it certainly does not stem, as with the Mansons, from outward affection. Every person in this picture is a wholly separate and unique individual, with a highly developed sense of personal distance and a well-established awareness of roles.

It is interesting that in addition to the consciousness of individual roles these people seem to project, I detect, besides, a pronounced feeling of the distinction between "masculine" and "feminine" roles. Might this partially account for the significance in the fact that the orientation and gaze of all the women in this photo is directed into the camera, while that of the men is directed uniformly right of centre?

What we know of these people, Jacob Hunter Todd family, tends to bear out what we have learned from their portrait. J. H. Todd came to British Columbia in 1862 from the farmlands of Brampton, Ontario, drawn by the prospect of fortune in the Cariboo gold fields. He found no fortune in gold, but his great drive and ambition forged for him within a few years the beginnings of what became a modest business and financial empire, J. H. Todd & Sons, Ltd., the name behind mining ventures and Horseshoe brand canned salmon. The firm was well known to British Columbians for its shrewd dealings and strict businss practices. Todd's wife, Anna Fox, died after only a few short years of marriage, leaving him two surviving children, the eldest of whom, Charles Fox Todd, became his father's astute business partner. Following a brief visit to his old home in Ontario in 1872, Todd returned to Victoria with a new wife, Rosanna Wigley, a Brampton schoolteacher. She bore him his second family, two sons and two daughters, whom we see in the Todd portrait.

Comparison of the Manson and Todd family portraits is an example of only one of the ways in which a wealth of information can be extracted from old photographs and visual records. With careful perception and imagination, the viewer should be able to find many more.

214

No matter whether we are looking at the image of a single individual, a group, a scenic view, or an inanimate object like a building, the key to unlocking its store of information is the same—observation. Learn to read a photograph as you would a book, go over it again and again, and you are bound to discover things you hadn't seen before each time you return to it. Never accept a picture at its "face value". So often, we look but do not see. Keep these things in mind when you are viewing the many photographs you will find in this book. Remember that all pictures, as the ancient Chinese knew well, tells a story of one kind or another. If you will but learn to read these stories, you may find you have increased your potential knowledge ten thousand-fold.

J. R. DAVIDSON
Archivist, Provincial Archives of British Columbia

BIBLIOGRAPHY

Abraham, Dorothy
    Lone Cone: A Journal of Life on the West Coast of Vancouver Island. Victoria: Abraham, 1961.

    Tu Whit Tu Whoo: Hoots From a Brown Owl. Victoria: Abraham, 1973.

Balf, Mary
    Kamloops: A History of the District up to 1914. Kamloops: Kamloops Museum, 1969.

Bancroft, H. H.
    History of British Columbia, 1792-1887. The Works of Hubert Howe Bancroft, vol. 32. New York-Toronto: Arno Press in cooperation with McGraw-Hill, 1967.

    History of the Northwest Coast. The Works of Hubert Howe Bancroft, vols. 27, 28. New York-Toronto: Arno Press in cooperation with McGraw-Hill.

Bilsland, W. W.
    Atlin, 1898-1910: The Story of a Gold Boom. Atlin: Atlin Centennial Committee, 1971.

Barnett, Homer
    Coast Salish of British Columbia. Eugene: University of Oregon, 1955.

Boas, Franz
    The Religion of the Kwakiutl Indians. New York: AMS Press, 1969. 2 vols.

Borradaile, John
    "Lady of Culzeal", Mayne Island. Borradaile, 1971.

Bowes, Gordon
    Peace River Chronicles. Victoria: Morriss Printing, 1971.

Carr, Emily
    Book of Small. Toronto: Clark, Irwin, 1971.

    Growing Pains. Toronto: Clark, Irwin, 1971.

    The Heart of a Peacock. Toronto: Oxford University Press, 1943.

    House of All Sorts. Toronto: Clarke, Irwin, 1971.

    Hundreds and Thousands: The Journals of Emily Carr. Toronto: Clarke, Irwin, 1966.

Cheadle, Walter Butler; Viscount Milton
    The North-west Passage by Land: Being the Narrative of an Expedition from the Atlantic to the Pacific. Reprint. Toronto: Coles Publishing, 1970.

Chittenden, Newton H.
    Settlers, Prospectors, and Tourist Guides; or Travels Through British Columbia. Circular 10 "The World's Guide for Home, Health, and Pleasure Seekers . . .". Victoria, 1882.

Codere, Helen
    Fighting with Property: A Study of Kwakiutl Potlatching and Warfare, 1792-1930. Seattle: Univ. of Washington Press, 1966.

Collier, Eric
    Three Against the Wilderness. New York: E. P. Dutton, 1964.

Cook, James
 The Voyage of the Resolution and Discovery, 1776-1780. Edited by J. C. Beaglehole. The Journals of Captain James Cook on His Voyages of Discovery, vol. 3. Cambridge, Eng.: Hakluyt Society, 1967. 2 vol.

Cornwallis, Kinahan
 The New El Dorado, or, British Columbia. Toronto: Arno Press, 1973.

Cronin, Kay
 Cross in the Wilderness. Vancouver: Mitchell Press, 1960.

Curtis, Edward
 The North American Indian, being a Series of volumes picturing and describing the Indians of the United States and Alaska. Reprint. New York: Johnson Reprint, 1970.

Davies, Marguerite; Ventress, Cora; Kyllo, Edith
 The Peacemakers of the North Peace. Davies, 1973.

Duff, Wilson
 The Impact of White Man. The Indian History of British Columbia, vol. 1. 2nd edition. Anthropology in British Columbia, Memoir No. 5. Victoria: Provincial Museum of Natural History and Anthropology, 1969.

 Histories, Territories and Laws of the Kitwancool. Anthropology in British Columbia Memoir No. 4. Victoria: Provincial Museum of Natural History and Anthropology, 1959.

Downs, Art
 Paddlewheels on the Frontier: The Story of the British Columbia and Yukon Sternwheel Steamers. Victoria: Gray's Publishing, 1972.

 Wagon Road North. Victoria: Gray's Publishing, 1969.

Drucker, Philip
 Cultures of the North Pacific Coast. San Francisco: Chandler Publishing, 1965.

 The Northern and Central Nootkan Tribes. Bulletin No. 144, U.S. Bureau of American Ethnology, Washington: U.S. Government Printing Office, 1951.

Florin, Lambert
 Ghost Towns: Alaska, Yukon and British Columbia. Seattle: Superior Publishing, 1971.

Forbes, Elizabeth
 Wild Roses at Their Feet: Pioneer Women of Vancouver Island. Vancouver: British Columbia Centennial Committee, 1971.

Forbes, Molly
 Lac La Hache: Historical Notes on the Early Settlers. Quesnel: Big Country Printers, 1970(?).

Fraser, Simon
 The Letters and Journals of Simon Fraser. Edited and with an introduction by W. Kaye Lamb. Pioneer Books. Toronto: Macmillan, 1960.

Gilroy, Marion; Samuel Rothstein, eds.
 As We Remember It: Interviews with Pioneer Librarians of British Columbia. Vancouver: School of Librarianship, University of British Columbia, 1970.

Gosnell, R. E.
 The Year Book of British Columbia and Manual of Provincial Information. 1897. Reprint. Toronto: Canadiana House, 1973.

Grant, George E.
 Ocean to Ocean: Sanford Fleming's Expedition Through Canada in 1872. Edmonton: M. G. Hurtig, 1967

Harmon, D. W.
 Sixteen Years in the Indian Country: the Journal of D. W. Harmon, 1800-1816. Edited by W. Kaye Lamb. Pioneer Books. Toronto: Macmillan, 1957.

Gunther, Erna

    Indian Life on the Northwest Coast of North America as seen by the Early Explorers and Fur Traders during the last decades of the Eighteenth Century. University of Chicago Press, 1972.

Howay, Frederick

    The Early History of the Fraser River Mines. Archives of British Columbia Memoir No. 6. Victoria, 1926.

Johnson, E. Pauline

    Legends of Vancouver. Toronto: McClelland and Stewart, 1973.

Johnson, F. Henry

    John Jessop: Gold Seeker and Educator. Vancouver: Mitchell Press, 1971.

Kelly, Nora

    Quest for a Profession: The History of the Vancouver General Hospital School for Nursing. Vancouver: Alumnae Assoc. of the Vancouver General Hospital School for Nursing, 1973.

Johnston, Jean

    Wilderness Women: Canada's Forgotten History. Toronto: Peter Martin Associates, 1973.

Krause, Aurel

    The Tlingit Indians: Results of a Trip to the Northwest Coast of America and the Bering Straits. Translated by Erna Gunther. Seattle: University of Washington Press, 1956.

Lindsay, F. W.

    The Cariboo Story. Quesnel: Quesnel Advertiser, 1958.

Ludditt, F. W.

    Barkerville Days. Vancouver: Mitchell Press, 1969.

MacDonald, D. G. F.

    British Columbia and Vancouver's Island. London, 1862.

McFeat, Tom

    Indians of the North Pacific Coast: Studies in Selected Topics. Toronto: McClelland and Stewart, 1966.

MacGill, Elsie

    My Mother the Judge, a Biography of Judge Helen Gregory MacGill. Toronto, 1955.

McNaughton, Margaret

    Overland to Cariboo: An Eventful Journal of Canadian Pioneers to the Gold Fields of British Columbia in 1862. Reprint. Introduction by Victor G. Hopwood. Northwest Library, vol. 3. Vancouver: J. J. Douglas, 1973.

McKelvie, B. A.

    Fort Langley: Outpost of Empire. Vancouver, 1947.

Mayne, R. C.

    Four Years in British Columbia and Vancouver Island. London, 1862.

Morice, Rev. A. G., O.M.I.

    The History of the Northern Interior of British Columbia Formerly New Caledonia. (1660 to 1880). Toronto: W. Briggs, 1904.

Ormsby, Margaret A.

    British Columbia: A History. Toronto: Macmillan, 1958.

Pethick, Derek

    James Douglas: Servant of Two Empires. Vancouver: Mitchell Press, 1969.

    S.S. Beaver, The Ship That Saved the West. Vancouver: Mitchell Press, 1970.

    Victoria: The Fort. Vancouver: Mitchell Press, 1968.

    British Columbia Recalled. Victoria: Hancock House, 1974.

Ramsey, Bruce
Barkerville: A Guide in Word and Picture to the Fabulous Gold Camp of the Cariboo. Vancouver: Mitchell Press, 1961.

Ghost Towns of British Columbia. Vancouver: Mitchell Press, 1970.

Rattray, Alexander
Vancouver Island and British Columbia: Where They Are, And What They May Become: A Sketch of Their History, Topography, Climate, Resources, Capabilities, and Advantages, Especially as Colonies for Settlement. London, 1862.

Scott, David; Hanic, Edna
Nelson, Queen City of the Kootenays. Vancouver: Mitchell Press, 1972.

Ross, Alexander
The Fur Traders of the Far West. Norman: University of Oklahoma Press, 1956.

Scott, Irene
The Trek of the Overlanders. Toronto: Burns and MacEachern, 1968.

Smith, Dorothy Blakey
James Douglas: Father of British Columbia. Toronto: Oxford University Press, 1971.

Street, Margaret
Watchfires on the Mountain: the Life and Writings of Ethel Johns. Toronto: University of Toronto Press, 1973.

Teit, James A.
Mythology of the Thompson Indians. 1912. Reprint. The Jesup North Pacific Expedition Publications, vol. 8, part 2. New York: AMS Press, 1973.

Thompson, David
Travels in Western North America, 1784-1812. Edited by Victor G. Hopwood. Toronto: Macmillan, 1971.

Thornton, Mildred V.
Indian Lives and Legends. Vancouver: Mitchell Press, 1966.

Wade, Mark Sweeten
The Overlanders of '62. Edited by John Hosie. Archives of British Columbia, Memoir No. 9. Victoria, 1931.

Walkem, W. W.
Stories of Early British Columbia. Vancouver: News-Advertiser, 1914.

Newspapers:
British Columbian (New Westminster)
Burnaby Columbian
Cariboo Sentinel (1874-75)
Chilliwack Progress
Colonist, the Daily (also was known as
    British Colonist and Victoria Daily Colonist)
Cranbrook Courier
Dawson Creek Peace River Block News
Fort Nelson News
Fort St. James Caledonia Courier
Fort St. John Alaska Highway News
Grand Forks Gazette
Gulf Islands Driftwood
Kamloops Daily Sentinel
Kelowna Courier
Lake News, Lake Cowichan
Langley Advance
Lillooet-Bridge River Lillooet News
Nanaimo Free Press
Nelson Daily News
One Hundred Mile Free Press
Penticton Herald

Port Hardy North Island Gazette
Prince George Citizen
Prince Rupert Daily News
Quesnel Cariboo Observer
Salmon Arm Observer
Surrey Leader
Terrace Herald
The Prospector, Fort Steele
Vanderhoof Nechako Chronicle
Vernon News
Vancouver Sun
Vancouver Province
Victoria Daily Times

Periodicals:
The Beaver
British Columbia Historical Quarterly
B.C. Library Quarterly
B.C. Studies
Canadian Historical Review
Canadian Geographical Journal
Malahat Review
Pacific Historical Review
Oregon Historical Quarterly

PHOTO CREDITS

The following sources kindly contributed photographs to this publication: AF Agnes Flett Pictures' AM A. Mathers, ASS Archives of Sisters of St. Ann, BC B.C. Provincial Archives, BH, Blanche Hipkiss, BT Bessie Tang family album' CAU Cauldwell album, CB CBC, CC Cecil Clark, CPA Canadian Pacific Airlines' DA Drummond album, DC All Dane Campbell, DE B.C. Dept. of Education, EC Edward Curtis collection, EG Ed Gould, ES Eve Smith album, FE Florrie Evans, FS B.C. Forest Service, GA Goossen album, GE Georgeson album, GG Girl Guides Association, GR Garrood album, GS G. Shepherd album, GU Guest album, HM Harriet Morrison family album, IM Ian McRain, IO Imperial Oil, JH J. Hart family album, JP Juli Porter, JR Jim Ryan photograph, JW Jessie Wharf, KF Krebs family album, KM Kamloops Museum, LA Liversidge album, LAR Larremouille photograph, LE Leppington album, LH L. Holdridge album, MAX Maxwell album, MB Mary Backlund album, MBL Ml. Blake, MD Marguerite Davies album, MF Molly Forbes family album, MH M. Holloman album, MT Dept. of Marine Transport, MU Klaus Muenter, PF Peterson family album, PG Prince George Citizen, PM B.C. Provincial Museum, Ethnology division, RF Reid family album, RJH Royal Jubilee Hospital archives, TG Tom Gore, TI B.C. Dept. of Travel Industry, UV UVic Relations office, VGH Vancouver General Hospital archives, VS Vancouver Sun, WA Wood Album, V. Wood photograph, YL'Yim-L Leong.

8 TI; 9A-EC, B-BC; 10A-PM, B-BC, C-BC; 11-BC; 12A-BC, B-EC, C-JP, D-EG, E-TI; 13A-BC, B-BC, C-PM; 14-PM; 15-BC; 16A-BC, B-KM, C-BC, D-BC; 17-BC; 18-BC; 19A-TI, B-BC, C-BC; 20A-BC, B-BC, C-EG, D-BC, E-BC; 21A-BC, B-KM; 23A-EG, B-TI; 24A-JW, B-TI; 25-TI; 26-BC; 28-BC; 29-BC; 30A-BC, B-JW; 33-BC; 34-BC; 35-BC; 36-BC; 37-BC; 40-BC; 41-BC; 42-BC; 43-BC; 45-BC; 46-BC; 47-BC; 49-BC; 50-BC; 53A-BC, B-BC, C-JW; 54-BC; 55-BC; 57-BC; 58-TI; 59A-PG, B-BC; 60-BC; 62-JW; 63A-KM, B-EG; 64-BC; 65A-BC, B-BC, C-TI; 66A-TI, B-TI, C-BC, D-BC, E-BC; 67-BC; 69-BC; 70-TI; 71-EG; 72A-EG, B-TI; 73-TI; 74A-BC, B-ES, C-BC; 75-TI; 76-PF; 78-TI; 79-FE; 80-JP; 81A-RF, B-EG, C-RF; 82A-BH, B-VW; 83-GA; 84-TI; 85A-BC; B-BC, C-EG, D-TI; 86A-TI; B-BC; 87-BC; 88-KM; 89-BC; 90-BC; 91-EG; 92-BC; 93A-BC, B-KM, C-BC, D-BC; 94A-BC, B-TI, C-TI, D-TI; 95A-TI, B-BT; 96-MF; 97A-JW, B-HM, C-TI; 98A-LF, B-BC, C-BC; 99-JW; 100-ES; 101A-JH, B-BC, C-RF, D-BC; 102A-BC, B-RF, C-JP; 103A-TI, B-MD; 104-TI; 105A-BC, B-MD; 106A-MH, B-FS; 107-BC; 108-BC; 109A-BC, B-TI; 110A-KM, B-BC, C-HM; 111-MBL; 112-LH; 113-LH; 114A-AM, B-GS; 115-MF; 116-TI; 118-ES; 119A-GA, B-MB; 120A-LAR, B-LE, C-MD; 123A-TI, B-TI, C-EG; 124-BC; 125-BC; 126-BC; 127-BC; 128-BC; 131A-JW, B-BC, C-BC; D-BC; 132A-TI, B-BC; 135-BC; 136-BC; 137-BC; 139-BC; 140A-BC, B-BC, C-JW; 141-BC; 142-MT; 144-MT; 145-MT; 146A-TI; B-MT, C-GE; 147-GE; 148-MD; 149-BC; 150-TI; 153-KF; 154-KF; 155-TI; 157-TI; 158A-ASS, B-BC, C-BC; 159-BC; 160A-TI, B-BC; 161-RJH; 162A-RJH, B-ASS, C-ASS; 163-LA; 164-KM; 165A-VGH, B-RJH, C-VGH; 166A-DA, B-DA, C-BC, D-BC; 167-BC; 169-BC; 170A-BC, B-BC, C-GR; 171-MD; 172-GU; 173-JR; 174-BC; 175-BC; 176-BC; 177-BC; 178-BC; 179-EG; 180-DC; 181A-BC, B-JR, C-CB; 182-BC; 184-BC; 185A-KM, B-BC; 186-BC; 187A-CC, B-MB; 188-WA; 189A-IO, B-GG, C-BC, D-BC; 190A-BC, B-BC, C-CPA, D-BC; 191-MAX; 192-BC; 193-BC; 194-BC; 195-BC; 196A-JP, B-BC, C-MU; 199A-IM, B-TG, C-VS; D-VS; 200-CAU; 201-BC; 202A-YL, B-BC, C-BC, D-VS, E-DE; 203-JR; 204-VS; 206A-BC, B-TI; 207-MD; 209A-TI, B-AF, C-UV; 210A-TI, B-JR, C-IM; 211-UV.

INDEX